The Algorithmic
Foundations of
Differential Privacy

The Algorithmic Foundations of Differential Privacy

Cynthia Dwork
Microsoft Research, USA
dwork@microsoft.com

Aaron Roth
University of Pennsylvania, USA
aaroth@gmail.com

Boston — Delft

Foundations and Trends® in Theoretical Computer Science

Published, sold and distributed by:
now Publishers Inc.
PO Box 1024
Hanover, MA 02339
United States
Tel. +1-781-985-4510
www.nowpublishers.com
sales@nowpublishers.com

Outside North America:
now Publishers Inc.
PO Box 179
2600 AD Delft
The Netherlands
Tel. +31-6-51115274

The preferred citation for this publication is

C. Dwork and A. Roth. *The Algorithmic Foundations of Differential Privacy.*
Foundations and Trends® in Theoretical Computer Science, vol. 9, nos. 3–4,
pp. 211–407, 2013.

*This Foundations and Trends® issue was typeset in LATEX using a class file designed
by Neal Parikh. Printed on acid-free paper.*

ISBN: 978-1-60198-818-8
© 2014 C. Dwork and A. Roth

Foundations and Trends® in Theoretical Computer Science
Volume 9, Issues 3–4, 2013
Editorial Board

Editorial Scope

Topics

Foundations and Trends® in Theoretical Computer Science publishes surveys and tutorials on the foundations of computer science. The scope of the series is broad. Articles in this series focus on mathematical approaches to topics revolving around the theme of efficiency in computing. The list of topics below is meant to illustrate some of the coverage, and is not intended to be an exhaustive list.

- Algorithmic game theory
- Computational algebra
- Computational aspects of combinatorics and graph theory
- Computational aspects of communication
- Computational biology
- Computational complexity
- Computational geometry
- Computational learning
- Computational Models and Complexity
- Computational Number Theory
- Cryptography and information security
- Data structures
- Database theory
- Design and analysis of algorithms
- Distributed computing
- Information retrieval
- Operations research
- Parallel algorithms
- Quantum computation
- Randomness in computation

Information for Librarians

Foundations and Trends® in Theoretical Computer Science, 2013, Volume 9, 4 issues. ISSN paper version 1551-305X. ISSN online version 1551-3068. Also available as a combined paper and online subscription.

Foundations and Trends® in
Theoretical Computer Science
Vol. 9, Nos. 3–4 (2013) 211–407
© 2014 C. Dwork and A. Roth
DOI: 10.1561/0400000042

The Algorithmic Foundations
of Differential Privacy

Cynthia Dwork
Microsoft Research, USA
dwork@microsoft.com

Aaron Roth
University of Pennsylvania, USA
aaroth@gmail.com

Contents

Preface   **3**

1   The Promise of Differential Privacy   5
   1.1   Privacy-preserving data analysis   6
   1.2   Bibliographic notes   10

2   Basic Terms   11
   2.1   The model of computation   11
   2.2   Towards defining private data analysis   12
   2.3   Formalizing differential privacy   15
   2.4   Bibliographic notes   26

3   Basic Techniques and Composition Theorems   29
   3.1   Useful probabilistic tools   29
   3.2   Randomized response   30
   3.3   The laplace mechanism   31
   3.4   The exponential mechanism   38
   3.5   Composition theorems   42
   3.6   The sparse vector technique   56
   3.7   Bibliographic notes   65

4 Releasing Linear Queries with Correlated Error   **67**

   4.1 An offline algorithm: SmallDB 71
   4.2 An online mechanism: private multiplicative weights 77
   4.3 Bibliographical notes 87

5 Generalizations   **89**

   5.1 Mechanisms via α-nets 90
   5.2 The iterative construction mechanism 92
   5.3 Connections 110
   5.4 Bibliographical notes 116

6 Boosting for Queries   **119**

   6.1 The boosting for queries algorithm 121
   6.2 Base synopsis generators 132
   6.3 Bibliographical notes 141

7 When Worst-Case Sensitivity is Atypical   **143**

   7.1 Subsample and aggregate 143
   7.2 Propose-test-Release 146
   7.3 Stability and privacy 153

8 Lower Bounds and Separation Results   **161**

   8.1 Reconstruction attacks 162
   8.2 Lower bounds for differential privacy 167
   8.3 Bibliographic notes 173

9 Differential Privacy and Computational Complexity   **175**

   9.1 Polynomial time curators 177
   9.2 Some hard-to-Syntheticize distributions 180
   9.3 Polynomial time adversaries 188
   9.4 Bibliographic notes 190

10 Differential Privacy and Mechanism Design   **193**

   10.1 Differential privacy as a solution concept 195
   10.2 Differential privacy as a tool in mechanism design 197
   10.3 Mechanism design for privacy aware agents 208
   10.4 Bibliographical notes 217

11 Differential Privacy and Machine Learning 221
11.1 The sample complexity of differentially private
machine learning 224
11.2 Differentially private online learning 227
11.3 Empirical risk minimization 232
11.4 Bibliographical notes 235

12 Additional Models 237
12.1 The local model 238
12.2 Pan-private streaming model 243
12.3 Continual observation 246
12.4 Average case error for query release 254
12.5 Bibliographical notes 258

13 Reflections 261
13.1 Toward practicing privacy 261
13.2 The differential privacy lens 265

Appendices 267

A The Gaussian Mechanism 269
A.1 Bibliographic notes 274

B Composition Theorems for (ε, δ)-DP 275
B.1 Extension of Theorem 3.16 275

Acknowledgments 277

References 279

Abstract

The problem of privacy-preserving data analysis has a long history spanning multiple disciplines. As electronic data about individuals becomes increasingly detailed, and as technology enables ever more powerful collection and curation of these data, the need increases for a robust, meaningful, and mathematically rigorous definition of privacy, together with a computationally rich class of algorithms that satisfy this definition. Differential Privacy is such a definition.

After motivating and discussing the meaning of differential privacy, the preponderance of this monograph is devoted to fundamental techniques for achieving differential privacy, and application of these techniques in creative combinations, using the query-release problem as an ongoing example. A key point is that, by rethinking the computational goal, one can often obtain far better results than would be achieved by methodically replacing each step of a non-private computation with a differentially private implementation. Despite some astonishingly powerful computational results, there are still fundamental limitations — not just on what can be achieved with differential privacy but on what can be achieved with any method that protects against a complete breakdown in privacy. Virtually all the algorithms discussed herein maintain differential privacy against adversaries of arbitrary computational power. Certain algorithms are computationally intensive, others are efficient. Computational complexity for the adversary and the algorithm are both discussed.

We then turn from fundamentals to applications other than query-release, discussing differentially private methods for mechanism design and machine learning. The vast majority of the literature on differentially private algorithms considers a single, static, database that is subject to many analyses. Differential privacy in other models, including distributed databases and computations on data streams is discussed.

Finally, we note that this work is meant as a thorough introduction to the problems and techniques of differential privacy, but is not intended to be an exhaustive survey — there is by now a vast amount of work in differential privacy, and we can cover only a small portion of it.

C. Dwork and A. Roth. *The Algorithmic Foundations of Differential Privacy.* Foundations and Trends® in Theoretical Computer Science, vol. 9, nos. 3–4, pp. 211–407, 2013.

DOI: 10.1561/0400000042.

Preface

The problem of privacy-preserving data analysis has a long history spanning multiple disciplines. As electronic data about individuals becomes increasingly detailed, and as technology enables ever more powerful collection and curation of these data, the need increases for a robust, meaningful, and mathematically rigorous definition of privacy, together with a computationally rich class of algorithms that satisfy this definition. *Differential Privacy* is such a definition.

After motivating and discussing the meaning of differential privacy, the preponderance of the book is devoted to fundamental techniques for achieving differential privacy, and application of these techniques in creative combinations (Sections 3–7), using the *query-release* problem as an ongoing example. A key point is that, by rethinking the computational goal, one can often obtain far better results than would be achieved by methodically replacing each step of a non-private computation with a differentially private implementation.

Despite some astonishingly powerful computational results, there are still fundamental limitations — not just on what can be achieved with differential privacy but on what can be achieved with *any* method that protects against a complete breakdown in privacy (Section 8).

Virtually all the algorithms discussed in this book maintain differential privacy against adversaries of arbitrary computational power. Certain algorithms are computationally intensive, others are efficient. Computational complexity for the adversary and the algorithm are both discussed in Section 9.

In Sections 10 and 11 we turn from fundamentals to applications other than query-release, discussing differentially private methods for mechanism design and machine learning. The vast majority of the literature on differentially private algorithms considers a single, static, database that is subject to many analyses. Differential privacy in other models, including distributed databases and computations on data streams is discussed in Section 12.

Finally, we note that this book is meant as a thorough introduction to the problems and techniques of differential privacy, but is not intended to be an exhaustive survey — there is by now a vast amount of work in differential privacy, and we can cover only a small portion of it.

1

The Promise of Differential Privacy

"Differential privacy" describes a promise, made by a data holder, or *curator*, to a data subject: "You will not be affected, adversely or otherwise, by allowing your data to be used in any study or analysis, no matter what other studies, data sets, or information sources, are available." At their best, differentially private database mechanisms can make confidential data widely available for accurate data analysis, without resorting to data clean rooms, data usage agreements, data protection plans, or restricted views. Nonetheless, data utility will eventually be consumed: the Fundamental Law of Information Recovery states that overly accurate answers to too many questions will destroy privacy in a spectacular way.[1] The goal of algorithmic research on differential privacy is to postpone this inevitability as long as possible.

Differential privacy addresses the paradox of learning nothing about an individual while learning useful information about a population. A medical database may teach us that smoking causes cancer, affecting an insurance company's view of a smoker's long-term medical costs. Has the smoker been harmed by the analysis? Perhaps — his insurance

---

[1]This result, proved in Section 8.1, applies to *all* techniques for privacy-preserving data analysis, and not just to differential privacy.

premiums may rise, if the insurer knows he smokes. He may also be helped — learning of his health risks, he enters a smoking cessation program. Has the smoker's privacy been compromised? It is certainly the case that more is known about him after the study than was known before, but was his information "leaked"? Differential privacy will take the view that it was not, with the rationale that the impact on the smoker is the same *independent of whether or not he was in the study.* It is the *conclusions reached* in the study that affect the smoker, not his presence or absence in the data set.

Differential privacy ensures that the same conclusions, for example, smoking causes cancer, will be reached, independent of whether any individual opts into or opts out of the data set. Specifically, it ensures that any sequence of outputs (responses to queries) is "essentially" equally likely to occur, independent of the presence or absence of any individual. Here, the probabilities are taken over random choices made by the privacy mechanism (something controlled by the data curator), and the term "essentially" is captured by a parameter, ε. A smaller ε will yield better privacy (and less accurate responses).

Differential privacy is a *definition,* not an algorithm. For a given computational task T and a given value of ε there will be many differentially private algorithms for achieving T in an ε-differentially private manner. Some will have better accuracy than others. When ε is small, finding a highly accurate ε-differentially private algorithm for T can be difficult, much as finding a numerically stable algorithm for a specific computational task can require effort.

1.1 Privacy-preserving data analysis

Differential privacy is a definition of privacy tailored to the problem of privacy-preserving data analysis. We briefly address some concerns with other approaches to this problem.

Data Cannot be Fully Anonymized and Remain Useful. Generally speaking, the richer the data, the more interesting and useful it is. This has led to notions of "anonymization" and "removal of personally identifiable information," where the hope is that portions of the data records can be suppressed and the remainder published and used for analysis. However, the richness of the data enables "naming" an individual by a sometimes surprising collection of fields, or attributes, such as the combination of zip code, date of birth, and sex, or even the names of three movies and the approximate dates on which an individual watched these movies. This "naming" capability can be used in a *linkage attack* to match "anonymized" records with non-anonymized records in a different dataset. Thus, the medical records of the governor of Massachussetts were identified by matching anonymized medical encounter data with (publicly available) voter registration records, and Netflix subscribers whose viewing histories were contained in a collection of anonymized movie records published by Netflix as training data for a competition on recommendation were identified by linkage with the Internet Movie Database (IMDb).

Differential privacy neutralizes linkage attacks: since being differentially private is a property of the data access mechanism, and is unrelated to the presence or absence of auxiliary information available to the adversary, access to the IMDb would no more permit a linkage attack to someone whose history is in the Netflix training set than to someone not in the training set.

Re-Identification of "Anonymized" Records is Not the Only Risk. Re-identification of "anonymized" data records is clearly undesirable, not only because of the re-identification *per se*, which certainly reveals membership in the data set, but also because the record may contain compromising information that, were it tied to an individual, could cause harm. A collection of medical encounter records from a specific urgent care center on a given date may list only a small number of distinct complaints or diagnoses. The additional information that a neighbor visited the facility on the date in question gives a fairly narrow range of possible diagnoses for the neighbor's condition. The fact that it may not be possible to match a specific record to the neighbor provides minimal privacy protection to the neighbor.

Queries Over Large Sets are Not Protective. Questions about specific individuals cannot be safely answered with accuracy, and indeed one might wish to reject them out of hand (were it computationally feasible to recognize them). Forcing queries to be over large sets is not a panacea, as shown by the following *differencing attack*. Suppose it is known that Mr. X is in a certain medical database. Taken together, the answers to the two large queries "How many people in the database have the sickle cell trait?" and "How many people, not named X, in the database have the sickle cell trait?" yield the sickle cell status of Mr. X.

Query Auditing Is Problematic. One might be tempted to *audit* the sequence of queries and responses, with the goal of interdicting any response if, in light of the history, answering the current query would compromise privacy. For example, the auditor may be on the lookout for pairs of queries that would constitute a differencing attack. There are two difficulties with this approach. First, it is possible that *refusing* to answer a query is itself disclosive. Second, query auditing can be computationally infeasible; indeed if the query language is sufficiently rich there may not even exist an algorithmic procedure for deciding if a pair of queries constitutes a differencing attack.

Summary Statistics are Not "Safe." In some sense, the failure of summary statistics as a privacy solution concept is immediate from the differencing attack just described. Other problems with summary statistics include a variety of *reconstruction attacks* against a database in which each individual has a "secret bit" to be protected. The utility goal may be to permit, for example, questions of the form "How many people satisfying property P have secret bit value 1?" The goal of the adversary, on the other hand, is to significantly increase his chance of guessing the secret bits of individuals. The reconstruction attacks described in Section 8.1 show the difficulty of protecting against even a *linear* number of queries of this type: unless sufficient inaccuracy is introduced almost all the secret bits can be reconstructed.

A striking illustration of the risks of releasing summary statistics is in an application of a statistical technique, originally intended for confirming or refuting the presence of an individual's DNA in a forensic mix, to ruling an individual in or out of a genome-wide association study. According to a Web site of the Human Genome Project, "Single nucleotide polymorphisms, or SNPs (pronounced "snips"), are DNA sequence variations that occur when a single nucleotide (A,T,C, or G) in the genome sequence is altered. For example a SNP might change the DNA sequence AAGGCTAA to ATGGCTAA." In this case we say there are two alleles: A and T. For such a SNP we can ask, given a particular reference population, what are the frequencies of each of the two possible alleles? Given the allele frequencies for SNPs in the reference population, we can examine how these frequencies may differ for a subpopulation that has a particular disease (the "case" group), looking for alleles that are associated with the disease. For this reason, genome-wide association studies may contain the allele frequencies of the case group for large numbers of SNPs. By definition, these allele frequencies are only aggregated statistics, and the (erroneous) assumption has been that, by virtue of this aggregation, they preserve privacy. However, given the genomic data of an individual, it is theoretically possible to determine if the individual is in the case group (and, therefore, has the disease). In response, the National Institutes of Health and Wellcome Trust terminated public access to aggregate frequency data from the studies they fund.

This is a challenging problem even for differential privacy, due to the large number — hundreds of thousands or even one million — of measurements involved and the relatively small number of individuals in any case group.

"Ordinary" Facts are Not "OK." Revealing "ordinary" facts, such as purchasing bread, may be problematic if a data subject is followed over time. For example, consider Mr. T, who regularly buys bread, year after year, until suddenly switching to rarely buying bread. An analyst might conclude Mr. T most likely has been diagnosed with Type 2 diabetes. The analyst might be correct, or might be incorrect; either way Mr. T is harmed.

"Just a Few." In some cases a particular technique may in fact provide privacy protection for "typical" members of a data set, or more generally, "most" members. In such cases one often hears the argument that the technique is adequate, as it compromises the privacy of "just a few" participants. Setting aside the concern that outliers may be precisely those people for whom privacy is most important, the "just a few"

philosophy is not intrinsically without merit: there is a social judgment, a weighing of costs and benefits, to be made. A well-articulated definition of privacy consistent with the "just a few" philosophy has yet to be developed; however, for a single data set, "just a few" privacy can be achieved by randomly selecting a subset of rows and releasing them in their entirety (Lemma 4.3, Section 4). Sampling bounds describing the quality of statistical analysis that can be carried out on random subsamples govern the number of rows to be released. Differential privacy provides an alternative when the "just a few" philosophy is rejected.

1.2 Bibliographic notes

Sweeney [81] linked voter registration records to "anonymized" medical encounter data; Narayanan and Shmatikov carried out a linkage attack against anonymized ranking data published by Netflix [65]. The work on presence in a forensic mix is due to Homer et al. [46]. The first reconstruction attacks were due to Dinur and Nissim [18].

2

Basic Terms

This section motivates and presents the formal definition of differential privacy, and enumerates some of its key properties.

2.1 The model of computation

We assume the existence of a trusted and trustworthy *curator* who holds the data of *individuals* in a database D, typically comprised of some number n of rows. The intuition is that each row contains the data of a single individual, and, still speaking intuitively, the privacy goal is to simultaneously protect every individual row while permitting statistical analysis of the database as a whole.

In the *non-interactive*, or *offline*, model the curator produces some kind of object, such as a "synthetic database," collection of summary statistics, or "sanitized database" once and for all. After this *release* the curator plays no further role and the original data may be destroyed.

A *query* is a function to be applied to a database. The *interactive*, or *online*, model permits the data analyst to ask queries adaptively, deciding which query to pose next based on the observed responses to previous queries.

The trusted curator can be replaced by a protocol run by the set of individuals, using the cryptographic techniques for secure multi-party protocols, but for the most part we will not be appealing to cryptographic assumptions. Section 12 describes this and other models studied in the literature.

When all the queries are known in advance the non-interactive model should give the best accuracy, as it is able to correlate noise knowing the structure of the queries. In contrast, when no information about the queries is known in advance, the non-interactive model poses severe challenges, as it must provide answers to all possible queries. As we will see, to ensure privacy, or even to prevent privacy catastrophes, accuracy will necessarily deteriorate with the number of questions asked, and providing accurate answers to all possible questions will be infeasible.

A *privacy mechanism*, or simply a *mechanism*, is an algorithm that takes as input a database, a universe $\mathcal{X}$ of data types (the set of all possible database rows), random bits, and, optionally, a set of queries, and produces an output string. The hope is that the output string can be decoded to produce relatively accurate answers to the queries, if the latter are present. If no queries are presented then we are in the non-interactive case, and the hope is that the output string can be interpreted to provide answers to future queries.

In some cases we may require that the output string be a *synthetic database*. This is a multiset drawn from the universe $\mathcal{X}$ of possible database rows. The decoding method in this case is to carry out the query on the synthetic database and then to apply some sort of simple transformation, such as multiplying by a scaling factor, to obtain an approximation to the the true answer to the query.

2.2 Towards defining private data analysis

A natural approach to defining privacy in the context of data analysis is to require that the analyst knows no more about any individual in the data set after the analysis is completed than she knew before the analysis was begun. It is also natural to formalize this goal by requiring that the adversary's prior and posterior views about an individual (i.e., before and after having access to the database) shouldn't be "too different," or that access to the database shouldn't change the adversary's views about any individual "too much." However, if the database teaches anything at all, this notion of privacy is unachievable. For example, suppose the adversary's (incorrect) prior view is that everyone has 2 left feet. Access to the statistical database teaches that almost everyone has one left foot and one right foot. The adversary now has a very different view of whether or not any given respondent has two left feet.

Part of the appeal of before/after, or "nothing is learned," approach to defining privacy is the intuition that if nothing is learned about an individual then the individual cannot be harmed by the analysis. However, the "smoking causes cancer" example shows this intuition to be flawed; the culprit is auxiliary information (Mr. X smokes).

The "nothing is learned" approach to defining privacy is reminiscent of semantic security for a cryptosystem. Roughly speaking, semantic security says that nothing is learned about the plaintext (the unencrypted message) from the ciphertext. That is, anything known about the plaintext after seeing the ciphertext was known before seeing the ciphertext. So if there is auxiliary information saying that the ciphertext is an encryption of either "dog" or "cat," then the ciphertext leaks no further information about which of "dog" or "cat" has been encrypted. Formally, this is modeled by comparing the ability of the eavesdropper to guess which of "dog" and "cat" has been encrypted to the ability of a so-called *adversary simulator*, who has the auxiliary information but does not have access to the ciphertext, to guess the same thing. If for every eavesdropping adversary, and all auxiliary information (to which both the adversary and the simulator are privy), the adversary simulator has essentially the same odds of guessing as does the eavesdropper, then the system enjoys semantic security. Of course, for the system to be useful, the legitimate receiver must be able to correctly decrypt the message; otherwise semantic security can be achieved trivially.

We know that, under standard computational assumptions, semantically secure cryptosystems exist, so why can we not build semantically secure private database mechanisms that yield answers to queries while keeping individual rows secret?

First, the analogy is not perfect: in a semantically secure cryptosystem there are three parties: the message sender (who encrypts the plaintext message), the message receiver (who decrypts the ciphertext), and the eavesdropper (who is frustrated by her inability to learn anything about the plaintext that she did not already know before it was sent). In contrast, in the setting of private data analysis there are only two parties: the curator, who runs the privacy mechanism (analogous to the sender) and the data analyst, who receives the informative responses to queries (like the message receiver) and also tries to squeeze out privacy-compromising information about individuals (like the eavesdropper). Because the legitimate receiver is the same party as the snooping adversary, the analogy to encryption is flawed: denying all information to the adversary means denying all information to the data analyst.

Second, as with an encryption scheme, we require the privacy mechanism to be useful, which means that it teaches the analyst something she did not previously know. This teaching is unavailable to an adversary simulator; that is, no simulator can "predict" what the analyst has learned. We can therefore look at the database as a weak source of random (unpredictable) bits, from which we can extract some very high quality randomness to be used as a *random pad*. This can be used in an encryption technique in which a secret message is added to a random value (the "random pad") in order to produce a string that information-theoretically hides the secret. Only someone knowing the random pad can learn the secret; any party that knows nothing about the pad learns nothing at all about the secret, no matter his or her computational power. Given access to the database, the analyst can learn the random pad, but the adversary simulator, not given access to the database, learns nothing at all about the pad. Thus, given as auxiliary information the encryption of a secret using the random pad, the analyst can decrypt the secret, but the adversary simulator learns nothing at all about the secret. This yields a huge disparity between the ability of the adversary/analyst to learn the secret and the ability of the adversary simulator to do the same thing, eliminating all hope of anything remotely resembling semantic security.

The obstacle in both the smoking causes cancer example and the hope for semantic security is auxiliary information. Clearly, to be meaningful, a privacy guarantee must hold even in the context of "reasonable" auxiliary knowledge, but separating reasonable from arbitrary auxiliary knowledge is problematic. For example, the analyst using a government database might be an employee at a major search engine company. What are "reasonable" assumptions about the auxiliary knowledge information available to such a person?

2.3 Formalizing differential privacy

We will begin with the technical definition of differential privacy, and then go on to interpret it. Differential privacy will provide privacy by *process*; in particular it will introduce randomness. An early example of privacy by randomized process is *randomized response*, a technique developed in the social sciences to collect statistical information about embarassing or illegal behavior, captured by having a property P. Study participants are told to report whether or not they have property P as follows:

1. Flip a coin.
2. If **tails**, then respond truthfully.
3. If **heads**, then flip a second coin and respond "Yes" if heads and "No" if tails.

"Privacy" comes from the plausible deniability of any outcome; in particular, if having property P corresponds to engaging in illegal behavior, even a "Yes" answer is not incriminating, since this answer occurs with probability at least 1/4 whether or not the respondent actually has property P. Accuracy comes from an understanding of the noise generation procedure (the introduction of spurious "Yes" and "No" answers from the randomization): The expected number of "Yes" answers is 1/4 times the number of participants who do not have property P plus 3/4 the number having property P. Thus, if p is the true fraction of participants having property P, the expected number of "Yes" answers is $(1/4)(1-p)+(3/4)p = (1/4)+p/2$. Thus, we can estimate p as twice the fraction answering "Yes" minus $1/2$, that is, $2((1/4)+p/2)-1/2$.

Randomization is essential; more precisely, any *non-trivial* privacy guarantee that holds regardless of all present or even future sources of auxiliary information, including other databases, studies, Web sites, on-line communities, gossip, newspapers, government statistics, and so on, requires randomization. This follows from a simple hybrid argument, which we now sketch. Suppose, for the sake of contradiction, that we have a non-trivial deterministic algorithm. Non-triviality says that there exists a query and two databases that yield different outputs under this query. Changing one row at a time we see there exists a pair of databases differing only in the value of a single row, on which the same query yields different outputs. An adversary knowing that the database is one of these two almost identical databases learns the value of the data in the unknown row.

We will therefore need to discuss the input and output space of randomized algorithms. Throughout this monograph we work with discrete probability spaces. Sometimes we will describe our algorithms as sampling from continuous distributions, but these should always be discretized to finite precision in an appropriately careful way (see Remark 2.1 below). In general, a randomized algorithm with domain A and (discrete) range B will be associated with a mapping from A to the probability simplex over B, denoted $\Delta(B)$:

Definition 2.1 (Probability Simplex). Given a discrete set B, the *probability simplex* over B, denoted $\Delta(B)$ is defined to be:

$$\Delta(B) = \left\{ x \in \mathbb{R}^{|B|} : x_i \geq 0 \text{ for all } i \text{ and } \sum_{i=1}^{|B|} x_i = 1 \right\}$$

Definition 2.2 (Randomized Algorithm). A randomized algorithm $\mathcal{M}$ with domain A and discrete range B is associated with a mapping $M : A \to \Delta(B)$. On input $a \in A$, the algorithm $\mathcal{M}$ outputs $\mathcal{M}(a) = b$ with probability $(M(a))_b$ for each $b \in B$. The probability space is over the coin flips of the algorithm $\mathcal{M}$.

We will think of databases x as being collections of records from a universe $\mathcal{X}$. It will often be convenient to represent databases by their histograms: $x \in \mathbb{N}^{|\mathcal{X}|}$, in which each entry x_i represents the number of elements in the database x of *type* $i \in \mathcal{X}$ (we abuse notation slightly, letting the symbol $\mathbb{N}$ denote the set of all non-negative integers, including zero). In this representation, a natural measure of the distance between two databases x and y will be their ℓ_1 distance:

Definition 2.3 (Distance Between Databases). The ℓ_1 norm of a database x is denoted $\|x\|_1$ and is defined to be:

$$\|x\|_1 = \sum_{i=1}^{|\mathcal{X}|} |x_i|.$$

The ℓ_1 distance between two databases x and y is $\|x - y\|_1$

Note that $\|x\|_1$ is a measure of the *size* of a database x (i.e., the number of records it contains), and $\|x - y\|_1$ is a measure of how many records *differ* between x and y.

Databases may also be represented by multisets of *rows* (elements of $\mathcal{X}$) or even ordered lists of rows, which is a special case of a set, where the row number becomes part of the name of the element. In this case distance between databases is typically measured by the Hamming distance, i.e., the number of rows on which they differ.

However, unless otherwise noted, we will use the histogram representation described above. (Note, however, that even when the histogram notation is more mathematically convenient, in actual implementations, the multiset representation will often be much more concise).

We are now ready to formally define *differential privacy*, which intuitively will guarantee that a randomized algorithm behaves similarly on similar input databases.

Definition 2.4 (Differential Privacy). A randomized algorithm $\mathcal{M}$ with domain $\mathbb{N}^{|\mathcal{X}|}$ is (ε, δ)-differentially private if for all $\mathcal{S} \subseteq \text{Range}(\mathcal{M})$ and for all $x, y \in \mathbb{N}^{|\mathcal{X}|}$ such that $\|x - y\|_1 \leq 1$:

$$\Pr[\mathcal{M}(x) \in \mathcal{S}] \leq \exp(\varepsilon) \Pr[\mathcal{M}(y) \in \mathcal{S}] + \delta,$$

where the probability space is over the coin flips of the mechanism $\mathcal{M}$. If $\delta = 0$, we say that $\mathcal{M}$ is ε-differentially private.

Typically we are interested in values of δ that are less than the inverse of any polynomial in the size of the database. In particular, values of δ on the order of $1/\|x\|_1$ are very dangerous: they permit "preserving privacy" by publishing the complete records of a small number of database participants — precisely the "just a few" philosophy discussed in Section 1.

Even when δ is negligible, however, there are theoretical distinctions between $(\varepsilon, 0)$- and (ε, δ)-differential privacy. Chief among these is what amounts to a switch of quantification order. $(\varepsilon, 0)$-differential privacy ensures that, for *every* run of the mechanism $\mathcal{M}(x)$, the output observed is (almost) equally likely to be observed on *every* neighboring database, simultaneously. In contrast (ε, δ)-differential privacy says that for every pair of neighboring databases x, y, it is extremely unlikely that, *ex post facto* the observed value $\mathcal{M}(x)$ will be much more or much less likely to be generated when the database is x than when the database is y. However, given an output $\xi \sim \mathcal{M}(x)$ it may be possible to find a database y such that ξ is much more likely to be produced on y than it is when the database is x. That is, the mass of ξ in the distribution $\mathcal{M}(y)$ may be substantially larger than its mass in the distribution $\mathcal{M}(x)$.

The quantity

$$\mathcal{L}^{(\xi)}_{\mathcal{M}(x)\|\mathcal{M}(y)} = \ln\left(\frac{\Pr[\mathcal{M}(x) = \xi]}{\Pr[\mathcal{M}(y) = \xi]}\right)$$

is important to us; we refer to it as the *privacy loss* incurred by observing ξ. This loss might be positive (when an event is more likely under x than under y) or it might be negative (when an event is more likely under y than under x). As we will see in Lemma 3.17, (ε, δ)-differential privacy ensures that for all adjacent x, y, the absolute value of the privacy loss will be bounded by ε with probability at least $1 - \delta$. As always, the probability space is over the coins of the mechanism $\mathcal{M}$.

Differential privacy is immune to *post-processing*: A data analyst, without additional knowledge about the private database, cannot compute a function of the output of a private algorithm $\mathcal{M}$ and make it less differentially private. That is, if an algorithm protects an individual's privacy, then a data analyst cannot increase privacy loss — either under the formal definition or even in any intuitive sense — simply by sitting in a corner and *thinking about* the output of the algorithm. Formally, the composition of a data-independent mapping f with an (ε, δ)-differentially private algorithm $\mathcal{M}$ is also (ε, δ) differentially private:

Proposition 2.1 (Post-Processing). Let $\mathcal{M} : \mathbb{N}^{|\mathcal{X}|} \to R$ be a randomized algorithm that is (ε, δ)-differentially private. Let $f : R \to R'$ be an arbitrary randomized mapping. Then $f \circ \mathcal{M} : \mathbb{N}^{|\mathcal{X}|} \to R'$ is (ε, δ)-differentially private.

Proof. We prove the proposition for a deterministic function $f : R \to R'$. The result then follows because any randomized mapping can be decomposed into a convex combination of deterministic functions, and a convex combination of differentially private mechanisms is differentially private.

Fix any pair of neighboring databases x, y with $\|x - y\|_1 \leq 1$, and fix any event $S \subseteq R'$. Let $T = \{r \in R : f(r) \in S\}$. We then have:

$$
\begin{aligned}
\Pr[f(\mathcal{M}(x)) \in S] &= \Pr[\mathcal{M}(x) \in T] \\
&\leq \exp(\epsilon) \Pr[\mathcal{M}(y) \in T] + \delta \\
&= \exp(\epsilon) \Pr[f(\mathcal{M}(y)) \in S] + \delta
\end{aligned}
$$

which was what we wanted. □

It follows immediately from Definition 2.4 that $(\varepsilon, 0)$-differential privacy composes in a straightforward way: the composition of two $(\varepsilon, 0)$-differentially private mechanisms is $(2\varepsilon, 0)$-differentially private. More generally (Theorem 3.16), "the epsilons and the deltas add up": the composition of k differentially private mechanisms, where the ith mechanism is $(\varepsilon_i, \delta_i)$-differentially private, for $1 \leq i \leq k$, is $(\sum_i \varepsilon_i, \sum_i \delta_i)$-differentially private.

Group privacy for $(\varepsilon, 0)$-differentially private mechanisms also follows immediately from Definition 2.4, with the strength of the privacy guarantee drops linearly with the size of the group.

Theorem 2.2. Any $(\varepsilon, 0)$-differentially private mechanism $\mathcal{M}$ is $(k\varepsilon, 0)$-differentially private for groups of size k. That is, for all $\|x - y\|_1 \leq k$ and all $\mathcal{S} \subseteq \mathrm{Range}(\mathcal{M})$

$$\Pr[\mathcal{M}(x) \in \mathcal{S}] \leq \exp(k\varepsilon) \Pr[\mathcal{M}(y) \in \mathcal{S}],$$

where the probability space is over the coin flips of the mechanism $\mathcal{M}$.

This addresses, for example, the question of privacy in surveys that include multiple family members.[1]

More generally, composition and group privacy are not the same thing and the improved composition bounds in Section 3.5.2 (Theorem 3.20), which substantially improve upon the factor of k, do not — and cannot — yield the same gains for group privacy, even when $\delta = 0$.

2.3.1 What differential privacy promises

An Economic View. Differential privacy promises to protect individuals from any *additional* harm that they might face due to their data being in the private database x that they would not have faced had their data not been part of x. Although individuals may indeed face harm once the results $\mathcal{M}(x)$ of a differentially private mechanism $\mathcal{M}$ have been released, differential privacy promises that the probability of harm was not significantly increased by their choice to participate. This is a very utilitarian definition of privacy, because when an individual is deciding whether or not to include her data in a database that will be used in a differentially private manner, it is exactly this difference that she is considering: the probability of harm given that she participates, as compared to the probability of harm given that she does not participate. She has no control over the remaining contents of the database. Given the promise of differential privacy, she is assured that she should

---

[1]However, as the group gets larger, the privacy guarantee deteriorates, and this is what we want: clearly, if we replace an entire surveyed population, say, of cancer patients, with a completely different group of respondents, say, healthy teenagers, we *should* get different answers to queries about the fraction of respondents who regularly run three miles each day. Although something similar holds for (ε, δ)-differential privacy, the approximation term δ takes a big hit, and we only obtain $(k\varepsilon, ke^{(k-1)\varepsilon}\delta)$-differential privacy for groups of size k.

be almost indifferent between participating and not, from the point of view of future harm. Given any incentive — from altruism to monetary reward — differential privacy may convince her to allow her data to be used. This intuition can be formalized in a utility-theoretic sense, which we here briefly sketch.

Consider an individual i who has arbitrary preferences over the set of all possible future events, which we denote by $\mathcal{A}$. These preferences are expressed by a utility function $u_i : \mathcal{A} \rightarrow \mathbb{R}_{\geq 0}$, and we say that individual i experiences utility $u_i(a)$ in the event that $a \in \mathcal{A}$ comes to pass. Suppose that $x \in \mathbb{N}^{|\mathcal{X}|}$ is a data-set containing individual is private data, and that $\mathcal{M}$ is an ε-differentially private algorithm. Let y be a data-set that is identical to x except that it does not include the data of individual i (in particular, $\|x - y\|_1 = 1$), and let $f : \text{Range}(\mathcal{M}) \rightarrow \Delta(\mathcal{A})$ be the (arbitrary) function that determines the distribution over future events $\mathcal{A}$, conditioned on the output of mechanism $\mathcal{M}$. By the guarantee of differential privacy, together with the resilience to arbitrary post-processing guaranteed by Proposition 2.1, we have:

$$
\begin{aligned}
\mathbb{E}_{a \sim f(\mathcal{M}(x))}[u_i(a)] &= \sum_{a \in \mathcal{A}} u_i(a) \cdot \Pr_{f(\mathcal{M}(x))}[a] \\
&\leq \sum_{a \in \mathcal{A}} u_i(a) \cdot \exp(\varepsilon) \Pr_{f(\mathcal{M}(y))}[a] \\
&= \exp(\varepsilon) \mathbb{E}_{a \sim f(\mathcal{M}(y))}[u_i(a)]
\end{aligned}
$$

Similarly,

$$
\mathbb{E}_{a \sim f(\mathcal{M}(x))}[u_i(a)] \geq \exp(-\varepsilon) \mathbb{E}_{a \sim f(\mathcal{M}(y))}[u_i(a)].
$$

Hence, by promising a guarantee of ε-differential privacy, a data analyst can promise an individual that his expected future utility will not be harmed by more than an $\exp(\varepsilon) \approx (1 + \varepsilon)$ factor. Note that this promise holds *independently* of the individual is utility function u_i, and holds *simultaneously* for multiple individuals who may have completely different utility functions.

2.3.2   What differential privacy does not promise

As we saw in the Smoking Causes Cancer example, while differential privacy is an extremely strong guarantee, it does not promise unconditional freedom from harm. Nor does it create privacy where none previously exists. More generally, differential privacy does not guarantee that what one believes to be one's secrets will remain secret. It merely ensures that one's participation in a survey will not in itself be disclosed, nor will participation lead to disclosure of any specifics that one has contributed to the survey. It is very possible that conclusions drawn from the survey may reflect statistical information about an individual. A health survey intended to discover early indicators of a particular ailment may produce strong, even conclusive results; that these conclusions hold for a given individual is not evidence of a differential privacy violation; the individual may not even have participated in the survey (again, differential privacy ensures that these conclusive results would be obtained with very similar probability whether or not the individual participated in the survey). In particular, if the survey teaches us that specific *private* attributes correlate strongly with *publicly observable* attributes, this is not a violation of differential privacy, since this same correlation would be observed with almost the same probability independent of the presence or absence of any respondent.

Qualitative Properties of Differential Privacy. Having introduced and formally defined differential privacy, we recaptiluate its key desirable qualities.

1. *Protection against arbitrary risks*, moving beyond protection against re-identification.

2. *Automatic neutralization of linkage attacks*, including all those attempted with all past, present, *and future* datasets and other forms and sources of auxiliary information.

3. *Quantification of privacy loss.* Differential privacy is not a binary concept, and has a measure of privacy loss. This permits comparisons among different techniques: for a fixed bound on privacy loss, which technique provides better accuracy? For a fixed accuracy, which technique provides better privacy?

4. *Composition.* Perhaps most crucially, the quantification of loss also permits the analysis and control of cumulative privacy loss over multiple computations. Understanding the behavior of differentially private mechanisms under composition enables the design and analysis of complex differentially private algorithms from simpler differentially private building blocks.

5. *Group Privacy.* Differential privacy permits the analysis and control of privacy loss incurred by groups, such as families.

6. *Closure Under Post-Processing* Differential privacy is immune to post-processing: A data analyst, without additional knowledge about the private database, cannot compute a function of the output of a differentially private algorithm M and make it less differentially private. That is, a data analyst cannot increase privacy loss, either under the formal definition or even in any intuitive sense, simply by sitting in a corner and thinking about the output of the algorithm, *no matter what auxiliary information is available.*

These are the signal attributes of differential privacy. Can we prove a converse? That is, do these attributes, or some subset thereof, imply differential privacy? Can differential privacy be weakened in these respects and still be meaningful? These are open questions.

2.3.3   Final remarks on the definition

The Granularity of Privacy.   Claims of differential privacy should be carefully scrutinized to ascertain the level of granularity at which privacy is being promised. Differential privacy promises that the behavior of an algorithm will be roughly unchanged even if a single entry in the database is modified. But what constitutes a single entry in the database? Consider for example a database that takes the form of a *graph.* Such a database might encode a social network: each individual $i \in [n]$ is represented by a vertex in the graph, and friendships between individuals are represented by edges.

We could consider differential privacy at a level of granularity corresponding to individuals: that is, we could require that differentially private algorithms be insensitive to the addition or removal of any *vertex* from the graph. This gives a strong privacy guarantee, but might in fact be stronger than we need. the addition or removal of a single vertex could after all add or remove up to n edges in the graph. Depending on what it is we hope to learn from the graph, insensitivity to n edge removals might be an impossible constraint to meet.

We could on the other hand consider differential privacy at a level of granularity corresponding to edges, and ask our algorithms to be insensitive only to the addition or removal of single, or small numbers of, *edges* from the graph. This is of course a weaker guarantee, but might still be sufficient for some purposes. Informally speaking, if we promise ε-differential privacy at the level of a single edge, then no data analyst should be able to conclude anything about the existence of any subset of $1/\varepsilon$ edges in the graph. In some circumstances, large groups of social contacts might not be considered sensitive information: for example, an individual might not feel the need to hide the fact that the majority of his contacts are with individuals in his city or workplace, because where he lives and where he works are public information. On the other hand, there might be a small number of social contacts whose existence is highly sensitive (for example a prospective new employer, or an intimate friend). In this case, edge privacy should be sufficient to protect sensitive information, while still allowing a fuller analysis of the data than vertex privacy. Edge privacy will protect such an individual's sensitive information provided that he has fewer than $1/\varepsilon$ such friends.

As another example, a differentially private movie recommendation system can be designed to protect the data in the training set at the "event" level of single movies, hiding the viewing/rating of any single movie but not, say, hiding an individual's enthusiasm for cowboy westerns or gore, or at the "user" level of an individual's entire viewing and rating history.

All Small Epsilons Are Alike. When ε is small, $(\varepsilon, 0)$-differential privacy asserts that for all pairs of adjacent databases x, y and all outputs o, an adversary cannot distinguish which is the true database on the basis of observing o. When ε is small, *failing* to be $(\varepsilon, 0)$-differentially private is not necessarily alarming — for example, the mechanism may be $(2\varepsilon, 0)$-differentially private. The nature of the privacy guarantees with differing but small epsilons are quite similar. But what of large values for ϵ? Failure to be $(15, 0)$-differentially private merely says there exist neighboring databases and an output o for which the ratio of probabilities of observing o conditioned on the database being, respectively, x or y, is large. An output of o might be very unlikely (this is addressed by (ε, δ)-differential privacy); databases x and y might be terribly contrived and ulikely to occur in the "real world"; the adversary may not have the right auxiliary information to recognize that a revealing output has occurred; or may not know enough about the database(s) to determine the value of their symmetric difference. Thus, much as a weak cryptosystem may leak anything from only the least significant bit of a message to the complete decryption key, the failure to be $(\varepsilon, 0)$- or (ε, δ)-differentially private may range from effectively meaningless privacy breaches to complete revelation of the entire database. A large epsilon is large after its own fashion.

A Few Additional Formalisms. Our privacy mechanism $\mathcal{M}$ will often take some auxiliary parameters w as input, in addition to the database x. For example, w may specify a query q_w on the database x, or a collection $\mathcal{Q}_w$ of queries. The mechanism $\mathcal{M}(w, x)$ might (respectively) respond with a differentially private approximation to $q_w(x)$ or to some or all of the queries in $\mathcal{Q}_w$. For all $\delta \geq 0$, we say that a mechanism $\mathcal{M}(\cdot, \cdot)$ satisfies (ε, δ)-differential privacy if for every w, $\mathcal{M}(w, \cdot)$ satisfies (ε, δ)-differential privacy.

Another example of a parameter that may be included in w is a *security parameter* κ to govern how small $\delta = \delta(\kappa)$ should be. That is, $\mathcal{M}(\kappa, \cdot)$ should be $(\varepsilon, \delta(\kappa))$ differentially private for all κ. Typically, and throughout this monograph, we require that δ be a negligible function in κ, i.e., $\delta = \kappa^{-\omega(1)}$. Thus, we think of δ as being cryptographically small, whereas ε is typically thought of as a moderately small constant.

In the case where the auxiliary parameter w specifies a collection $\mathcal{Q}_w = \{q : \mathcal{X}^n \to \mathbb{R}\}$ of queries, we call the mechanism $\mathcal{M}$ a *synopsis generator.* A synopsis generator outputs a (differentially private) synopsis $\mathcal{A}$ which can be used to compute answers to all the queries in $\mathcal{Q}_w$. That is, we require that there exists a reconstruction procedure R such that for each input v specifying a query $q_v \in \mathcal{Q}_w$, the reconstruction procedure outputs $R(\mathcal{A}, v) \in \mathbb{R}$. Typically, we will require that with high probability $\mathcal{M}$ produces a synopsis $\mathcal{A}$ such that the reconstruction procedure, using $\mathcal{A}$, computes accurate answers. That is, for all or most (weighted by some distribution) of the queries $q_v \in \mathcal{Q}_w$, the error $|R(\mathcal{A}, v) - q_v(x)|$ will be bounded. We will occasionally abuse notation and refer to the reconstruction procedure taking as input the actual query q (rather than some representation v of it), and outputting $R(\mathcal{A}, q)$.

A special case of a synopsis is a *synthetic database.* As the name suggests, the rows of a synthetic database are of the same type as rows of the original database. An advantage to synthetic databases is that they may be analyzed using the same software that the analyst would use on the original database, obviating the need for a special reconstruction procedure R.

Remark 2.1. Considerable care must be taken when programming real-valued mechanisms, such as the Laplace mechanism, due to subtleties in the implementation of floating point numbers. Otherwise differential privacy can be destroyed, as outputs with non-zero probability on a database x, may, because of rounding, have zero probability on adjacent databases y. This is just one way in which the implementation of floating point requires scrutiny in the context of differential privacy, and it is not unique.

2.4 Bibliographic notes

The definition of differential privacy is due to Dwork et al. [23]; the precise formulation used here and in the literature first appears in [20] and is due to Dwork and McSherry. The term "differential privacy" was coined by Michael Schroeder. The impossibility of semantic security is due to Dwork and Naor [25]. Composition and group privacy for $(\varepsilon, 0)$-differentially private mechanisms is first addressed in [23].

Composition for (ε, δ)-differential privacy was first addressed in [21] (but see the corrected proof in Appendix B, due to Dwork and Lei [22]). The vulnerability of differential privacy to inappropriate implementations of floating point numbers was observed by Mironov, who proposed a mitigation [63].

3

Basic Techniques and Composition Theorems

After reviewing a few probabilistic tools, we present the Laplace mechanism, which gives differential privacy for real (vector) valued queries. An application of this leads naturally to the exponential mechanism, which is a method for differentially private selection from a discrete set of candidate outputs. We then analyze the cumulative privacy loss incurred by composing multiple differentially private mechanisms. Finally we give a method — the sparse vector technique — for privately reporting the outcomes of a potentially very large number of computations, provided that only a few are "significant."

In this section, we describe some of the most basic techniques in differential privacy that we will come back to use again and again. The techniques described here form the basic building blocks for all of the other algorithms that we will develop.

3.1   Useful probabilistic tools

The following concentration inequalities will frequently be useful. We state them in easy to use forms rather than in their strongest forms.

Theorem 3.1 (Additive Chernoff Bound). Let $X_1, \ldots, X_m$ be independent random variables bounded such that $0 \le X_i \le 1$ for all i. Let $S = \frac{1}{m} \sum_{i=1}^{m} X_i$ denote their mean, and let $\mu = \mathbb{E}[S]$ denote their expected mean. Then:

$$\Pr[S > \mu + \varepsilon] \le e^{-2m\varepsilon^2}$$

$$\Pr[S < \mu - \varepsilon] \le e^{-2m\varepsilon^2}$$

Theorem 3.2 (Multiplicative Chernoff Bound). Let $X_1, \ldots, X_m$ be independent random variables bounded such that $0 \le X_i \le 1$ for all i. Let $S = \frac{1}{m} \sum_{i=1}^{m} X_i$ denote their mean, and let $\mu = \mathbb{E}[S]$ denote their expected mean. Then:

$$\Pr[S > (1 + \varepsilon)\mu] \le e^{-m\mu\varepsilon^2/3}$$

$$\Pr[S < (1 - \varepsilon)\mu] \le e^{-m\mu\varepsilon^2/2}$$

When we do not have independent random variables, all is not lost. We may still apply Azuma's inequality:

Theorem 3.3 (Azuma's Inequality). Let f be a function of m random variables $X_1, \ldots, X_m$, each X_i taking values from a set A_i such that $\mathbb{E}[f]$ is bounded. Let c_i denote the maximum effect of X_i on f — i.e., for all $a_i, a_i' \in A_i$:

$$|\mathbb{E}[f|X_1, \ldots, X_{i-1}, X_i = a_i] - \mathbb{E}[f|X_1, \ldots, X_{i-1}, X_i = a_i']| \le c_i$$

Then:

$$\Pr[f(X_1, \ldots, X_m) \ge \mathbb{E}[f] + t] \le \exp\left(-\frac{2t^2}{\sum_{i=1}^{m} c_i^2}\right)$$

Theorem 3.4 (Stirling's Approximation). $n!$ can be approximated by $\sqrt{2n\pi}(n/e)^n$:

$$\sqrt{2n\pi}(n/e)^n e^{1/(12n+1)} < n! < \sqrt{2n\pi}(n/e)^n e^{1/(12n)}.$$

3.2 Randomized response

Let us recall the simple randomized response mechanism, described in Section 2, for evaluating the frequency of embarrassing or illegal behaviors. Let XYZ be such an activity. Faced with the query, "Have you engaged in XYZ in the past week?" the respondent is instructed to perform the following steps:

1. Flip a coin.
2. If **tails**, then respond truthfully.
3. If **heads**, then flip a second coin and respond "Yes" if heads and "No" if tails.

The intuition behind randomized response is that it provides "plausible deniability." For example, a response of "Yes" may have been offered because the first and second coin flips were both Heads, which occurs with probability 1/4. In other words, *privacy is obtained by process*, there are no "good" or "bad" responses. The process by which the responses are obtained affects how they may legitimately be interpreted. As the next claim shows, randomized response is differentially private.

Claim 3.5. The version of randomized response described above is $(\ln 3, 0)$-differentially private.

Proof. Fix a respondent. A case analysis shows that $\Pr[\text{Response} = \text{Yes}|\text{Truth} = \text{Yes}] = 3/4$. Specifically, when the truth is "Yes" the outcome will be "Yes" if the first coin comes up tails (probability 1/2) or the first and second come up heads (probability 1/4)), while $\Pr[\text{Response} = \text{Yes}|\text{Truth} = \text{No}] = 1/4$ (first comes up heads and second comes up tails; probability 1/4). Applying similar reasoning to the case of a "No" answer, we obtain:

$$\frac{\Pr[\text{Response} = \text{Yes}|\text{Truth} = \text{Yes}]}{\Pr[\text{Response} = \text{Yes}|\text{Truth} = \text{No}]}$$

$$= \frac{3/4}{1/4} = \frac{\Pr[\text{Response} = \text{No}|\text{Truth} = \text{No}]}{\Pr[\text{Response} = \text{No}|\text{Truth} = \text{Yes}]} = 3.$$

$\square$

3.3 The laplace mechanism

Numeric queries, functions $f : \mathbb{N}^{|\mathcal{X}|} \to \mathbb{R}^k$, are one of the most fundamental types of database queries. These queries map databases to k

real numbers. One of the important parameters that will determine just how accurately we can answer such queries is their ℓ_1 sensitivity:

Definition 3.1 (ℓ_1-sensitivity). The ℓ_1-sensitivity of a function f : $\mathbb{N}^{|\mathcal{X}|} \to \mathbb{R}^k$ is:

$$\Delta f = \max_{\substack{x,y \in \mathbb{N}^{|\mathcal{X}|} \\ \|x-y\|_1 = 1}} \|f(x) - f(y)\|_1.$$

The ℓ_1 sensitivity of a function f captures the magnitude by which a single individual's data can change the function f in the worst case, and therefore, intuitively, the uncertainty in the response that we must introduce in order to hide the participation of a single individual. Indeed, we will formalize this intuition: the sensitivity of a function gives an upper bound on how much we must perturb its output to preserve privacy. One noise distribution naturally lends itself to differential privacy.

Definition 3.2 (The Laplace Distribution). The Laplace Distribution (centered at 0) with scale b is the distribution with probability density function:

$$\mathrm{Lap}(x|b) = \frac{1}{2b} \exp\left(-\frac{|x|}{b}\right).$$

The variance of this distribution is $\sigma^2 = 2b^2$. We will sometimes write $\mathrm{Lap}(b)$ to denote the Laplace distribution with scale b, and will sometimes abuse notation and write $\mathrm{Lap}(b)$ simply to denote a random variable $X \sim \mathrm{Lap}(b)$.

The Laplace distribution is a symmetric version of the exponential distribution.

We will now define the *Laplace Mechanism*. As its name suggests, the Laplace mechanism will simply compute f, and perturb each coordinate with noise drawn from the Laplace distribution. The scale of the noise will be calibrated to the sensitivity of f (divided by ε).[1]

---

[1]Alternately, using Gaussian noise with variance calibrated to $\Delta f \ln(1/\delta)/\varepsilon$, one can achieve (ε, δ)-differential privacy (see Appendix A). Use of the Laplace mechanism is cleaner and the two mechanisms behave similarly under composition (Theorem 3.20).

Definition 3.3 (The Laplace Mechanism). Given any function f : $\mathbb{N}^{|\mathcal{X}|} \to \mathbb{R}^k$, the Laplace mechanism is defined as:

$$\mathcal{M}_L(x, f(\cdot), \varepsilon) = f(x) + (Y_1, \ldots, Y_k)$$

where Y_i are i.i.d. random variables drawn from $\text{Lap}(\Delta f / \varepsilon)$.

Theorem 3.6. The Laplace mechanism preserves $(\varepsilon, 0)$-differential privacy.

Proof. Let $x \in \mathbb{N}^{|\mathcal{X}|}$ and $y \in \mathbb{N}^{|\mathcal{X}|}$ be such that $\|x - y\|_1 \le 1$, and let $f(\cdot)$ be some function $f : \mathbb{N}^{|\mathcal{X}|} \to \mathbb{R}^k$. Let p_x denote the probability density function of $\mathcal{M}_L(x, f, \varepsilon)$, and let p_y denote the probability density function of $\mathcal{M}_L(y, f, \varepsilon)$. We compare the two at some arbitrary point $z \in \mathbb{R}^k$

$$
\begin{aligned}
\frac{p_x(z)}{p_y(z)} &= \prod_{i=1}^{k} \left(\frac{\exp(-\frac{\varepsilon |f(x)_i - z_i|}{\Delta f})}{\exp(-\frac{\varepsilon |f(y)_i - z_i|}{\Delta f})} \right) \\
&= \prod_{i=1}^{k} \exp\left(\frac{\varepsilon(|f(y)_i - z_i| - |f(x)_i - z_i|)}{\Delta f} \right) \\
&\le \prod_{i=1}^{k} \exp\left(\frac{\varepsilon |f(x)_i - f(y)_i|}{\Delta f} \right) \\
&= \exp\left(\frac{\varepsilon \cdot \|f(x) - f(y)\|_1}{\Delta f} \right) \\
&\le \exp(\varepsilon),
\end{aligned}
$$

where the first inequality follows from the triangle inequality, and the last follows from the definition of sensitivity and the fact that $\|x - y\|_1 \le 1$. That $\frac{p_x(z)}{p_y(z)} \ge \exp(-\varepsilon)$ follows by symmetry. □

Example 3.1 (Counting Queries). Counting queries are queries of the form "How many elements in the database satisfy Property P?" We will return to these queries again and again, sometimes in this pure form, sometimes in fractional form ("What fraction of the elements in the databases...?"), sometimes with weights (linear queries), and sometimes in slightly more complex forms (e.g., apply $h : \mathbb{N}^{|\mathcal{X}|} \to [0, 1]$ to each element in the database and sum the results). Counting is an extremely powerful primitive. It captures everything learnable in the statistical queries learning model, as well as many standard datamining tasks and basic statistics. Since the sensitivity of a counting query is 1 (the addition or deletion of a single individual can change a count by at most 1), it is an immediate consequence of Theorem 3.6 that $(\varepsilon, 0)$-differential privacy can be achieved for counting queries by the addition of noise scaled to $1/\varepsilon$, that is, by adding noise drawn from $\mathrm{Lap}(1/\varepsilon)$. The expected distortion, or error, is $1/\varepsilon$, independent of the size of the database.

A fixed but arbitrary list of m counting queries can be viewed as a vector-valued query. Absent any further information about the set of queries a worst-case bound on the sensitivity of this vector-valued query is m, as a single individual might change every count. In this case $(\varepsilon, 0)$-differential privacy can be achieved by adding noise scaled to m/ε to the true answer to each query.

We sometimes refer to the problem of responding to large numbers of (possibly arbitrary) queries as the *query release problem*.

Example 3.2 (Histogram Queries). In the special (but common) case in which the queries are structurally disjoint we can do much better — we don't necessarily have to let the noise scale with the number of queries. An example is the *histogram query*. In this type of query the universe $\mathbb{N}^{|\mathcal{X}|}$ is partitioned into cells, and the query asks how many database elements lie in each of the cells. Because the cells are disjoint, the addition or removal of a single database element can affect the count in exactly one cell, and the difference to that cell is bounded by 1, so histogram queries have sensitivity 1 and can be answered by adding independent draws from $\mathrm{Lap}(1/\varepsilon)$ to the true count in each cell.

To understand the accuracy of the Laplace mechanism for general queries we use the following useful fact:

Fact 3.7. If $Y \sim \mathrm{Lap}(b)$, then:

$$\Pr[|Y| \geq t \cdot b] = \exp(-t).$$

This fact, together with a union bound, gives us a simple bound on the accuracy of the Laplace mechanism:

Theorem 3.8. Let $f : \mathbb{N}^{|\mathcal{X}|} \to \mathbb{R}^k$, and let $y = \mathcal{M}_L(x, f(\cdot), \varepsilon)$. Then $\forall \delta \in (0, 1]$:

$$\Pr\left[\|f(x) - y\|_\infty \geq \ln\left(\frac{k}{\delta}\right) \cdot \left(\frac{\Delta f}{\varepsilon}\right)\right] \leq \delta$$

Proof. We have:

$$\Pr\left[\|f(x) - y\|_\infty \geq \ln\left(\frac{k}{\delta}\right) \cdot \left(\frac{\Delta f}{\varepsilon}\right)\right] = \Pr\left[\max_{i \in [k]} |Y_i| \geq \ln\left(\frac{k}{\delta}\right) \cdot \left(\frac{\Delta f}{\varepsilon}\right)\right]$$

$$\leq k \cdot \Pr\left[|Y_i| \geq \ln\left(\frac{k}{\delta}\right) \cdot \left(\frac{\Delta f}{\varepsilon}\right)\right]$$

$$= k \cdot \left(\frac{\delta}{k}\right)$$

$$= \delta$$

where the second to last inequality follows from the fact that each $Y_i \sim \text{Lap}(\Delta f / \varepsilon)$ and Fact 3.7. $\square$

Example 3.3 (First Names). Suppose we wish to calculate which first names, from a list of 10,000 potential names, were the most common among participants of the 2010 census. This question can be represented as a query $f : \mathbb{N}^{|\mathcal{X}|} \to \mathbb{R}^{10000}$. This is a histogram query, and so has sensitivity $\Delta f = 1$, since every person can only have at most one first name. Using the above theorem, we see that we can simultaneously calculate the frequency of all $10,000$ names with $(1,0)$-differential privacy, and with probability 95%, no estimate will be off by more than an additive error of $ln(10000/.05) \approx 12.2$. That's pretty low error for a nation of more than $300,000,000$ people!

Differentially Private Selection. The task in Example 3.3 is one of *differentially private selection*: the space of outcomes is discrete and the task is to produce a "best" answer, in this case the most populous histogram cell.

Example 3.4 (Most Common Medical Condition). Suppose we wish to know which condition is (approximately) the most common in the medical histories of a set of respondents, so the set of questions is, for each condition under consideration, whether the individual has ever received a diagnosis of this condition. Since individuals can experience many conditions, the sensitivity of this set of questions can be high. Nonetheless, as we next describe, this task can be addressed using addition of $\text{Lap}(1/\varepsilon)$ noise to each of the counts (note the small scale of the noise, which is independent of the total number of conditions). Crucially, the m noisy counts themselves will *not* be released (although the "winning" count can be released at no extra privacy cost).

Report Noisy Max. Consider the following simple algorithm to determine which of m counting queries has the highest value: Add independently generated Laplace noise $\text{Lap}(1/\varepsilon)$ to each count and return the index of the largest noisy count (we ignore the possibility of a tie). Call this algorithm Report Noisy Max.

Note the "information minimization" principle at work in the Report Noisy Max algorithm: rather than releasing all the noisy counts and allowing the analyst to find the max and its index, only the index corresponding to the maximum is made public. Since the data of an individual can affect all counts, the vector of counts has high ℓ_1-sensitivity, specifically, $\Delta f = m$, and much more noise would be needed if we wanted to release all of the counts using the Laplace mechanism.

Claim 3.9. The Report Noisy Max algorithm is $(\varepsilon, 0)$-differentially private.

Proof. Fix $D = D' \cup \{a\}$. Let c, respectively c', denote the vector of counts when the database is D, respectively D'. We use two properties:

1. *Monotonicity of Counts.* For all $j \in [m]$, $c_j \geq c'_j$; and
2. *Lipschitz Property.* For all $j \in [m]$, $1 + c'_j \geq c_j$.

Fix any $i \in [m]$. We will bound from above and below the ratio of the probabilities that i is selected with D and with D'.

Fix r_{-i}, a draw from $[\text{Lap}(1/\varepsilon)]^{m-1}$ used for all the noisy counts except the ith count. We will argue for each r_{-i} independently. We use the notation $\Pr[i|\xi]$ to mean the probability that the output of the Report Noisy Max algorithm is i, conditioned on ξ.

We first argue that $\Pr[i|D, r_{-i}] \leq e^{\varepsilon} \Pr[i|D', r_{-i}]$. Define

$$r^* = \min_{r_i} : c_i + r_i > c_j + r_j \ \forall j \neq i.$$

Note that, having fixed r_{-i}, i will be the output (the argmax noisy count) when the database is D if and only if $r_i \geq r^*$.

We have, for all $1 \leq j \neq i \leq m$:

$$c_i + r^* > c_j + r_j$$
$$\Rightarrow (1 + c'_i) + r^* \geq c_i + r^* > c_j + r_j \geq c'_j + r_j$$
$$\Rightarrow c'_i + (r^* + 1) > c'_j + r_j.$$

Thus, if $r_i \geq r^* + 1$, then the ith count will be the maximum when the database is D' and the noise vector is (r_i, r_{-i}). The probabilities below are over the choice of $r_i \sim \text{Lap}(1/\varepsilon)$.

$$\Pr[r_i \geq 1 + r^*] \geq e^{-\varepsilon} \Pr[r_i \geq r^*] = e^{-\varepsilon} \Pr[i|D, r_{-i}]$$
$$\Rightarrow \Pr[i|D', r_{-i}] \geq \Pr[r_i \geq 1 + r^*] \geq e^{-\varepsilon} \Pr[r_i \geq r^*] = e^{-\varepsilon} \Pr[i|D, r_{-i}],$$

which, after multiplying through by e^{ε}, yields what we wanted to show: $\Pr[i|D, r_{-i}] \leq e^{\varepsilon} \Pr[i|D', r_{-i}]$.

We now argue that $\Pr[i|D', r_{-i}] \leq e^{\varepsilon} \Pr[i|D, r_{-i}]$. Define

$$r^* = \min_{r_i} : c'_i + r_i > c'_j + r_j \ \forall j \neq i.$$

Note that, having fixed r_{-i}, i will be the output (argmax noisy count) when the database is D' if and only if $r_i \geq r^*$.

We have, for all $1 \leq j \neq i \leq m$:

$$c'_i + r^* > c'_j + r_j$$
$$\Rightarrow 1 + c'_i + r^* > 1 + c'_j + r_j$$
$$\Rightarrow c'_i + (r^* + 1) > (1 + c'_j) + r_j$$
$$\Rightarrow c_i + (r^* + 1) \geq c'_i + (r^* + 1) > (1 + c'_j) + r_j \geq c_j + r_j.$$

Thus, if $r_i \geq r^* + 1$, then i will be the output (the argmax noisy count) on database D with randomness (r_i, r_{-i}). We therefore have, with probabilities taken over choice of r_i:

$$\Pr[i|D, r_{-i}] \geq \Pr[r_i \geq r^* + 1] \geq e^{-\varepsilon} \Pr[r_i \geq r^*] = e^{-\varepsilon} \Pr[i|D', r_{-i}],$$

which, after multiplying through by e^ε, yields what we wanted to show: $\Pr[i|D', r_{-i}] \leq e^\varepsilon \Pr[i|D, r_{-i}]$.   □

The proof is easiy extended to show that the release of the maximum noisy count, and not just its index, incurs no further loss of privacy.

3.4   The exponential mechanism

In both the "most common name" and "most common condition" examples the "utility" of a response (name or medical condition, respectively) we estimated counts using Laplace noise and reported the noisy maximum. In both examples the utility of the response is directly related to the noise values generated; that is, the popularity of the name or condition is appropriately measured on the same scale and in the same units as the magnitude of the noise.

The *exponential mechanism* was designed for situations in which we wish to choose the "best" response but adding noise directly to the computed quantity can completely destroy its value, such as setting a price in an auction, where the goal is to maximize revenue, and adding a small amount of positive noise to the optimal price (in order to protect the privacy of a bid) could dramatically reduce the resulting revenue.

Example 3.5 (Pumpkins.). Suppose we have an abundant supply of pumpkins and four bidders: A, F, I, K, where A, F, I each bid \$1.00 and K bids \$3.01. What is the optimal price? At \$3.01 the revenue is \$3.01, at \$3.00 and at \$1.00 the revenue is \$3.00, but at \$3.02 the revenue is zero!

The exponential mechanism is the natural building block for answering queries with arbitrary utilities (and arbitrary non-numeric range), while preserving differential privacy. Given some arbitrary range $\mathcal{R}$, the exponential mechanism is defined with respect to some utility function $u : \mathbb{N}^{|\mathcal{X}|} \times \mathcal{R} \to \mathbb{R}$, which maps database/output pairs to utility scores. Intuitively, for a fixed database x, the user prefers that the mechanism outputs some element of $\mathcal{R}$ with the maximum possible utility score. Note that when we talk about the sensitivity of the utility score $u : \mathbb{N}^{|\mathcal{X}|} \times \mathcal{R} \to \mathbb{R}$, we care only about the sensitivity of u with respect to its database argument; it can be arbitrarily sensitive in its range argument:

$$\Delta u \equiv \max_{r \in \mathcal{R}} \max_{x,y: \|x-y\|_1 \leq 1} |u(x,r) - u(y,r)|.$$

The intuition behind the exponential mechanism is to output each possible $r \in \mathcal{R}$ with probability proportional to $\exp(\varepsilon u(x,r)/\Delta u)$ and so the privacy loss is approximately:

$$\ln \left(\frac{\exp(\varepsilon u(x,r)/\Delta u)}{\exp(\varepsilon u(y,r)/\Delta u)} \right) = \varepsilon[u(x,r) - u(y,r)]/\Delta u) \leq \varepsilon.$$

This intuitive view overlooks some effects of a normalization term which arises when an additional person in the database causes the utilities of some elements $r \in \mathcal{R}$ to decrease and others to increase. The actual mechanism, defined next, reserves half the privacy budget for changes in the normalization term.

Definition 3.4 (The Exponential Mechanism). The exponential mechanism $\mathcal{M}_E(x, u, \mathcal{R})$ selects and outputs an element $r \in \mathcal{R}$ with probability proportional to $\exp(\frac{\varepsilon u(x,r)}{2\Delta u})$.

The exponential mechanism can define a complex distribution over a large arbitrary domain, and so it may not be possible to implement the exponential mechanism efficiently when the range of u is super-polynomially large in the natural parameters of the problem.

Returning to the pumpkin example, utility for a price p on database x is simply the profit obtained when the price is p and the demand curve is as described by x. It is important that the range of *potential* prices is independent of the actual bids. Otherwise there would exist a price with non-zero weight in one dataset and zero weight in a neighboring set, violating differential privacy.

Theorem 3.10. The exponential mechanism preserves $(\varepsilon, 0)$-differential privacy.

Proof. For clarity, we assume the range $\mathcal{R}$ of the exponential mechanism is finite, but this is not necessary. As in all differential privacy proofs, we consider the ratio of the probability that an instantiation of the exponential mechanism outputs some element $r \in \mathcal{R}$ on two neighboring databases $x \in \mathbb{N}^{|\mathcal{X}|}$ and $y \in \mathbb{N}^{|\mathcal{X}|}$ (i.e., $\|x - y\|_1 \leq 1$).

$$\frac{\Pr[\mathcal{M}_E(x, u, \mathcal{R}) = r]}{\Pr[\mathcal{M}_E(y, u, \mathcal{R}) = r]} = \frac{\left(\frac{\exp(\frac{\varepsilon u(x,r)}{2\Delta u})}{\sum_{r' \in \mathcal{R}} \exp(\frac{\varepsilon u(x,r')}{2\Delta u})}\right)}{\left(\frac{\exp(\frac{\varepsilon u(y,r)}{2\Delta u})}{\sum_{r' \in \mathcal{R}} \exp(\frac{\varepsilon u(y,r')}{2\Delta u})}\right)}$$

$$= \left(\frac{\exp(\frac{\varepsilon u(x,r)}{2\Delta u})}{\exp(\frac{\varepsilon u(y,r)}{2\Delta u})}\right) \cdot \left(\frac{\sum_{r' \in \mathcal{R}} \exp(\frac{\varepsilon u(y,r')}{2\Delta u})}{\sum_{r' \in \mathcal{R}} \exp(\frac{\varepsilon u(x,r')}{2\Delta u})}\right)$$

$$= \exp\left(\frac{\varepsilon(u(x,r') - u(y,r'))}{2\Delta u}\right)$$

$$\cdot \left(\frac{\sum_{r' \in \mathcal{R}} \exp(\frac{\varepsilon u(y,r')}{2\Delta u})}{\sum_{r' \in \mathcal{R}} \exp(\frac{\varepsilon u(x,r')}{2\Delta u})}\right)$$

$$\leq \exp\left(\frac{\varepsilon}{2}\right) \cdot \exp\left(\frac{\varepsilon}{2}\right) \cdot \left(\frac{\sum_{r' \in \mathcal{R}} \exp(\frac{\varepsilon u(x,r')}{2\Delta u})}{\sum_{r' \in \mathcal{R}} \exp(\frac{\varepsilon u(x,r')}{2\Delta u})}\right)$$

$$= \exp(\varepsilon).$$

Similarly, $\frac{\Pr[\mathcal{M}_E(y,u)=r]}{\Pr[\mathcal{M}_E(x,u)=r]} \geq \exp(-\varepsilon)$ by symmetry. $\square$

The exponential mechanism can often give strong utility guarantees, because it discounts outcomes exponentially quickly as their quality score falls off. For a given database x and a given utility measure $u :$ $\mathbb{N}^{|\mathcal{X}|} \times \mathcal{R} \to \mathbb{R}$, let $\text{OPT}_u(x) = \max_{r \in \mathcal{R}} u(x, r)$ denote the maximum utility score of any element $r \in \mathcal{R}$ with respect to database x. We will bound the probability that the exponential mechanism returns a "good" element of $\mathcal{R}$, where good will be measured in terms of $\text{OPT}_u(x)$. The result is that it will be highly unlikely that the returned element r has a utility score that is inferior to $\text{OPT}_u(x)$ by more than an additive factor of $O((\Delta u/\varepsilon) \log |\mathcal{R}|)$.

Theorem 3.11. Fixing a database x, let $\mathcal{R}_{\text{OPT}} = \{r \in \mathcal{R} : u(x, r) = \text{OPT}_u(x)\}$ denote the set of elements in $\mathcal{R}$ which attain utility score

$\mathrm{OPT}_u(x)$. Then:

$$\Pr\left[u(\mathcal{M}_E(x, u, \mathcal{R})) \leq \mathrm{OPT}_u(x) - \frac{2\Delta u}{\varepsilon}\left(\ln\left(\frac{|\mathcal{R}|}{|\mathcal{R}_{\mathrm{OPT}}|}\right) + t\right)\right] \leq e^{-t}$$

Proof.

$$\Pr[u(\mathcal{M}_E(x, u, \mathcal{R})) \leq c] \leq \frac{|\mathcal{R}|\exp(\varepsilon c/2\Delta u)}{|\mathcal{R}_{\mathrm{OPT}}|\exp(\varepsilon \mathrm{OPT}_u(x)/2\Delta u)}$$

$$= \frac{|\mathcal{R}|}{|\mathcal{R}_{\mathrm{OPT}}|}\exp\left(\frac{\varepsilon(c - \mathrm{OPT}_u(x))}{2\Delta u}\right).$$

The inequality follows from the observation that each $r \in \mathcal{R}$ with $u(x, r) \leq c$ has un-normalized probability mass at most $\exp(\varepsilon c/2\Delta u)$, and hence the entire set of such "bad" elements r has total un-normalized probability mass at most $|\mathcal{R}|\exp(\varepsilon c/2\Delta u)$. In contrast, we know that there exist at least $|\mathcal{R}_{\mathrm{OPT}}| \geq 1$ elements with $u(x, r) = \mathrm{OPT}_u(x)$, and hence un-normalized probability mass $\exp(\varepsilon \mathrm{OPT}_u(x)/2\Delta u)$, and so this is a lower bound on the normalization term.

The theorem follows from plugging in the appropriate value for c. □

Since we always have $|\mathcal{R}_{\mathrm{OPT}}| \geq 1$, we can more commonly make use of the following simple corollary:

Corollary 3.12. Fixing a database x, we have:

$$\Pr\left[u(\mathcal{M}_E(x, u, \mathcal{R})) \leq \mathrm{OPT}_u(x) - \frac{2\Delta u}{\varepsilon}\left(\ln\left(|\mathcal{R}|\right) + t\right)\right] \leq e^{-t}$$

As seen in the proofs of Theorem 3.11 and Corollary 3.12, the Exponential Mechanism can be particularly easy to analyze.

Example 3.6 (Best of Two). Consider the simple question of determining which of exactly two medical conditions A and B is more common. Let the two true counts be 0 for condition A and $c > 0$ for condition B. Our notion of utility will be tied to the actual counts, so that conditions with bigger counts have higher utility and $\Delta u = 1$. Thus, the utility of A is 0 and the utility of B is c. Using the Exponential Mechanism we can immediately apply Corollary 3.12 to see that the probability of observing (wrong) outcome A is at most $2e^{-c(\varepsilon/(2\Delta u))} = 2e^{-c\varepsilon/2}$.

Analyzing Report Noisy Max appears to be more complicated, as it requires understanding what happens in the (probability 1/4) case when the noise added to the count for A is positive and the noise added to the count for B is negative.

A function is *monotonic in the data set* if the addition of an element to the data set cannot cause the value of the function to decrease. Counting queries are monotonic; so is the revenue obtained by offering a fixed price to a collection of buyers.

Consider the *Report One-Sided Noisy Arg-Max* mechanism, which adds noise to the *utility* of each potential output drawn from the *one-sided* exponential distribution with parameter $\varepsilon/\Delta u$ in the case of a monotonic utility, or parameter $\varepsilon/2\Delta u$ for the case of a non-monotonic utility, and reports the resulting arg-max.

With this algorithm, whose privacy proof is almost identical to that of Report Noisy Max (but loses a factor of two when the utility is non-monotonic), we immediately obtain in Example 3.6 above that outcome A is exponentially in $c(\varepsilon/\Delta u) = c\varepsilon$ less likely to be selected than outcome B.

Theorem 3.13. Report One-Sided Noisy Arg-Max, when run with parameter $\varepsilon/2\Delta u$ yields the same distribution on outputs as the exponential mechanism.

Note that, in contrast to the case with Report Noisy Max, we *cannot* report the noisy utility value itself when we use Report One-Sided Noisy Arg-Max. To see this, suppose that in database x the count for medical condition B is c and in adjacent y the count is $c - 1$, and consider a small interval $I = [c - 1, c - 1 + \eta]$, for $\eta < 1$. Then on database x the probability of an outcome in I is zero, while on database y it is non-zero, a violation of $(\varepsilon, 0)$-differential privacy.

3.5 Composition theorems

Now that we have several building blocks for designing differentially private algorithms, it is important to understand how we can combine them to design more sophisticated algorithms. In order to use these tools, we would like that the combination of two differentially private algorithms be differentially private itself. Indeed, as we will see, this is the case. Of course the parameters ε and δ will necessarily degrade — consider repeatedly computing the same statistic using the Laplace mechanism, scaled to give ε-differential privacy each time. The average of the answer given by each instance of the mechanism will eventually converge to the true value of the statistic, and so we cannot avoid that the strength of our privacy guarantee will degrade with repeated use. In this section we give theorems showing how exactly the parameters ε and δ compose when differentially private subroutines are combined.

Let us first begin with an easy warm up: we will see that the independent use of an $(\varepsilon_1, 0)$-differentially private algorithm and an $(\varepsilon_2, 0)$-differentially private algorithm, when taken together, is $(\varepsilon_1 + \varepsilon_2, 0)$-differentially private.

Theorem 3.14. Let $\mathcal{M}_1 : \mathbb{N}^{|\mathcal{X}|} \to \mathcal{R}_1$ be an ε_1-differentially private algorithm, and let $\mathcal{M}_2 : \mathbb{N}^{|\mathcal{X}|} \to \mathcal{R}_2$ be an ε_2-differentially private algorithm. Then their combination, defined to be $\mathcal{M}_{1,2} : \mathbb{N}^{|\mathcal{X}|} \to \mathcal{R}_1 \times \mathcal{R}_2$ by the mapping: $\mathcal{M}_{1,2}(x) = (\mathcal{M}_1(x), \mathcal{M}_2(x))$ is $\varepsilon_1 + \varepsilon_2$-differentially private.

Proof. Let $x, y \in \mathbb{N}^{|\mathcal{X}|}$ be such that $\|x - y\|_1 \leq 1$. Fix any $(r_1, r_2) \in \mathcal{R}_1 \times \mathcal{R}_2$. Then:

$$\frac{\Pr[\mathcal{M}_{1,2}(x) = (r_1, r_2)]}{\Pr[\mathcal{M}_{1,2}(y) = (r_1, r_2)]} = \frac{\Pr[\mathcal{M}_1(x) = r_1]\Pr[\mathcal{M}_2(x) = r_2]}{\Pr[\mathcal{M}_1(y) = r_1]\Pr[\mathcal{M}_2(y) = r_2]}$$

$$= \left(\frac{\Pr[\mathcal{M}_1(x) = r_1]}{\Pr[\mathcal{M}_1(y) = r_1]}\right)\left(\frac{\Pr[\mathcal{M}_2(x) = r_1]}{\Pr[\mathcal{M}_2(y) = r_1]}\right)$$

$$\leq \exp(\varepsilon_1)\exp(\varepsilon_2)$$

$$= \exp(\varepsilon_1 + \varepsilon_2)$$

By symmetry, $\frac{\Pr[\mathcal{M}_{1,2}(x)=(r_1,r_2)]}{\Pr[\mathcal{M}_{1,2}(y)=(r_1,r_2)]} \geq \exp(-(\varepsilon_1 + \varepsilon_2))$. $\square$

The composition theorem can be applied repeatedly to obtain the following corollary:

Corollary 3.15. Let $\mathcal{M}_i : \mathbb{N}^{|\mathcal{X}|} \to \mathcal{R}_i$ be an $(\varepsilon_i, 0)$-differentially private algorithm for $i \in [k]$. Then if $\mathcal{M}_{[k]} : \mathbb{N}^{|\mathcal{X}|} \to \prod_{i=1}^k \mathcal{R}_i$ is defined to be $\mathcal{M}_{[k]}(x) = (\mathcal{M}_1(x), \ldots, \mathcal{M}_k(x))$, then $\mathcal{M}_{[k]}$ is $(\sum_{i=1}^k \varepsilon_i, 0)$-differentially private.

A proof of the generalization of this theorem to (ε, δ)-differential privacy appears in Appendix B:

Theorem 3.16. Let $\mathcal{M}_i : \mathbb{N}^{|\mathcal{X}|} \to \mathcal{R}_i$ be an $(\varepsilon_i, \delta_i)$-differentially private algorithm for $i \in [k]$. Then if $\mathcal{M}_{[k]} : \mathbb{N}^{|\mathcal{X}|} \to \prod_{i=1}^k \mathcal{R}_i$ is defined to be $\mathcal{M}_{[k]}(x) = (\mathcal{M}_1(x), \ldots, \mathcal{M}_k(x))$, then $\mathcal{M}_{[k]}$ is $(\sum_{i=1}^k \varepsilon_i, \sum_{i=1}^k \delta_i)$-differentially private.

It is a strength of differential privacy that composition is "automatic," in that the bounds obtained hold without any special effort by the database curator.

3.5.1   Composition: some technicalities

In the remainder of this section, we will prove a more sophisticated composition theorem. To this end, we will need some definitions and lemmas, rephrasing differential privacy in terms of distance measures between distributions. In the fractional quantities below, if the denominator is zero, then we define the value of the fraction to be infinite (the numerators will always be positive).

Definition 3.5 (KL-Divergence). The KL-Divergence, or Relative Entropy, between two random variables Y and Z taking values from the same domain is defined to be:

$$D(Y\|Z) = \mathbb{E}_{y \sim Y} \left[\ln \frac{\Pr[Y = y]}{\Pr[Z = y]} \right].$$

It is known that $D(Y\|Z) \geq 0$, with equality if and only if Y and Z are identically distributed. However, D is not symmetric, does not satisfy the triangle inequality, and can even be infinite, specifically when $\mathrm{Supp}(Y)$ is not contained in $\mathrm{Supp}(Z)$.

Definition 3.6 (Max Divergence). The Max Divergence between two random variables Y and Z taking values from the same domain is defined to be:

$$D_\infty(Y\|Z) = \max_{S\subseteq\text{Supp}(Y)} \left[\ln \frac{\Pr[Y \in S]}{\Pr[Z \in S]}\right].$$

The δ-Approximate Max Divergence between Y and Z is defined to be:

$$D_\infty^\delta(Y\|Z) = \max_{S\subseteq\text{Supp}(Y):\Pr[Y\in S]\geq\delta} \left[\ln \frac{\Pr[Y \in S] - \delta}{\Pr[Z \in S]}\right]$$

Remark 3.1. Note that a mechanism $\mathcal{M}$ is

1. ε-differentially private if and only if on every two neighboring databases x and y, $D_\infty(\mathcal{M}(x)\|\mathcal{M}(y)) \leq \varepsilon$ and $D_\infty(\mathcal{M}(y)\|\mathcal{M}(x)) \leq \varepsilon$; and is

2. (ε, δ)-differentially private if and only if on every two neighboring databases x, y: $D_\infty^\delta(\mathcal{M}(x)\|\mathcal{M}(y)) \leq \varepsilon$ and $D_\infty^\delta(\mathcal{M}(y)\| \mathcal{M}(x)) \leq \varepsilon$.

One other distance measure that will be useful is the *statistical distance* between two random variables Y and Z, defined as

$$\Delta(Y, Z) \stackrel{\text{def}}{=} \max_S |\Pr[Y \in S] - \Pr[Z \in S]|.$$

We say that Y and Z are δ-*close* if $\Delta(Y, Z) \leq \delta$.

We will use the following reformulations of approximate maxdivergence in terms of exact max-divergence and statistical distance:

Lemma 3.17.

1. $D_\infty^\delta(Y\|Z) \leq \varepsilon$ if and only if there exists a random variable Y' such that $\Delta(Y, Y') \leq \delta$ and $D_\infty(Y'\|Z) \leq \varepsilon$.

2. We have both $D_\infty^\delta(Y\|Z) \leq \varepsilon$ and $D_\infty^\delta(Z\|Y) \leq \varepsilon$ if and only if there exist random variables Y', Z' such that $\Delta(Y, Y') \leq \delta/(e^\varepsilon + 1)$, $\Delta(Z, Z') \leq \delta/(e^\varepsilon + 1)$, and $D_\infty(Y'\|Z') \leq \varepsilon$.

Proof. For Part 1, suppose there exists Y' δ-close to Y such that $D_\infty(Y\|Z) \leq \varepsilon$. Then for every S,

$$\Pr[Y \in S] \leq \Pr[Y' \in S] + \delta \leq e^\varepsilon \cdot \Pr[Z \in S] + \delta,$$

and thus $D_\infty^\delta(Y\|Z) \leq \varepsilon$.

Conversely, suppose that $D_\infty^\delta(Y\|Z) \le \varepsilon$. Let $S = \{y : \Pr[Y = y] > e^\varepsilon \cdot \Pr[Z = y]\}$. Then

$$\sum_{y \in S} (\Pr[Y = y] - e^\varepsilon \cdot \Pr[Z = y]) = \Pr[Y \in S] - e^\varepsilon \cdot \Pr[Z \in S] \le \delta.$$

Moreover, if we let $T = \{y : \Pr[Y = y] < \Pr[Z = y]\}$, then we have

$$\begin{aligned}
\sum_{y \in T} (\Pr[Z = y] - \Pr[Y = y]) &= \sum_{y \notin T} (\Pr[Y = y] - \Pr[Z = y]) \\
&\ge \sum_{y \in S} (\Pr[Y = y] - \Pr[Z = y]) \\
&\ge \sum_{y \in S} (\Pr[Y = y] - e^\varepsilon \cdot \Pr[Z = y])/
\end{aligned}$$

Thus, we can obtain Y' from Y by lowering the probabilities on S and raising the probabilities on T to satisfy:

1. For all $y \in S$, $\Pr[Y' = y] = e^\varepsilon \cdot \Pr[Z = y] < \Pr[Y = y]$.
2. For all $y \in T$, $\Pr[Y = y] \le \Pr[Y' = y] \le \Pr[Z = y]$.
3. For all $y \notin S \cup T$, $\Pr[Y' = y] = \Pr[Y = y] \le e^\varepsilon \cdot \Pr[Z = y]$.

Then $D_\infty(Y'\|Z) \le \varepsilon$ by inspection, and

$$\Delta(Y, Y') = \Pr[Y \in S] - \Pr[Y' \in S] = \Pr[Y \in S] - e^\varepsilon \cdot \Pr[Z \in S] \le \delta.$$

We now prove Part 2. Suppose there exist random variables Y' and Z' as stated. Then, for every set S,

$$\begin{aligned}
\Pr[Y \in S] &\le \Pr[Y' \in S] + \frac{\delta}{e^\varepsilon + 1} \\
&\le e^\varepsilon \cdot \Pr[Z' \in S] + \frac{\delta}{e^\varepsilon + 1} \\
&\le e^\varepsilon \cdot \left(\Pr[Z \in S] + \frac{\delta}{e^\varepsilon + 1}\right) + \frac{\delta}{e^\varepsilon + 1} \\
&= e^\varepsilon \cdot \Pr[Z \in S] + \delta.
\end{aligned}$$

Thus $D_\infty^\delta(Y\|Z) \le \varepsilon$, and by symmetry, $D_\infty^\delta(Z\|Y) \le \varepsilon$.

Conversely, given Y and Z such that $D_\infty^\delta(Y\|Z) \le \varepsilon$ and $D_\infty^\delta(Z\|Y) \le \varepsilon$, we proceed similarly to Part 1. However, instead of simply decreasing the probability mass of Y on S to obtain Y' and eliminate the gap with $e^\varepsilon \cdot Z$, we also increase the probability mass of Z on S. Specifically, for every $y \in S$, we'll take

$$\Pr[Y' = y] = e^\varepsilon \cdot \Pr[Z' = y]$$

$$= \frac{e^\varepsilon}{1 + e^\varepsilon} \cdot (\Pr[Y = y] + \Pr[Z = y])$$

$$\in [e^\varepsilon \cdot \Pr[Z = y], \Pr[Y = y]].$$

This also implies that for $y \in S$, we have:

$$\Pr[Y = y] - \Pr[Y' = y]$$

$$= \Pr[Z' = y] - \Pr[Z = y] \frac{\Pr[Y = y] - e^\varepsilon \cdot \Pr[Z = y]}{e^\varepsilon + 1},$$

and thus

$$\alpha \stackrel{\text{def}}{=} \sum_{y \in S} (\Pr[Y = y] - \Pr[Y' = y])$$

$$= \sum_{y \in S} (\Pr[Z' = y] - \Pr[Z = y])$$

$$= \frac{\Pr[Y \in S] - e^\varepsilon \cdot \Pr[Z \in S]}{e^\varepsilon + 1}$$

$$\leq \frac{\delta}{e^\varepsilon + 1}.$$

Similarly on the set $S' = \{y : \Pr[Z = y] > e^\varepsilon \cdot \Pr[Y = y]\}$, we can decrease the probability mass of Z and increase the probability mass of Y by a total of some $\alpha' \leq \delta/(e^\varepsilon + 1)$ so that for every $y \in S'$, we have $\Pr[Z' = y] = e^\varepsilon \cdot \Pr[Y' = y]$.

If $\alpha = \alpha'$, then we can take $\Pr[Z' = y] = \Pr[Z = y]$ and $\Pr[Y' = y] = \Pr[Y = y]$ for all $y \notin S \cup S'$, giving $D_\infty(Y\|Z) \leq \varepsilon$ and $\Delta(Y, Y') = \Delta(Z, Z') = \alpha$. If $\alpha \neq \alpha'$, say $\alpha > \alpha'$, then we need to still increase the probability mass of Y' and decrease the mass of Z' by a total of $\beta = \alpha - \alpha'$ on points outside of $S \cup S'$ in order to ensure that the probabilities sum to 1. That is, if we try to take the "mass functions" $\Pr[Y' = y]$ and $\Pr[Z' = y]$ as defined above, then while we do have the property that for every y, $\Pr[Y' = y] \leq e^\varepsilon \cdot \Pr[Z' = y]$ and $\Pr[Z' = y] \leq e^\varepsilon \cdot \Pr[Y' = y]$ we also have $\sum_y \Pr[Y' = y] = 1 - \beta$

and $\sum_y \Pr[Z' = y] = 1 + \beta$. However, this means that if we let $R = \{y : \Pr[Y' = y] < \Pr[Z' = y]\}$, then

$$\sum_{y \in R} (\Pr[Z' = y] - \Pr[Y' = y]) \geq \sum_y (\Pr[Z' = y] - \Pr[Y' = y]) = 2\beta.$$

So we can increase the probability mass of Y' on points in R by a total of β and decrease the probability mass of Z' on points in R by a total of β, while retaining the property that for all $y \in R$, $\Pr[Y' = y] \leq \Pr[Z' = y]$. The resulting Y' and Z' have the properties we want: $D_\infty(Y', Z') \leq \varepsilon$ and $\Delta(Y, Y'), \Delta(Z, Z') \leq \alpha$. □

Lemma 3.18. Suppose that random variables Y and Z satisfy $D_\infty(Y \| Z) \leq \varepsilon$ and $D_\infty(Z \| Y) \leq \varepsilon$. Then $D(Y \| Z) \leq \varepsilon \cdot (e^\varepsilon - 1)$.

Proof. We know that for any Y and Z it is the case that $D(Y \| Z) \geq 0$ (via the "log-sum inequality"), and so it suffices to bound $D(Y \| Z) + D(Z \| Y)$. We get:

$$D(Y \| Z) \leq D(Y \| Z) + D(Z \| Y)$$
$$= \sum_y \Pr[Y = y] \cdot \left(\ln \frac{\Pr[Y = y]}{\Pr[Z = y]} + \ln \frac{\Pr[Z = y]}{\Pr[Y = y]} \right)$$
$$+ (\Pr[Z = y] - \Pr[Y = y]) \cdot \left(\ln \frac{\Pr[Z = y]}{\Pr[Y = y]} \right)$$
$$\leq \sum_y [0 + |\Pr[Z = y] - \Pr[Y = y]| \cdot \varepsilon]$$
$$= \varepsilon \cdot \sum_y [\max\{\Pr[Y = y], \Pr[Z = y]\}$$
$$- \min\{\Pr[Y = y], \Pr[Z = y]\}]$$
$$\leq \varepsilon \cdot \sum_y [(e^\varepsilon - 1) \cdot \min\{\Pr[Y = y], \Pr[Z = y]\}]$$
$$\leq \varepsilon \cdot (e^\varepsilon - 1).$$ □

Lemma 3.19 (Azuma's Inequality). Let $C_1, \ldots, C_k$ be real-valued random variables such that for every $i \in [k]$, $\Pr[|C_i| \leq \alpha] = 1$, and for every $(c_1, \ldots, c_{i-1}) \in \mathrm{Supp}(C_1, \ldots, C_{i-1})$, we have

$$\mathbb{E}[C_i | C_1 = c_1, \ldots, C_{i-1} = c_{i-1}] \leq \beta.$$

Then for every $z > 0$, we have

$$\Pr\left[\sum_{i=1}^{k} C_i > k\beta + z\sqrt{k} \cdot \alpha\right] \leq e^{-z^2/2}.$$

3.5.2 Advanced composition

In addition to allowing the parameters to degrade more slowly, we would like our theorem to be able to handle more complicated forms of composition. However, before we begin, we must discuss what exactly we mean by composition. We would like our definitions to cover the following two interesting scenarios:

1. Repeated use of differentially private algorithms on the same database. This allows both the repeated use of the same mechanism multiple times, as well as the modular construction of differentially private algorithms from arbitrary private building blocks.

2. Repeated use of differentially private algorithms on *different* databases that may nevertheless contain information relating to the same individual. This allows us to reason about the cumulative privacy loss of a single individual whose data might be spread across multiple data sets, each of which may be used independently in a differentially private way. Since new databases are created all the time, and the adversary may actually influence the makeup of these new databases, this is a fundamentally different problem than repeatedly querying a single, fixed, database.

We want to model composition where the adversary can adaptively affect the databases being input to future mechanisms, as well as the queries to those mechanisms. Let $\mathcal{F}$ be a family of database access mechanisms. (For example $\mathcal{F}$ could be the set of all ε-differentially private mechanisms.) For a probabilistic adversary A, we consider two experiments, Experiment 0 and Experiment 1, defined as follows.

Experiment b for family $\mathcal{F}$ and adversary A:

For $i = 1, \ldots, k$:

1. A outputs two adjacent databases x_i^0 and x_i^1, a mechanism $\mathcal{M}_i \in \mathcal{F}$, and parameters w_i.
2. A receives $y_i \in_R \mathcal{M}_i(w_i, x_{i,b})$.

We allow the adversary A above to be stateful throughout the experiment, and thus it may choose the databases, mechanisms, and the parameters adaptively depending on the outputs of previous mechanisms. We define A's *view* of the experiment to be A's coin tosses and all of the mechanism outputs $(y_1, \ldots, y_k)$. (The x_i^j's, $\mathcal{M}_i$'s, and w_i's can all be reconstructed from these.)

For intuition, consider an adversary who always chooses x_i^0 to hold Bob's data and x_i^1 to differ only in that Bob's data are deleted. Then experiment 0 can be thought of as the "real world," where Bob allows his data to be used in many data releases, and Experiment 1 as an "ideal world," where the outcomes of these data releases do not depend on Bob's data. Our definitions of privacy still require these two experiments to be "close" to each other, in the same way as required by the definitions of differential privacy. The intuitive guarantee to Bob is that the adversary "can't tell", given the output of all k mechanisms, whether Bob's data was ever used.

Definition 3.7. We say that the family $\mathcal{F}$ of database access mechanisms satisfies ε-*differential privacy under k-fold adaptive composition* if for every adversary A, we have $D_\infty(V^0 \| V^1) \le \varepsilon$ where V^b denotes the view of A in k-fold Composition Experiment b above.

(ε, δ)-*differential privacy under k-fold adaptive composition* instead requires that $D_\infty^\delta(V^0 \| V^1) \le \varepsilon$.

Theorem 3.20 (Advanced Composition). For all $\varepsilon, \delta, \delta' \ge 0$, the class of (ε, δ)-differentially private mechanisms satisfies $(\varepsilon', k\delta + \delta')$-differential privacy under k-fold adaptive composition for:

$$\varepsilon' = \sqrt{2k \ln(1/\delta')}\varepsilon + k\varepsilon(e^\varepsilon - 1).$$

Proof. A view of the adversary A consists of a tuple of the form $v = (r, y_1, \ldots, y_k)$, where r is the coin tosses of A and $y_1, \ldots, y_k$ are the outputs of the mechanisms $\mathcal{M}_1, \ldots, \mathcal{M}_k$. Let

$$B = \{v : \Pr[V^0 = v] > e^{\varepsilon'} \cdot \Pr[V^1 = v]\}.$$

We will show that $\Pr[V^0 \in B] \le \delta$, and hence for every set S, we have

$$\Pr[V^0 \in S] \le \Pr[V^0 \in B] + \Pr[V^0 \in (S \setminus B)] \le \delta + e^{\varepsilon'} \cdot \Pr[V^1 \in S].$$

This is equivalent to saying that $D_\infty^\delta(V^0 \| V^1) \le \varepsilon'$.

It remains to show $\Pr[V^0 \in B] \le \delta$. Let random variable $V^0 = (R^0, Y_1^0, \ldots, Y_k^0)$ denote the view of A in Experiment 0 and $V^1 = (R^1, Y_1^1, \ldots, Y_k^1)$ the view of A in Experiment 1. Then for a fixed view $v = (r, y_1, \ldots, y_k)$, we have

$$
\begin{aligned}
&\ln\left(\frac{\Pr[V^0 = v]}{\Pr[V^1 = v]}\right) \\
&= \ln\left(\frac{\Pr[R^0 = r]}{\Pr[R^1 = r]} \cdot \prod_{i=1}^k \frac{\Pr[Y_i^0 = y_i | R^0 = r, Y_1^0 = y_1, \ldots, Y_{i-1}^0 = y_{i-1}]}{\Pr[Y_i^1 = y_i | R^1 = r, Y_1^1 = y_1, \ldots, Y_{i-1}^1 = y_{i-1}]}\right) \\
&= \sum_{i=1}^k \ln\left(\frac{\Pr[Y_i^0 = y_i | R^0 = r, Y_1^0 = y_1, \ldots, Y_{i-1}^0 = y_{i-1}]}{\Pr[Y_i^1 = y_i | R^1 = r, Y_1^1 = y_1, \ldots, Y_{i-1}^1 = y_{i-1}]}\right) \\
&\overset{\text{def}}{=} \sum_{i=1}^k c_i(r, y_1, \ldots, y_i).
\end{aligned}
$$

Now for every prefix $(r, y_1, \ldots, y_{i-1})$ we condition on $R^0 = r$, $Y_1^0 = y_1, \ldots, Y_{i-1}^0 = y_{i-1}$, and analyze the expectation and maximum possible value of the random variable $c_i(R^0, Y_1^0, \ldots, Y_i^0) = c_i(r, y_1, \ldots, y_{i-1}, Y_i^0)$. Once the prefix is fixed, the next pair of databases x_i^0 and x_i^1, the mechanism $\mathcal{M}_i$, and parameter w_i output by A are also determined (in both Experiment 0 and 1). Thus Y_i^0 is distributed according to $\mathcal{M}_i(w_i, x_i^0)$. Moreover for any value y_i, we have

$$c_i(r, y_1, \ldots, y_{i-1}, y_i) = \ln\left(\frac{\Pr[\mathcal{M}_i(w_i, x_i^0) = y_i]}{\Pr[\mathcal{M}_i(w_i, x_i^1) = y_i]}\right).$$

By ε-differential privacy this is bounded by ε. We can also reason as follows:

$$|c_i(r, y_1, \ldots, y_{i-1}, y_i)|$$
$$\leq \max\{D_\infty(\mathcal{M}_i(w_i, x_i^0)\|\mathcal{M}_i(w_i, x_i^1)),$$
$$D_\infty(\mathcal{M}_i(w_i, x_i^1)\|\mathcal{M}_i(w_i, x_i^0))\}$$
$$= \varepsilon.$$

By Lemma 3.18, we have:

$$\mathbb{E}[c_i(R^0, Y_1^0, \ldots, Y_i^0)|R^0 = r, Y_1^0 = y_1, \ldots, Y_{i-1}^0 = y_{i-1}]$$
$$= D(\mathcal{M}_i(w_i, x_i^0)\|\mathcal{M}_i(w_i, x_i^1))$$
$$\leq \varepsilon(e^\varepsilon - 1).$$

Thus we can apply Azuma's Inequality to the random variables $C_i = c_i(R^0, Y_1^0, \ldots, Y_i^0)$ with $\alpha = \varepsilon$, $\beta = \varepsilon \cdot \varepsilon_0$, and $z = \sqrt{2\ln(1/\delta)}$, to deduce that

$$\Pr[V^0 \in B] = \Pr\left[\sum_i C_i > \varepsilon'\right] < e^{-z^2/2} = \delta,$$

as desired.

To extend the proof to composition of (ε, δ)-differentially private mechanisms, for $\delta > 0$, we use the characterization of approximate max-divergence from Lemma 3.17 (Part 2) to reduce the analysis to the same situation as in the case of $(\varepsilon, 0)$-indistinguishable sequences. Specifically, using Lemma 3.17, Part 2 for each of the differentially private mechanisms selected by the adversary A and the triangle inequality for statistical distance, it follows that that V^0 is $k\delta$-close to a random variable $W = (R, Z_1, \ldots, Z_k)$ such that for every prefix $r, y_1, \ldots, y_{i-1}$, if we condition on $R = R^1 = r, Z_1 = Y_1^1 = y_1, \ldots, Z_{i-1} = Y_{i-1}^1 = y_{i-1}$, then it holds that $D_\infty(Z_i\|Y_i^1) \leq \varepsilon$ and $D_\infty(Y_i^1\|Z_i) \leq \varepsilon$.

This suffices to show that $D_\infty^{\delta'}(W\|V^1) \leq \varepsilon'$. Since V^0 is $k\delta$-close to W, Lemma 3.17, Part 1 gives $D_\infty^{\delta'+k\delta}(V^0\|W) \leq \varepsilon'$. $\square$

An immediate and useful corollary tells us a safe choice of ε for each of k mechanisms if we wish to ensure $(\varepsilon', k\delta + \delta')$-differential privacy for a given ε', δ'.

Corollary 3.21. Given target privacy parameters $0 < \varepsilon' < 1$ and $\delta' > 0$, to ensure $(\varepsilon', k\delta + \delta')$ cumulative privacy loss over k mechanisms, it suffices that each mechanism is (ε, δ)-differentially private, where

$$\varepsilon = \frac{\varepsilon'}{2\sqrt{2k \ln(1/\delta')}}.$$

Proof. Theorem 3.20 tells us the composition will be $(\varepsilon^*, k\delta + \delta')$ for all δ', where $\varepsilon^* = \sqrt{2k \ln(1/\delta')} \cdot \varepsilon + k\varepsilon^2$. When $\varepsilon' < 1$, we have that $\varepsilon^* \leq \varepsilon'$ as desired. □

Note that the above corollary gives a rough guide for how to set ε to get desired privacy parameters under composition. When one cares about optimizing constants (which one does when dealing with actual implementations), ε can be set more tightly by appealing directly to the composition theorem.

Example 3.7. Suppose, over the course of his lifetime, Bob is a member of $k = 10,000$ $(\varepsilon_0, 0)$-differentially private databases. Assuming no coordination among these databases — the administrator of any given database may not even be aware of the existence of the other databases — what should be the value of ε_0 so that, over the course of his lifetime, Bob's cumulative privacy loss is bounded by $\varepsilon = 1$ with probability at least $1 - e^{-32}$? Theorem 3.20 says that, taking $\delta' = e^{-32}$ it suffices to have $\varepsilon_0 \leq 1/801$. This turns out to be essentially optimal against an arbitrary adversary, assuming no coordination among distinct differentially private databases.

So how many queries can we answer with non-trivial accuracy? On a database of size n let us say the accuracy is non-trivial if the error is of order $o(n)$. Theorem 3.20 says that for fixed values of ε and δ, it is possible to answer close to n^2 counting queries with non-trivial accuracy. Similarly, one can answer close to n queries while still having noise $o(\sqrt{n})$ — that is, noise less than the sampling error. We will see that it is possible to dramatically improve on these results, handling, in some cases, even an exponential number of queries with noise only slightly larger than $\sqrt{n}$, by coordinating the noise added to the individual responses. It turns out that such coordination is essential: without coordination the bound in the advanced composition theorem is almost tight.

3.5.3 Laplace versus Gauss

An alternative to adding Laplacian noise is to add Gaussian noise. In this case, rather than scaling the noise to the ℓ_1 sensitivity Δf, we instead scale to the ℓ_2 sensitivity:

Definition 3.8 (ℓ_2-sensitivity). The ℓ_2-sensitivity of a function $f : \mathbb{N}^{|\mathcal{X}|} \to \mathbb{R}^k$ is:

$$\Delta_2(f) = \max_{\substack{x,y \in \mathbb{N}^{|\mathcal{X}|} \\ \|x-y\|_1=1}} \|f(x) - f(y)\|_2.$$

The *Gaussian Mechanism* with parameter b adds zero-mean Gaussian noise with variance b in each of the k coordinates. The following theorem is proved in Appendix A.

Theorem 3.22. Let $\varepsilon \in (0,1)$ be arbitrary. For $c^2 > 2\ln(1.25/\delta)$, the Gaussian Mechanism with parameter $\sigma \geq c\Delta_2(f)/\varepsilon$ is (ε, δ)-differentially private.

Among the advantages to Gaussian noise is that the noise added for privacy is of the same type as other sources of noise; moreover, the sum of two Gaussians is a Gaussian, so the effects of the privacy mechanism on the statistical analysis may be easier to understand and correct for.

The two mechanisms yield the same cumulative loss under composition, so even though the privacy guarantee is weaker for each individual computation, the cumulative effects over many computations are comparable. Also, if δ is sufficiently (e.g., subpolynomially) small, in practice we will never experience the weakness of the guarantee.

That said, there is a theoretical disadvantage to Gaussian noise, relative to what we experience with Laplace noise. Consider Report Noisy Max (with Laplace noise) in a case in which every candidate output has the same quality score on database x as on its neighbor y. Independent of the number of candidate outputs, the mechanism yields $(\varepsilon, 0)$-differential privacy. If instead we use Gaussian noise and report the max, and if the number of candidates is large compared to $1/\delta$, then we will exactly select for the events with large Gaussian noise — noise that occurs with probability less than δ. When we are this far out on the tail of the Gaussian we no longer have a guarantee that the observation is within an $e^{\pm\varepsilon}$ factor as likely to occur on x as on y.

3.5.4 Remarks on composition

The ability to analyze cumulative privacy loss under composition gives us a handle on what a world of differentially private databases can offer. A few observations are in order.

Weak Quantification. Assume that the adversary always chooses x_i^0 to hold Bob's data, and x_i^1 to be the same database but with Bob's data deleted. Theorem 3.20, with appropriate choise of parameters, tells us that an adversary — including one that knows or even selects(!) the database pairs — has little advantage in determining the value of $b \in \{0, 1\}$. This is an inherently weak quantification. We can ensure that the adversary is unlikely to distinguish reality from any given alternative, but we cannot ensure this simultaneously for all alternatives. If there are one zillion databases but Bob is a member of only 10,000 of these, then we are not simultaneously protecting Bob's *absence* from all zillion minus ten thousand. This is analogous to the quantification in the definition of (ε, δ)-differential privacy, where we fix in advance a pair of adjacent databases and argue that with high probability the output will be almost equally likely with these two databases.

Humans and Ghosts. Intuitively, an $(\epsilon, 0)$-differentially private database with a small number of bits per record is less protective than a differentially private database with the same choice of ϵ that contains our entire medical histories. So in what sense is our principle privacy measure, ϵ, telling us the same thing about databases that differ radically in the complexity and sensitivity of the data they store? The answer lies in the composition theorems. Imagine a world inhabited by two types of beings: ghosts and humans. Both types of beings behave the same, interact with others in the same way, write, study, work, laugh, love, cry, reproduce, become ill, recover, and age in the same fashion. The only difference is that ghosts have no records in databases, while humans do. The goal of the privacy adversary is to determine whether a given 50-year old, the "target," is a ghost or a human. Indeed, the adversary is given all 50 years to do so. The adversary does not need to remain passive, for example, she can organize clinical trials and enroll patients of her choice, she can create humans to populate databases, effectively creating the worst-case (for privacy) databases, she can expose the target to chemicals at age 25 and again at 35, and so on. She can know everything about the target that could possibly be entered into any database. She can know which databases the target would be in, were the target human. The composition theorems tell us that the privacy guarantees of each database — regardless of the data type, complexity, and sensitivity — give comparable protection for the human/ghost bit.

3.6 The sparse vector technique

The Laplace mechanism can be used to answer adaptively chosen low sensitivity queries, and we know from our composition theorems that the privacy parameter degrades proportionally to the number of queries answered (or its square root). Unfortunately, it will often happen that we have a very large number of questions to answer — too many to yield a reasonable privacy guarantee using independent perturbation techniques, even with the advanced composition theorems of Section 3.5. In some situations however, we will only care to know the identity of the queries that lie above a certain threshold. In this case, we can hope to gain over the naïve analysis by discarding the numeric answer to queries that lie significantly below the threshold, and merely reporting that they do indeed lie below the threshold. (We will be able to get the numeric values of the above-threshold queries as well, at little additional cost, if we so choose). This is similar to what we did in the Report Noisy Max mechanism in section 3.3, and indeed iterating either that algorithm or the exponential mechanism would be an option for the non-interactive, or offline, case.

In this section, we show how to analyze a method for this in the online setting. The technique is simple — add noise and report only whether the noisy value exceeds the threshold — and our emphasis is on the analysis, showing that privacy degrades only with the number of queries which actually lie above the threshold, rather than with the total number of queries. This can be a huge savings if we know that the set of queries that lie above the threshold is much smaller than the total number of queries — that is, if the answer vector is *sparse*.

In a little more detail, we will consider a sequence of events — one for each query — which occur if a query evaluated on the database exceeds a given (known, public) threshold. Our goal will be to release a bit vector indicating, for each event, whether or not it has occurred. As each query is presented, the mechanism will compute a noisy response, compare it to the (publicly known) threshold, and, if the threshold is exceeded, reveal this fact. For technical reasons in the proof of privacy (Theorem 3.24), the algorithm works with a noisy version $\hat{T}$ of the threshold T. While T is public the noisy version $\hat{T}$ is not.

Rather than incurring a privacy loss for each *possible* query, the analysis below will result in a privacy cost only for the query values that are near or above the threshold.

The Setting. Let m denote the total number of sensitivity 1 queries, which may be chosen adaptively. Without loss of generality, there is a single threshold T fixed in advance (alternatively, each query can have its own threshold, but the results are unchanged). We will be adding noise to query values and comparing the results to T. A *positive* outcome means that a noisy query value exceeds the threshold. We expect a small number c of noisy values to exceed the threshold, and we are releasing only the noisy values above the threshold. The algorithm will use c in its stopping condition.

We will first analyze the case in which the algorithm halts after $c = 1$ above-threshold query, and show that this algorithm is ϵ-differentially private no matter how long the *total* sequence of queries is. We will then analyze the case of $c > 1$ by using our composition theorems, and derive bounds both for $(\epsilon, 0)$ and (ϵ, δ)-differential privacy.

We first argue that AboveThreshold, the algorithm specialized to the case of only one above-threshold query, is private and accurate.

Algorithm 1 Input is a private database D, an adaptively chosen stream of sensitivity 1 queries $f_1, \ldots$, and a threshold T. Output is a stream of responses $a_1, \ldots$

AboveThreshold$(D, \{f_i\}, T, \epsilon)$

   Let $\hat{T} = T + \text{Lap}\left(\frac{2}{\epsilon}\right)$.

   for Each query i **do**

      Let $\nu_i = \text{Lap}(\frac{4}{\epsilon})$

      if $f_i(D) + \nu_i \geq \hat{T}$ **then**

         Output $a_i = \top$.

         Halt.

      else

         Output $a_i = \bot$.

      end if

   end for

Theorem 3.23. AboveThreshold is $(\epsilon, 0)$-differentially private.

Proof. Fix any two neighboring databases D and D'. Let A denote the random variable representing the output of **AboveThreshold**$(D, \{f_i\}, T, \epsilon)$ and let A' denote the random variable representing the output of **AboveThreshold**$(D', \{f_i\}, T, \epsilon)$. The output of the algorithm is some realization of these random variables, $a \in \{\top, \bot\}^k$ and has the form that for all $i < k$, $a_i = \bot$ and $a_k = \top$. There are two types of random variables internal to the algorithm: the noisy threshold $\hat{T}$ and the perturbations to each of the k queries, $\{\nu_i\}_{i=1}^k$. For the following analysis, we will fix the (arbitrary) values of $\nu_1, \ldots, \nu_{k-1}$ and take probabilities over the randomness of ν_k and $\hat{T}$. Define the following quantity representing the maximum noisy value of any query $f_1, \ldots, f_{k-1}$ evaluated on D:

$$g(D) = \max_{i<k} \left(f_i(D) + \nu_i \right)$$

In the following, we will abuse notation and write $\Pr[\hat{T} = t]$ as shorthand for the pdf of $\hat{T}$ evaluated at t (similarly for ν_k), and write $\mathbf{1}[x]$ to denote the indicator function of event x. Note that fixing the values of $\nu_1, \ldots, \nu_{k-1}$ (which makes $g(D)$ a deterministic quantity), we have:

$$
\Pr_{\hat{T},\nu_k}[A = a] = \Pr_{\hat{T},\nu_k}[\hat{T} > g(D) \text{ and } f_k(D) + \nu_k \geq \hat{T}]
$$

$$
= \Pr_{\hat{T},\nu_k}[\hat{T} \in (g(D), f_k(D) + \nu_k]]
$$

$$
= \int_{-\infty}^{\infty} \int_{-\infty}^{\infty} \Pr[\nu_k = v]
$$

$$
\cdot \Pr[\hat{T} = t] \mathbf{1}[t \in (g(D), f_k(D) + v]] dv dt
$$

$$
\doteq *
$$

We now make a change of variables. Define:

$$
\hat{v} = v + g(D) - g(D') + f_k(D') - f_k(D)
$$

$$
\hat{t} = t + g(D) - g(D')
$$

and note that for any D, D', $|\hat{v} - v| \leq 2$ and $|\hat{t} - t| \leq 1$. This follows because each query $f_i(D)$ is 1-sensitive, and hence the quantity $g(D)$ is 1-sensitive as well. Applying this change of variables, we have:

$$
* = \int_{-\infty}^{\infty} \int_{-\infty}^{\infty} \Pr[\nu_k = \hat{v}] \cdot \Pr[\hat{T} = \hat{t}] \mathbf{1}[(t + g(D) - g(D'))
$$

$$
\in (g(D), f_k(D') + v + g(D) - g(D')]] dv dt
$$

$$
= \int_{-\infty}^{\infty} \int_{-\infty}^{\infty} \Pr[\nu_k = \hat{v}] \cdot \Pr[\hat{T} = \hat{t}] \mathbf{1}[(t \in (g(D'), f_k(D') + v]] dv dt
$$

$$
\leq \int_{-\infty}^{\infty} \int_{-\infty}^{\infty} \exp(\epsilon/2) \Pr[\nu_k = v]
$$

$$
\cdot \exp(\epsilon/2) \Pr[\hat{T} = t] \mathbf{1}[(t \in (g(D'), f_k(D') + v]] dv dt
$$

$$
= \exp(\epsilon) \Pr_{\hat{T},\nu_k}[\hat{T} > g(D') \text{ and } f_k(D') + \nu_k \geq \hat{T}]
$$

$$
= \exp(\epsilon) \Pr_{\hat{T},\nu_k}[A' = a]
$$

where the inequality comes from our bounds on $|\hat{v} - v|$ and $|\hat{t} - t|$ and the form of the pdf of the Laplace distribution. $\square$

Definition 3.9 (Accuracy). We will say that an algorithm which outputs a stream of answers $a_1, \ldots, \in \{\top, \bot\}^*$ in response to a stream of k

queries $f_1, \ldots, f_k$ is (α, β)-accurate with respect to a threshold T if except with probability at most β, the algorithm does not halt before f_k, and for all $a_i = \top$:

$$f_i(D) \geq T - \alpha$$

and for all $a_i = \bot$:

$$f_i(D) \leq T + \alpha.$$

What can go wrong in Algorithm 1? The noisy threshold $\hat{T}$ can be very far from T, say, $|\hat{T} - T| > \alpha$. In addition a small count $f_i(D) < T - \alpha$ can have so much noise added to it that it is reported as above threshold (even when the threshold is close to correct), and a large count $f_i(D) > T + \alpha$ can be reported as below threshold. All of these happen with probability exponentially small in α. In summary, we can have a problem with the choice of the noisy threshold or we can have a problem with one or more of the individual noise values ν_i. Of course, we could have both kinds of errors, so in the analysis below we allocate $\alpha/2$ to each type.

Theorem 3.24. For any sequence of k queries $f_1, \ldots, f_k$ such that $|\{i < k : f_i(D) \geq T - \alpha\}| = 0$ (i.e. the only query close to being above threshold is possibly the last one), AboveThreshold$(D, \{f_i\}, T, \epsilon)$ is (α, β) accurate for:

$$\alpha = \frac{8(\log k + \log(2/\beta))}{\epsilon}.$$

Proof. Observe that the theorem will be proved if we can show that except with probability at most β:

$$\max_{i \in [k]} |\nu_i| + |T - \hat{T}| \leq \alpha$$

If this is the case, then for any $a_i = \top$, we have:

$$f_i(D) + \nu_i \geq \hat{T} \geq T - |T - \hat{T}|$$

or in other words:

$$f_i(D) \geq T - |T - \hat{T}| - |\nu_i| \geq T - \alpha$$

Similarly, for any $a_i = \perp$ we have:

$$f_i(D) < \hat{T} \leq T + |T - \hat{T}| + |\nu_i| \leq T + \alpha$$

We will also have that for any $i < k$: $f_i(D) < T - \alpha < T - |\nu_i| - |T - \hat{T}|$, and so: $f_i(D) + \nu_i \leq \hat{T}$, meaning $a_i = \perp$. Therefore the algorithm does not halt before k queries are answered.

We now complete the proof.

Recall that if $Y \sim \mathrm{Lap}(b)$, then: $\Pr[|Y| \geq t \cdot b] = \exp(-t)$. Therefore we have:

$$\Pr[|T - \hat{T}| \geq \frac{\alpha}{2}] = \exp\left(-\frac{\epsilon \alpha}{4}\right)$$

Setting this quantity to be at most $\beta/2$, we find that we require $\alpha \geq \frac{4\log(2/\beta)}{\epsilon}$

Similarly, by a union bound, we have:

$$\Pr[\max_{i \in [k]} |\nu_i| \geq \alpha/2] \leq k \cdot \exp\left(-\frac{\epsilon \alpha}{8}\right)$$

Setting this quantity to be at most $\beta/2$, we find that we require $\alpha \geq \frac{8(\log(2/\beta) + \log k)}{\epsilon}$ These two claims combine to prove the theorem. $\qquad\square$

We now show how to handle multiple "above threshold" queries using composition.

The Sparse algorithm can be thought of as follows: As queries come in, it makes repeated calls to AboveThreshold. Each time an above threshold query is reported, the algorithm simply restarts the remaining stream of queries on a new instantiation of AboveThreshold. It halts after it has restarted AboveThreshold c times (i.e. after c above threshold queries have appeared). Each instantiation of AboveThreshold is $(\epsilon, 0)$-private, and so the composition theorems apply.

Theorem 3.25. Sparse is (ϵ, δ)-differentially private.

Proof. We observe that Sparse is exactly equivalent to the following procedure: We run AboveThreshold$(D, \{f_i\}, T, \epsilon')$ on our stream of queries $\{f_i\}$ setting

$$\epsilon' = \begin{cases} \frac{\epsilon}{c}, & \text{If } \delta = 0; \\ \frac{\epsilon}{\sqrt{8c \ln \frac{1}{\delta}}}, & \text{Otherwise.} \end{cases}$$

Algorithm 2 Input is a private database D, an adaptively chosen stream of sensitivity 1 queries $f_1, \ldots$, a threshold T, and a cutoff point c. Output is a stream of answers $a_1, \ldots$

$\mathbf{Sparse}(D, \{f_i\}, T, c, \epsilon, \delta)$

   If $\delta = 0$ Let $\sigma = \frac{2c}{\epsilon}$. Else Let $\sigma = \frac{\sqrt{32c \ln \frac{1}{\delta}}}{\epsilon}$
   Let $\hat{T}_0 = T + \mathrm{Lap}(\sigma)$
   Let count $= 0$
   for Each query i **do**
      Let $\nu_i = \mathrm{Lap}(2\sigma)$
      if $f_i(D) + \nu_i \geq \hat{T}_{\mathrm{count}}$ **then**
         Output $a_i = \top$.
         Let count $=$ count $+1$.
         Let $\hat{T}_{\mathrm{count}} = T + \mathrm{Lap}(\sigma)$
      else
         Output $a_i = \bot$.
      end if
      if count $\geq c$ **then**
         Halt.
      end if
   end for

---

using the answers supplied by AboveThreshold. When AboveThreshold halts (after 1 above threshold query), we simply restart $\mathrm{Sparse}(D, \{f_i\}, T, \epsilon')$ on the remaining stream, and continue in this manner until we have restarted AboveThreshold c times. After the c'th restart of AboveThreshold halts, we halt as well. We have already proven that AboveThreshold$(D, \{f_i\}, T, \epsilon')$ is $(\epsilon', 0)$ differentially private. Finally, by the advanced composition theorem (Theorem 3.20), c applications of an $\epsilon' = \frac{\epsilon}{\sqrt{8c \ln \frac{1}{\delta}}}$-differentially private algorithm is (ϵ, δ)-differentially private, and c applications of an $\epsilon' = \epsilon/c$ differentially private algorithm is $(\epsilon, 0)$-private as desired. $\square$

   It remains to prove accuracy for Sparse, by again observing that Sparse consists only of c calls to AboveThreshold. We note that if each of these calls to AboveThreshold is $(\alpha, \beta/c)$-accurate, then Sparse will be (α, β)-accurate.

Theorem 3.26. For any sequence of k queries $f_1, \ldots, f_k$ such that $L(T) \equiv |\{i : f_i(D) \geq T - \alpha\}| \leq c$, if $\delta > 0$, Sparse is (α, β) accurate for:

$$\alpha = \frac{(\ln k + \ln \frac{2c}{\beta})\sqrt{512c \ln \frac{1}{\delta}}}{\epsilon}.$$

If $\delta = 0$, Sparse is (α, β) accurate for:

$$\alpha = \frac{8c(\ln k + \ln(2c/\beta))}{\epsilon}$$

Proof. We simply apply Theorem 3.24 setting β to be β/c, and ϵ to be $\frac{\epsilon}{\sqrt{8c \ln \frac{1}{\delta}}}$ and ϵ/c, depending on whether $\delta > 0$ or $\delta = 0$, respectively. $\square$

Finally, we give a version of Sparse that actually outputs the numeric values of the above threshold queries, which we can do with only a constant factor loss in accuracy. We call this algorithm NumericSparse, and it is simply a composition of Sparse with the Laplace mechanism. Rather than outputting a vector $a \in \{\top, \bot\}^*$, it outputs a vector $a \in (\mathbb{R} \cup \{\bot\})^*$.

We observe that NumericSparse is private:

Theorem 3.27. NumericSparse is (ϵ, δ)-differentially private.

Proof. Observe that if $\delta = 0$, NumericSparse$(D, \{f_i\}, T, c, \epsilon, 0)$ is simply the adaptive composition of Sparse$(D, \{f_i\}, T, c, \frac{8}{9}\epsilon, 0)$, together with the Laplace mechanism with privacy parameters $(\epsilon', \delta) = (\frac{1}{9}\epsilon, 0)$. If $\delta > 0$, then NumericSparse$(D, \{f_i\}, T, c, \epsilon, 0)$ is the composition of Sparse$(D, \{f_i\}, T, c, \frac{\sqrt{512}}{\sqrt{512}+1}\epsilon, \delta/2)$ together with the Laplace mechanism with privacy parameters $(\epsilon', \delta) = (\frac{1}{\sqrt{512}+1}\epsilon, \delta/2)$. Hence the privacy of NumericSparse follows from simple composition. $\square$

To discuss accuracy, we must define what we mean by the accuracy of a mechanism that outputs a stream $a \in (\mathbb{R} \cup \{\bot\})^*$ in response to a sequence of numeric valued queries:

Algorithm 3 Input is a private database D, an adaptively chosen stream of sensitivity 1 queries $f_1, \ldots$, a threshold T, and a cutoff point c. Output is a stream of answers $a_1, \ldots$

$\text{NumericSparse}(D, \{f_i\}, T, c, \epsilon, \delta)$

If $\delta = 0$ **Let** $\epsilon_1 \leftarrow \frac{8}{9}\epsilon$, $\epsilon_2 \leftarrow \frac{2}{9}\epsilon$. **Else Let** $\epsilon_1 = \frac{\sqrt{512}}{\sqrt{512}+1}\epsilon$, $\epsilon_2 = \frac{2}{\sqrt{512}+1}$

If $\delta = 0$ **Let** $\sigma(\epsilon) = \frac{2c}{\epsilon}$. **Else Let** $\sigma(\epsilon) = \frac{\sqrt{32c \ln \frac{2}{\delta}}}{\epsilon}$

Let $\hat{T}_0 = T + \text{Lap}(\sigma(\epsilon_1))$

Let count $= 0$

for Each query i **do**

    Let $\nu_i = \text{Lap}(2\sigma(\epsilon_1))$

    if $f_i(D) + \nu_i \geq \hat{T}_{\text{count}}$ **then**

        Let $\nu_i \leftarrow \text{Lap}(\sigma(\epsilon_2))$

        Output $a_i = f_i(D) + \nu_i$.

        Let count $=$ count $+1$.

        Let $\hat{T}_{\text{count}} = T + \text{Lap}(\sigma(\epsilon_1))$

    else

        Output $a_i = \perp$.

    end if

    if count $\geq c$ **then**

        Halt.

    end if

end for

Definition 3.10 (Numeric Accuracy). We will say that an algorithm which outputs a stream of answers $a_1, \ldots, \in (\mathbb{R} \cup \{\perp\})^*$ in response to a stream of k queries $f_1, \ldots, f_k$ is (α, β)-accurate with respect to a threshold T if except with probability at most β, the algorithm does not halt before f_k, and for all $a_i \in \mathbb{R}$:

$$|f_i(D) - a_i| \leq \alpha$$

and for all $a_i = \perp$:

$$f_i(D) \leq T + \alpha.$$

Theorem 3.28. For any sequence of k queries $f_1, \ldots, f_k$ such that $L(T) \equiv |\{i : f_i(D) \geq T - \alpha\}| \leq c$, if $\delta > 0$, Sparse is (α, β) accurate for:

$$\alpha = \frac{(\ln k + \ln \frac{4c}{\beta})\sqrt{c \ln \frac{2}{\delta}}(\sqrt{512} + 1)}{\epsilon}.$$

If $\delta = 0$, Sparse is (α, β) accurate for:

$$\alpha = \frac{9c(\ln k + \ln(4c/\beta))}{\epsilon}$$

Proof. Accuracy requires two conditions: first, that for all $a_i = \bot$: $f_i(D) \leq T + \alpha$. This holds with probability $1 - \beta/2$ by the accuracy theorem for Sparse. Next, for all $a_i \in \mathbb{R}$, it requires $|f_i(D) - a_i| \leq \alpha$. This holds for with probability $1 - \beta/2$ by the accuracy of the Laplace mechanism. $\square$

What did we show in the end? If we are given a sequence of queries together with a guarantee that only at most c of them have answers above $T - \alpha$, we can answer those queries that are above a given threshold T, up to error α. This accuracy is equal, up to constants and a factor of $\log k$, to the accuracy we would get, given the same privacy guarantee, if we knew the identities of these large above-threshold queries ahead of time, and answered them with the Laplace mechanism. That is, the sparse vector technique allowed us to fish out the identities of these large queries almost "for free", paying only logarithmically for the irrelevant queries. This is the same guarantee that we could have gotten by trying to find the large queries with the exponential mechanism and then answering them with the Laplace mechanism. This algorithm, however, is trivial to run, and crucially, allows us to choose our queries adaptively.

3.7 Bibliographic notes

Randomized Response is due to Warner [84] (predating differential privacy by four decades!). The Laplace mechanism is due to Dwork et al. [23]. The exponential mechanism was invented by McSherry and Talwar [60]. Theorem 3.16 (simple composition) was claimed in [21];

the proof appearing in Appendix B is due to Dwork and Lei [22]; McSherry and Mironov obtained a similar proof. The material in Sections 3.5.1 and 3.5.2 is taken almost verbatim from Dwork et al. [32]. Prior to [32] composition was modeled informally, much as we did for the simple composition bounds. For specific mechanisms applied on a single database, there are "evolution of confidence" arguments due to Dinur, Dwork, and Nissim [18, 31], (which pre-date the definition of differential privacy) showing that the privacy parameter in k-fold composition need only deteriorate like $\sqrt{k}$ if we are willing to tolerate a (negligible) loss in δ (for $k < 1/\varepsilon^2$). Theorem 3.20 generalizes those arguments to arbitrary differentially private mechanisms,

The claim that without coordination in the noise the bounds in the composition theorems are almost tight is due to Dwork, Naor, and Vadhan [29]. The sparse vector technique is an abstraction of a technique that was introduced, by Dwork, Naor, Reingold, Rothblum, and Vadhan [28] (indicator vectors in the proof of Lemma 4.4). It has subsequently found wide use (e.g. by Roth and Roughgarden [74], Dwork, Naor, Pitassi, and Rothblum [26], and Hardt and Rothblum [44]). In our presentation of the technique, the proof of Theorem 3.23 is due to Salil Vadhan.

4

Releasing Linear Queries with Correlated Error

One of the most fundamental primitives in private data analysis is the ability to answer numeric valued queries on a dataset. In the last section, we began to see tools that would allow us to do this by adding independently drawn noise to the query answers. In this section, we continue this study, and see that by instead adding carefully correlated noise, we can gain the ability to privately answer vastly more queries to high accuracy. Here, we see two specific mechanisms for solving this problem, which we will generalize in the next section.

In this section, we consider algorithms for solving the *query release* problem with better accuracy than we would get by simply using compositions of the Laplace mechanism. The improvements are possible because the set of queries is handled as a whole — even in the online setting! — permitting the noise on individual queries to be correlated. To immediately see that something along these lines might be possible, consider the pair of queries in the differencing attack described in Section 1: "How many people in the database have the sickle cell trait?" and "How many people, not named X, in the database have the sickle cell trait?" Suppose a mechanism answers the first question using the Laplace mechanism and then, when the second question is posed, responds "You already know the approximate answer, because you just asked me almost the exact same question." This coordinated response to the pair of questions incurs no more privacy loss than either question would do taken in isolation, so a (small) privacy savings has been achieved.

The query release problem is quite natural: given a class of queries $\mathcal{Q}$ over the database, we wish to release some answer a_i for each query $f_i \in \mathcal{Q}$ such that the error $\max_i |a_i - f_i(x)|$ is as low as possible, while still preserving differential privacy.[1] Recall that for any family of low sensitivity queries, we can apply the Laplace mechanism, which adds fresh, independent, noise to the answer to each query. Unfortunately, at a fixed privacy level, for $(\epsilon, 0)$-privacy guarantees, the magnitude of the noise that we must add with the Laplace mechanism scales with $|\mathcal{Q}|$ because this is the rate at which the sensitivity of the combined queries may grow. Similarly, for (ϵ, δ)-privacy guarantees, the noise scales with $\sqrt{|\mathcal{Q}| \ln(1/\delta)}$. For example, suppose that our class of queries $\mathcal{Q}$ consists only of many copies of the same query: $f_i = f^*$ for all i. If we use the Laplace mechanism to release the answers, it will add independent noise, and so each a_i will be an independent random variable with mean $f^*(x)$. Clearly, in this regime, the noise rate must grow with $|\mathcal{Q}|$ since otherwise the average of the a_i will converge to the true value $f^*(x)$, which would be a privacy violation. However, in this case, because $f_i = f^*$ for all i, it would make more sense to approximate f^* only once with $a^* \approx f^*(x)$ and release $a_i = a^*$ for all i. In this case, the noise rate would not have to scale with $|\mathcal{Q}|$ at all. In this section, we aim to design algorithms that are much more accurate than the Laplace mechanism (with error that scales with $\log |\mathcal{Q}|$) by adding non-independent noise as a function of the set of queries.

Recall that our universe is $\mathcal{X} = \{\chi_1, \chi_2, \ldots, \chi_{|\mathcal{X}|}\}$ and that databases are represented by histograms in $\mathbb{N}^{|\mathcal{X}|}$. A *linear query* is simply a counting query, but generalized to take values in the interval $[0, 1]$ rather than only boolean values. Specifically, a linear query f takes the

---

[1]It is the privacy constraint that makes the problem interesting. Without this constraint, the query release problem is trivially and optimally solved by just outputting exact answers for every query.

form $f : \mathcal{X} \to [0,1]$, and applied to a database x returns either the *sum* or *average* value of the query on the database (we will think of both, depending on which is more convenient for the analysis). When we think of linear queries as returning *average* values, we will refer to them as *normalized* linear queries, and say that they take value:

$$f(x) = \frac{1}{\|x\|_1} \sum_{i=1}^{|\mathcal{X}|} x_i \cdot f(\chi_i).$$

When we think of linear queries as returning *sum* values we will refer to them as *un-normalized* linear queries, and say that they take value:

$$f(x) = \sum_{i=1}^{|\mathcal{X}|} x_i \cdot f(\chi_i).$$

Whenever we state a bound, it should be clear from context whether we are speaking of normalized or un-normalized queries, because they take values in very different ranges. Note that normalized linear queries take values in $[0,1]$, whereas un-normalized queries take values in $[0, \|x\|_1]$.

Note that with this definition linear queries have sensitivity $\Delta f \leq 1$. Later sections will discuss arbitrary low-sensitivity queries.

We will present two techniques, one each for the offline and online cases. Surprisingly, and wonderfully, the offline technique is an immediate application of the exponential mechanism using well-known sampling bounds from learning theory! The algorithm will simply be to apply the exponential mechanism with range equal to the set of all *small* databases y and quality function $u(x, y)$ equal to minus the maximum approximation error incurred by querying y to obtain an approximation for $f(x)$:

$$u(x, y) = - \max_{f \in \mathcal{Q}} |f(x) - f(y)|. \tag{4.1}$$

Sampling bounds (see Lemma 4.3 below) tell us that a random subset of $\ln |\mathcal{Q}|/\alpha^2$ elements of x will very likely give us a good approximation for all $f(x)$ (specifically, with additive error bounded by α), so we know it is sufficient to restrict the set of possible outputs to small databases. We don't actually care that the potential output databases are small, only that they are not too numerous: their number plays a role in the proof of utility, which is an immediate application of the utility theorem for the exponential mechanism (Theorem 3.11). More specifically, if the total number of potential outputs is not too numerous then, in particular, the total number of low-utility outputs is not too numerous, and therefore the ratio of bad outputs to good outputs (there is at least one) is not too large.

The online mechanism, which, despite not knowing the entire set of queries in advance, will achieve the same accuracy as the offline mechanism, and will be a direct application of the sparse vector technique. As a result, privacy will be immediate, but utility will require a proof. The key will be to argue that, even for a very large set of counting queries, few queries are "significant"; that is, significant queries will be sparse. As with the sparse vector algorithms, we can scale noise according to the number of significant queries, with little dependence on the total number of queries.

Before we go on and present the mechanisms, we will give just one example of a useful class of linear queries.

Example 4.1. Suppose that elements of the database are represented by d *boolean* features. For example, the first feature may represent whether or not the individual is male or female, the second feature may represent whether or not they are a college graduate, the third feature may represent whether or not they are US citizens, etc. That is, our data universe is $\mathcal{X} = \{0, 1\}^d$. Given a subset of these attributes $S \subseteq \{1, \ldots, d\}$, we might like to know how many people in the dataset have these attributes. (e.g., "What fraction of the dataset consists of male college graduates with a family history of lung cancer?"). This naturally defines a query called a *monotone conjunction query*, parameterized by a subset of attributes S and defined as $f_S(z) = \prod_{i \in S} z_i$, for $z \in \mathcal{X}$. The class of *all* such queries is simply $\mathcal{Q} = \{f_S : S \subseteq \{1, \ldots, d\}\}$, and has size $|\mathcal{Q}| = 2^d$. A collection of answers to conjunctions is sometimes called a *contingency* or *marginal* table, and is a common method of releasing statistical information about a dataset. Often times, we may not be interested in the answers to *all* conjunctions, but rather just those that ask about subsets of features S of size $|S| = k$ for some fixed k. This class of queries $\mathcal{Q}_k = \{f_S : S \subseteq \{1, \ldots, d\}, |S| = k\}$ has size $\binom{d}{k}$.

This large and useful class of queries is just one example of the sorts of queries that can be accurately answered by the algorithms given in this section. (Note that if we wish to also allow (non-monotone) conjunctions which ask about *negated* attributes, we can do that as well — simply double the feature space from d to $2d$, and set $z_{d+i} = 1 - z_i$ for all $i \in \{1, \ldots, d\}$.)

4.1 An offline algorithm: SmallDB

In this section, we give an algorithm based on the idea of sampling a small database using the exponential mechanism. What we will show is that, for counting queries, it suffices to consider databases that are small: their size will only be a function of the query class, and our desired approximation accuracy α, and crucially *not* on $\|x\|_1$, the size of the private database. This is important because it will allow us to simultaneously guarantee, for all sufficiently large databases, that there is at least *one* database in the range of the exponential mechanism that well approximates x on queries in $\mathcal{Q}$, and that there are not *too many* databases in the range to dissipate the probability mass placed on this "good" database.

Algorithm 4 The Small Database Mechanism

SmallDB$(x, \mathcal{Q}, \varepsilon, \alpha)$

    Let $\mathcal{R} \leftarrow \{y \in \mathbb{N}^{|\mathcal{X}|} : \|y\|_1 = \frac{\log |\mathcal{Q}|}{\alpha^2}\}$
    Let $u : \mathbb{N}^{|\mathcal{X}|} \times \mathcal{R} \to \mathbb{R}$ be defined to be:

$$u(x, y) = - \max_{f \in \mathcal{Q}} |f(x) - f(y)|$$

    Sample And Output $y \in \mathcal{R}$ with the exponential mechanism $\mathcal{M}_E(x, u, \mathcal{R})$

We first observe that the Small Database mechanism preserves ε-differential privacy.

Proposition 4.1. The Small Database mechanism is $(\varepsilon, 0)$ differentially private.

Proof. The Small Database mechanism is simply an instantiation of the exponential mechanism. Therefore, privacy follows from Theorem 3.10.

□

We may similarly call on our analysis of the exponential mechanism to understand the utility guarantees of the Small Database mechanism. But first, we must justify our choice of range $\mathcal{R} = \{y \in \mathbb{N}^{|\mathcal{X}|} : \|y\|_1 = \frac{\log |\mathcal{Q}|}{\alpha^2}\}$, the set of all databases of size $\log |\mathcal{Q}|/\alpha^2$.

Theorem 4.2. For any finite class of linear queries $\mathcal{Q}$, if $\mathcal{R} = \{y \in \mathbb{N}^{|\mathcal{X}|} : \|y\|_1 = \frac{\log |\mathcal{Q}|}{\alpha^2}\}$ then for all $x \in \mathbb{N}^{|\mathcal{X}|}$, there exists a $y \in \mathcal{R}$ such that:

$$\max_{f \in \mathcal{Q}} |f(x) - f(y)| \leq \alpha$$

In other words, we will show that for any collection of linear queries $\mathcal{Q}$ and for any database x, there is a "small" database y of size $\|y\|_1 = \frac{\log |\mathcal{Q}|}{\alpha^2}$ that approximately encodes the answers to every query in $\mathcal{Q}$, up to error α.

Lemma 4.3 (Sampling Bounds). For any $x \in \mathbb{N}^{|\mathcal{X}|}$ and for any collection of linear queries $\mathcal{Q}$, there exists a database y of size

$$\|y\|_1 = \frac{\log |\mathcal{Q}|}{\alpha^2}$$

such that:

$$\max_{f \in \mathcal{Q}} |f(x) - f(y)| \leq \alpha$$

Proof. Let $m = \frac{\log |\mathcal{Q}|}{\alpha^2}$. We will construct a database y by taking m uniformly random samples from the elements of x. Specifically, for $i \in \{1, \ldots, m\}$, let X_i be a random variable taking value $\chi_j \in \mathcal{X}$ with probability $x_j/\|x\|_1$, and let y be the database containing elements $X_1, \ldots, X_m$. Now fix any $f \in \mathcal{Q}$ and consider the quantity $f(y)$. We have:

$$f(y) = \frac{1}{\|y\|_1} \sum_{i=1}^{|\mathcal{X}|} y_i \cdot f(\chi_i) = \frac{1}{m} \sum_{i=1}^{m} f(X_i).$$

We note that each term $f(X_i)$ of the sum is a bounded random variable taking values $0 \leq f(X_i) \leq 1$ with expectation

$$\mathbb{E}[f(X_i)] = \sum_{j=1}^{|\mathcal{X}|} \frac{x_j}{\|x\|_1} f(\chi_j) = f(x),$$

and that the expectation of $f(y)$ is:

$$\mathbb{E}[f(y)] = \frac{1}{m} \sum_{i=1}^{m} \mathbb{E}[f(X_i)] = f(x).$$

Therefore, we can apply the Chernoff bound stated in Theorem 3.1 which gives:

$$\Pr\left[|f(y) - f(x)| > \alpha\right] \leq 2e^{-2m\alpha^2}.$$

Taking a union bound over all of the linear queries $f \in \mathcal{Q}$, we get:

$$\Pr\left[\max_{f \in \mathcal{Q}} |f(y) - f(x)| > \alpha\right] \leq 2|\mathcal{Q}|e^{-2m\alpha^2}.$$

Plugging in $m = \frac{\log|\mathcal{Q}|}{\alpha^2}$ makes the right hand side smaller than 1 (so long as $|\mathcal{Q}| > 2$), proving that there exists a database of size m satisfying the stated bound, which completes the proof of the lemma. $\square$

The proof of Theorem 4.2 simply follows from the observation that $\mathcal{R}$ contains *all* databases of size $\frac{\log|\mathcal{Q}|}{\alpha^2}$.

Proposition 4.4. Let $\mathcal{Q}$ be any class of linear queries. Let y be the database output by SmallDB$(x, \mathcal{Q}, \varepsilon, \alpha)$. Then with probability $1 - \beta$:

$$\max_{f \in \mathcal{Q}} |f(x) - f(y)| \leq \alpha + \frac{2\left(\frac{\log|\mathcal{X}| \log|\mathcal{Q}|}{\alpha^2} + \log\left(\frac{1}{\beta}\right)\right)}{\varepsilon\|x\|_1}.$$

Proof. Applying the utility bounds for the exponential mechanism (Theorem 3.11) with $\Delta u = \frac{1}{\|x\|_1}$ and $\mathrm{OPT}_q(D) \leq \alpha$ (which follows from Theorem 4.2), we find:

$$\Pr\left[\max_{f \in \mathcal{Q}} |f(x) - f(y)| \geq \alpha + \frac{2}{\varepsilon\|x\|_1}\left(\log\left(|\mathcal{R}|\right) + t\right)\right] \leq e^{-t}.$$

We complete the proof by (1) noting that $\mathcal{R}$, which is the set of all databases of size at most $\log|\mathcal{Q}|/\alpha^2$, satisfies $|\mathcal{R}| \leq |\mathcal{X}|^{\log|\mathcal{Q}|/\alpha^2}$ and (2) by setting $t = \log\left(\frac{1}{\beta}\right)$. $\square$

Finally, we may now state the utility theorem for SmallDB.

Theorem 4.5. By the appropriate choice of α, letting y be the database output by $\mathrm{SmallDB}(x, \mathcal{Q}, \varepsilon, \frac{\alpha}{2})$, we can ensure that with probability $1 - \beta$:

$$\max_{f \in \mathcal{Q}} |f(x) - f(y)| \leq \left(\frac{16 \log |\mathcal{X}| \log |\mathcal{Q}| + 4 \log \left(\frac{1}{\beta} \right)}{\varepsilon \|x\|_1} \right)^{1/3}. \qquad (4.2)$$

Equivalently, for any database x with

$$\|x\|_1 \geq \frac{16 \log |\mathcal{X}| \log |\mathcal{Q}| + 4 \log \left(\frac{1}{\beta} \right)}{\varepsilon \alpha^3} \qquad (4.3)$$

with probability $1 - \beta$: $\max_{f \in \mathcal{Q}} |f(x) - f(y)| \leq \alpha$.

Proof. By Theorem 4.2, we get:

$$\max_{f \in \mathcal{Q}} |f(x) - f(y)| \leq \frac{\alpha}{2} + \frac{2 \left(\frac{4 \log |\mathcal{X}| \log |\mathcal{Q}|}{\alpha^2} + \log \left(\frac{1}{\beta} \right) \right)}{\varepsilon \|x\|_1}.$$

Setting this quantity to be at most α and solving for $\|x\|_1$ yields (4.3). Solving for α yields (4.4). $\qquad \square$

Note that this theorem states that for fixed α and ε, even with $\delta = 0$, it is possible to answer almost *exponentially* many queries in the size of the database.[2] This is in contrast to the Laplace mechanism, when we use it directly to answer linear queries, which can only answer *linearly* many.

Note also that in this discussion, it has been most convenient to think about normalized queries. However, we can get the corresponding bounds for unnormalized queries simply by multiplying by $\|x\|_1$:

Theorem 4.6 (Accuracy theorem for un-normalized queries). By the appropriate choice of α, letting y be the database output by

---

[2]Specifically, solving for k we find that the mechanism can answer k queries for:

$$k \leq \exp \left(O \left(\frac{\alpha^3 \epsilon \|x\|_1}{\log |\mathcal{X}|} \right) \right).$$

SmallDB$(x, \mathcal{Q}, \varepsilon, \frac{\alpha}{2})$, we can ensure that with probability $1 - \beta$:

$$\max_{f \in \mathcal{Q}} |f(x) - f(y)| \leq \|x\|_1^{2/3} \left(\frac{16 \log |\mathcal{X}| \log |\mathcal{Q}| + 4 \log \left(\frac{1}{\beta}\right)}{\varepsilon} \right)^{1/3} . \quad (4.4)$$

More Refined Bounds. We proved that *every* set of linear queries $\mathcal{Q}$ has a collection of databases of size at most $|\mathcal{X}|^{\log |\mathcal{Q}|/\alpha^2}$ that well-approximates every database x with respect to $\mathcal{Q}$ with error at most α. This is often an over-estimate however, since it completely ignores the structure of the queries. For example, if $\mathcal{Q}$ simply contains the same query repeated over and over again, each time in a different guise, then there is no reason that the size of the range of the exponential mechanism should grow with $|\mathcal{Q}|$. Similarly, there may even be classes of queries $\mathcal{Q}$ that have *infinite* cardinality, but nevertheless are well approximated by small databases. For example, queries that correspond to asking whether a point lies within a given interval on the real line form an infinitely large class $\mathcal{Q}$, since there are uncountably many intervals on the real line. Nevertheless, this class of queries exhibits very simple structure that causes it to be well approximated by small databases. By considering more refined structure of our query classes, we will be able to give bounds for differentially private mechanisms which improve over the simple sampling bounds (Lemma 4.3) and can be non-trivial even for doubly exponentially large classes of queries.[3] We will not fully develop these bounds here, but will instead state several results for the simpler class of *counting queries*. Recall that a counting query $f : \mathcal{X} \to \{0, 1\}$ maps database points to boolean values, rather than any value in the interval $[0, 1]$ as linear queries do.

Definition 4.1 (Shattering). A class of counting queries $\mathcal{Q}$ *shatters* a collection of points $S \subseteq \mathcal{X}$ if for every $T \subseteq S$, there exists an $f \in \mathcal{Q}$ such that $\{x \in S : f(x) = 1\} = T$. That is, $\mathcal{Q}$ shatters S if for every one of the $2^{|S|}$ subsets T of S, there is some function in $\mathcal{Q}$ that labels exactly

---

[3]In fact, our complexity measure for a class of queries can be finite even for *infinite* classes of queries, but here we are dealing with queries over a finite universe, so there do not exist infinitely many distinct queries.

those elements as positive, and does not label any of the elements in $S \setminus T$ as positive.

Note that for $\mathcal{Q}$ to shatter S it must be the case that $|\mathcal{Q}| \geq 2^{|S|}$ since $\mathcal{Q}$ must contain a function f for each subset $T \subseteq S$. We can now define our complexity measure for counting queries.

Definition 4.2 (Vapnik–Chervonenkis (VC) Dimension). A collection of counting queries $\mathcal{Q}$ has VC-dimension d if there exists some set $S \subseteq \mathcal{X}$ of cardinality $|S| = d$ such that $\mathcal{Q}$ shatters S, and $\mathcal{Q}$ does not shatter any set of cardinality $d+1$. We can denote this quantity by VC-DIM($\mathcal{Q}$).

Consider again the class of 1-dimensional intervals on the range $[0, \infty]$ defined over the domain $\mathcal{X} = \mathbb{R}$. The function $f_{a,b}$ corresponding to the interval $[a, b]$ is defined such that $f_{a,b}(x) = 1$ if and only if $x \in [a, b]$. This is an infinite class of queries, but its VC-dimension is 2. For any pair of distinct points $x < y$, there is an interval that contains neither point $(a, b < x)$, an interval that contains both points $(a < x < y < b)$, and an interval that contains each of the points but not the other ($a < x < b < y$ and $x < a < y < b$). However, for any 3 distinct points $x < y < z$, there is no interval $[a, b]$ such that $f_{a,b}[x] = f_{a,b}[z] = 1$ but $f_{a,b}[y] = 0$.

We observe that the VC-dimension of a finite concept class can never be too large.

Lemma 4.7. For any finite class $\mathcal{Q}$, VC-DIM($\mathcal{Q}$) $\leq \log |\mathcal{Q}|$.

Proof. If VC-DIM($\mathcal{Q}$) $= d$ then $\mathcal{Q}$ shatters some set of items $S \subseteq \mathcal{X}$ of cardinality $|S| = d$. But by the definition of shattering, since S has 2^d distinct subsets, $\mathcal{Q}$ must have at least 2^d distinct functions in it. $\square$

It will turn out that we can essentially replace the term $\log |\mathcal{Q}|$ with the term VC-DIM($\mathcal{Q}$) in our bounds for the SmallDB mechanism. By the previous lemma, this is can only be an improvement for finite classes $\mathcal{Q}$.

Theorem 4.8. For any finite class of linear queries $\mathcal{Q}$, if $\mathcal{R} = \{y \in \mathbb{N}^{|\mathcal{X}|} : \|y\| \in O\left(\frac{\text{VC-DIM}(\mathcal{Q})}{\alpha^2}\right)\}$ then for all $x \in \mathbb{N}^{|\mathcal{X}|}$, there exists a $y \in \mathcal{R}$

such that:

$$\max_{f \in \mathcal{Q}} |f(x) - f(y)| \leq \alpha$$

As a result of this theorem, we get the analogue of Theorem 4.5 with VC-dimension as our measure of query class complexity:

Theorem 4.9. Let y be the database output by SmallDB$(x, \mathcal{Q}, \varepsilon, \frac{\alpha}{2})$. Then with probability $1 - \beta$:

$$\max_{f \in \mathcal{Q}} |f(x) - f(y)| \leq O\left(\left(\frac{\log |\mathcal{X}| \text{VC-DIM}(\mathcal{Q}) + \log\left(\frac{1}{\beta}\right)}{\varepsilon \|x\|_1}\right)^{1/3}\right)$$

Equivalently, for any database x with

$$\|x\|_1 \geq O\left(\frac{\log |\mathcal{X}| \text{VC-DIM}(\mathcal{Q}) + \log\left(\frac{1}{\beta}\right)}{\varepsilon \alpha^3}\right)$$

with probability $1 - \beta$: $\max_{f \in \mathcal{Q}} |f(x) - f(y)| \leq \alpha$.

An analogous (although more cumbersome) measure of query complexity, the "Fat Shattering Dimension," defines the complexity of a class of linear queries, as opposed to simply counting queries. The Fat Shattering Dimension controls the size of the smallest "α-net" (Definition 5.2 in Section 5) for a class of linear queries $\mathcal{Q}$ as VC-dimension does for counting queries. This measure can similarly be used to give more refined bounds for mechanisms designed to privately release linear queries.

4.2 An online mechanism: private multiplicative weights

We will now give a mechanism for answering queries that arrive online and may be interactively chosen. The algorithm will be a simple combination of the sparse vector algorithm (which can answer threshold queries adaptively), and the exponentiated gradient descent algorithm for learning linear predictors online.

This latter algorithm is also known as Hedge or more generally the multiplicative weights technique. The idea is the following: When we view the database $D \in \mathbb{N}^{|\mathcal{X}|}$ as a histogram and are interested only in linear queries (i.e., linear functions of this histogram), then we can view the problem of answering linear queries as the problem of learning the linear function D that defines the query answers $\langle D, q \rangle$, given a query $q \in [0, 1]^{|\mathcal{X}|}$. If the learning algorithm only needs to access the data using privacy-preserving queries, then rather than having a privacy cost that grows with the number of queries we would like to answer, we can have a privacy cost that grows only with the number of queries the learning algorithm needs to make. The "multiplicative weights" algorithm which we present next is a classical example of such a learning algorithm: it can learn any linear predictor by making only a small number of queries. It maintains at all times a current "hypothesis predictor," and accesses the data only by requiring examples of queries on which its hypothesis predictor differs from the (true) private database by a large amount. Its guarantee is that it will always learn the target linear function up to small error, given only a small number of such examples. How can we find these examples? The sparse vector algorithm that we saw in the previous section allows us to do this on the fly, while paying for only those examples that have high error on the current multiplicative weights hypothesis. As queries come in, we ask whether the true answer to the query differs substantially from the answer to the query on the current multiplicative weights hypothesis. Note that this is a threshold query of the type handled by the sparse vector technique. If the answer is "no" — i.e., the difference, or error, is "below threshold," — then we can respond to the query using the publicly known hypothesis predictor, and have no further privacy loss. If the answer is "yes," meaning that the currently known hypothesis predictor gives rise to an error that is above threshold, then we have found an example appropriate to update our learning algorithm. Because "above threshold" answers correspond exactly to queries needed to update our learning algorithm, the total privacy cost depends only on the learning rate of the algorithm, and not on the total number of queries that we answer.

First we give the multiplicative weights update rule and prove a theorem about its convergence in the language of answering linear queries.

It will be convenient to think of databases x as being probability distributions over the data universe $\mathcal{X}$. That is, letting $\Delta([\mathcal{X}])$ denote the set of probability distributions over the set $[|\mathcal{X}|]$, we have $x \in \Delta([\mathcal{X}])$. Note that we can always scale a database to have this property without changing the normalized value of any linear query.

Algorithm 5 The Multiplicative Weights (MW) Update Rule. It is instantiated with a parameter $\eta \leq 1$. In the following analysis, we will take $\eta = \alpha/2$, where α is the parameter specifying our target accuracy.

$\mathbf{MW}(x^t, f_t, v_t)$:

    if $v_t < f_t(x^t)$ **then**
        Let $r_t = f_t$
    else
        Let $r_t = 1 - f_t$
        (i.e., for all χ_i, $r_t(\chi_i) = 1 - f_t[\chi_i]$)
    end if
    Update: For all $i \in [|\mathcal{X}|]$ Let

$$\hat{x}_i^{t+1} = \exp(-\eta r_t[i]) \cdot x_i^t$$

$$x_i^{t+1} = \frac{\hat{x}_i^{t+1}}{\sum_{j=1}^{|\mathcal{X}|} \hat{x}_j^{t+1}}$$

    Output x^{t+1}.

Theorem 4.10. Fix a class of linear queries $\mathcal{Q}$ and a database $x \in \Delta([\mathcal{X}])$, and let $x^1 \in \Delta([\mathcal{X}])$ describe the uniform distribution over $\mathcal{X}$: $x_i^1 = 1/|\mathcal{X}|$ for all i. Now consider a maximal length sequence of databases x^t for $t \in \{2, \ldots, L\}$ generated by setting $x^{t+1} = MW(x^t, f_t, v_t)$ as described in Algorithm 5, where for each t, $f_t \in \mathcal{Q}$ and $v_t \in \mathbb{R}$ are such that:

1. $|f_t(x) - f_t(x^t)| > \alpha$, and
2. $|f_t(x) - v_t| < \alpha$.

Then it must be that:

$$L \leq 1 + \frac{4 \log |\mathcal{X}|}{\alpha^2}.$$

Note that if we prove this theorem, we will have proven that for the last database x^{L+1} in the sequence it must be that for all $f \in \mathcal{Q}$: $|f(x) - f(x^{L+1})| \leq \alpha$, as otherwise it would be possible to extend the sequence, contradicting maximality. In other words, given *distinguishing queries* f^t, the multiplicative weights update rule learns the private database x with respect to any class of linear queries $\mathcal{Q}$, up to some tolerance α, in only a small number (L) of steps. We will use this theorem as follows. The Private Online Multiplicative Weights algorithm, described (twice!) below, will at all times t have a *public* approximation x^t to the database x. Given an input query f, the algorithm will compute a noisy approximation to the difference $|f(x) - f(x^t)|$. If the (noisy) difference is large, the algorithm will provide a noisy approximation $f(x) + \lambda_t$ to the true answer $f(x)$, where λ_t is drawn from some appropriately chosen Laplace distribution, and the Multiplicative Weights Update Rule will be invoked with parameters $(x^t, f, f(x) + \lambda_t)$. If the update rule is invoked only when the difference $|f(x) - f(x^t)|$ is truly large (Theorem 4.10, condition 1), and if the approximations $f(x) + \lambda_t$ are sufficiently accurate (Theorem 4.10, condition 2), then we can apply the theorem to conclude that updates are not so numerous (because L is not so large) *and* the resulting x^{L+1} gives accurate answers to all queries in $\mathcal{Q}$ (because no distinguishing query remains).

Theorem 4.10 is proved by keeping track of a potential function Ψ measuring the similarity between the hypothesis database x^t at time t, and the true database D. We will show:

1. The potential function does not start out too large.

2. The potential function decreases by a significant amount at each update round.

3. The potential function is always non-negative.

Together, these 3 facts will force us to conclude that there cannot be too many update rounds.

Let us now begin the analysis for the proof of the convergence theorem.

Proof. We must show that any sequence $\{(x^t, f_t, v_t)\}_{t=1,...,L}$ with the property that $|f_t(x^t) - f_t(x)| > \alpha$ and $|v_t - f_t(x)| < \alpha$ cannot have $L > \frac{4\log|\mathcal{X}|}{\alpha^2}$.

We define our potential function as follows. Recall that we here view the database as a probability distribution — i.e., we assume $\|x\|_1 = 1$. Of course this does not require actually modifying the real database. The potential function that we use is the relative entropy, or KL divergence, between x and x^t (when viewed as probability distributions):

$$\Psi_t \stackrel{\text{def}}{=} KL(x\|x^t) = \sum_{i=1}^{|\mathcal{X}|} x[i] \log\left(\frac{x[i]}{x^t[i]}\right).$$

We begin with a simple fact:

Proposition 4.11. For all t: $\Psi_t \geq 0$, and $\Psi_1 \leq \log|\mathcal{X}|$.

Proof. Relative entropy (KL-Divergence) is always a non-negative quantity, by the log-sum inequality, which states that if $a_1, \ldots, a_n$ and $b_1, \ldots, b_n$ are non-negative numbers, then

$$\sum_i a_i \log\frac{a_i}{b_i} \geq \left(\sum_i a_i\right)\frac{\sum_i a_i}{\sum_i b_i}.$$

To see that $\Psi_1 \leq \log|\mathcal{X}|$, recall that $x^1[i] = 1/|\mathcal{X}|$ for all i, and so $\Psi_1 = \sum_{i=1}^{|\mathcal{X}|} x[i]\log(|\mathcal{X}|x[i])$. Noting that x is a probability distribution, we see that this quantity is maximized when $x[1] = 1$ and $x[i] = 0$ for all $i > 1$, giving $\Psi_i = \log|\mathcal{X}|$. $\square$

We will now argue that at each step, the potential function drops by at least $\alpha^2/4$. Because the potential begins at $\log|\mathcal{X}|$, and must always be non-negative, we therefore know that there can be at most $L \leq 4\log|X|/\alpha^2$ steps in the database update sequence. To begin, let us see exactly how much the potential drops at each step:

Lemma 4.12.

$$\Psi_t - \Psi_{t+1} \geq \eta\left(\langle r_t, x^t\rangle - \langle r_t, x\rangle\right) - \eta^2$$

Proof. Recall that $\sum_{i=1}^{|\mathcal{X}|} x[i] = 1$.

$$
\Psi_t - \Psi_{t+1} = \sum_{i=1}^{|\mathcal{X}|} x[i] \log \left(\frac{x[i]}{x_i^t} \right) - \sum_{i=1}^{|\mathcal{X}|} x[i] \log \left(\frac{x[i]}{x_i^{t+1}} \right)
$$

$$
= \sum_{i=1}^{|\mathcal{X}|} x[i] \log \left(\frac{x_i^{t+1}}{x_i^t} \right)
$$

$$
= \sum_{i=1}^{|\mathcal{X}|} x[i] \log \left(\frac{\hat{x}_i^{t+1} / \sum_i \hat{x}_i^{t+1}}{x_i^t} \right)
$$

$$
= \sum_{i=1}^{|\mathcal{X}|} x[i] \left[\log \left(\frac{x_i^t \exp(-\eta r_t[i]))}{x_i^t} \right) - \log \left(\sum_{j=1}^{|\mathcal{X}|} \exp(-\eta r_t[j]) x_j^t \right) \right]
$$

$$
= - \left(\sum_{i=1}^{|\mathcal{X}|} x[i] \eta r_t[i] \right) - \log \left(\sum_{i=j}^{|\mathcal{X}|} \exp(-\eta r_t[j]) x_j^t \right)
$$

$$
= -\eta \langle r_t, x \rangle - \log \left(\sum_{j=1}^{|\mathcal{X}|} \exp(-\eta r_t[j]) x_j^t \right)
$$

$$
\geq -\eta \langle r_t, x \rangle - \log \left(\sum_{j=1}^{|\mathcal{X}|} x_j^t (1 + \eta^2 - \eta r_t[j]) \right)
$$

$$
= -\eta \langle r_t, x \rangle - \log \left(1 + \eta^2 - \eta \langle r_t, x^t \rangle \right)
$$

$$
\geq \eta \left(\langle r_t, x^t \rangle - \langle r_t, x \rangle \right) - \eta^2.
$$

The first inequality follows from the fact that:

$$
\exp(-\eta r_t[j]) \leq 1 - \eta r_t[j] + \eta^2 (r_t[j])^2 \leq 1 - \eta r_t[j] + \eta^2.
$$

The second inequality follows from the fact that $\log(1 + y) \leq y$ for $y > -1$. $\qquad \square$

The rest of the proof now follows easily. By the conditions of the database/query sequence (described in the hypothesis for Theorem 4.10 above), for every t,

1. $|f_t(x) - f_t(x^t)| \geq \alpha$ and
2. $|v_t - f_t(x)| < \alpha$.

Thus, $f_t(x) < f_t(x^t)$ if and only if $v_t < f_t(x^t)$. In particular, $r_t = f_t$ if $f_t(x^t) - f_t(x) \geq \alpha$, and $r_t = 1 - f_t$ if $f_t(x) - f_t(x^t) \geq \alpha$. Therefore, by Lemma 4.12 and the choice of $\eta = \alpha/2$ as described in the Update Rule,

$$\Psi_t - \Psi_{t+1} \geq \frac{\alpha}{2}\left(\langle r_t, x^t \rangle - \langle r_t, x \rangle\right) - \frac{\alpha^2}{4} \geq \frac{\alpha}{2}(\alpha) - \frac{\alpha^2}{4} = \frac{\alpha^2}{4}.$$

Finally we know:

$$0 \leq \Psi_L \leq \Psi_0 - L \cdot \frac{\alpha^2}{4} \leq \log |\mathcal{X}| - L\frac{\alpha^2}{4}.$$

Solving, we find: $L \leq \frac{4 \log |\mathcal{X}|}{\alpha^2}$. This completes the proof. $\square$

We can now combine the Multiplicative Weights Update Rule with the NumericSparse algorithm to give an interactive query release mechanism. For $(\epsilon, 0)$ privacy, we essentially (with somewhat worse constants) recover the bound for SmallDB. For (ϵ, δ)-differential privacy, we obtain better bounds, by virtue of being able to use the composition theorem. The queries to NumericSparse are asking whether the magnitude of the error given by estimating $f_i(x)$ by applying f_i to the current approximation x^t to x is above an appropriately chosen threshold T, that is, they are asking if $|f(x) - f(x^t)|$ is large. For technical reasons this is done by asking about $f(x) - f(x^t)$ (without the absolute value) and about $f(x^t) - f(x)$. Recall that the NumericSparse algorithm responds with either $\perp$ or some (positive) value exceeding T. We use the mnemonic E for the responses to emphasize that the query is asking about an error.

Theorem 4.13. The Online Multiplicative Weights Mechanism (via NumericSparse) is $(\epsilon, 0)$-differentially private.

Algorithm 6 The Online Multiplicative Weights Mechanism (via NumericSparse) takes as input a private database x, privacy parameters ϵ, δ, accuracy parameters α and β, and a stream of linear queries $\{f_i\}$ that may be chosen adaptively from a class of queries $\mathcal{Q}$. It outputs a stream of answers $\{a_i\}$.

OnlineMW via NumericSparse $(x, \{f_i\}, \epsilon, \delta, \alpha, \beta)$

Let $c \leftarrow \frac{4 \log |\mathcal{X}|}{\alpha^2}$,

if $\delta = 0$ **then**

    Let $T \leftarrow \frac{18c(\log(2|\mathcal{Q}|) + \log(4c/\beta))}{\epsilon \|x\|_1}$

else

    Let $T \leftarrow \frac{(2 + 32\sqrt{2})\sqrt{c \log \frac{2}{\delta}}(\log k + \log \frac{4c}{\beta})}{\epsilon \|x\|_1}$

end if

Initialize NumericSparse$(x, \{f_i'\}, T, c, \epsilon, \delta)$ with a stream of queries $\{f_i'\}$, outputting a stream of answers E_i.

Let $t \leftarrow 0$, and let $x^0 \in \Delta([\mathcal{X}])$ satisfy $x_i^0 = 1/|\mathcal{X}|$ for all $i \in [|\mathcal{X}|]$.

for each query f_i **do**

    Let $f_{2i-1}'(\cdot) = f_i(\cdot) - f_i(x^t)$.

    Let $f_{2i}'(\cdot) = f_i(x^t) - f_i(\cdot)$

    if $E_{2i-1} = \bot$ and $E_{2i} = \bot$ **then**

      Let $a_i = f_i(x^t)$

    else

      if $E_{2i-1} \in \mathbb{R}$ **then**

        Let $a_i = f_i(x^t) + E_{2i-1}$

      else

        Let $a_i = f_i(x^t) - E_{2i}$

      end if

      Let $x^{t+1} = MW(x^t, f_i, a_i)$

      Let $t \leftarrow t + 1$.

    end if

end for

Proof. This follows directly from the privacy analysis of NumericSparse, because the OnlineMW algorithm accesses the database only through NumericSparse. $\square$

Speaking informally, the proof of utility for the Online Multiplicative Weights Mechanism (via NumericSparse) uses the utility theorem for the NumericSparse (Theorem 3.28) to conclude that, with high probability, the Multiplicative Weights Update Rule is only invoked when the query f_t is truly a distinguishing query, meaning, $|f_i(x) - f_t(x^t)|$ is "large," *and* the released noisy approximations to $f_i(x)$ are "accurate." Under this assumption, we can apply the convergence theorem (Theorem 4.10) to conclude that the total number of updates is small and therefore the algorithm can answer all queries in $\mathcal{Q}$.

Theorem 4.14. For $\delta = 0$, with probability at least $1 - \beta$, for all queries f_i, the Online Multiplicative Weights Mechanism (via NumericSparse) returns an answer a_i such that $|f_i(x) - a_i| \leq 3\alpha$ for any α such that:

$$\alpha \geq \frac{32 \log |\mathcal{X}| \left(\log(|\mathcal{Q}|) + \log \left(\frac{32 \log |\mathcal{X}|}{\alpha^2 \beta}\right)\right)}{\epsilon \alpha^2 \|x\|_1}$$

Proof. Recall that, by Theorem 3.28, given k queries and a maximum number c of above-threshold queries, NumericSparse is (α, β)-accurate for any α such that:

$$\alpha \geq \frac{9c(\log k + \log(4c/\beta))}{\epsilon}.$$

In our case $c = 4 \log |\mathcal{X}|/\alpha^2$ and $k = 2|\mathcal{Q}|$, and we have been normalizing, which reduces α by a factor of $\|x\|_1$. With this in mind, we can take

$$\alpha = \frac{32 \log |\mathcal{X}| \left(\log(|\mathcal{Q}|) + \log \left(\frac{32 \log |\mathcal{X}|}{\alpha^2 \beta}\right)\right)}{\epsilon \alpha^2 \|x\|_1}$$

and note that with this value we get $T = 2\alpha$ for the case $\delta = 0$.

Assume we are in this high $(1 - \beta)$ probability case. Then for all i such that f_i triggers an update, $|f_i(x) - f_i(x^t)| \geq T - \alpha = \alpha$ (Theorem 4.10, condition 1). Thus, f_i, a_i form a valid pair of query/value updates as required in the hypothesis of Theorem 4.10 and so, by that theorem, there can be at most $c = \frac{4 \log |\mathcal{X}|}{\alpha^2}$ such update steps.

In addition, still by the accuracy properties of the Sparse Vector algorithm,

1. at most one of E_{2i-1}, E_{2i} will have value $\perp$;

2. for all i such that no update is triggered ($a_i = f_i(x^t)$) we have $|f_i(x) - f_i(x^t)| \leq T + \alpha = 3\alpha$; and

3. for all i such that an update is triggered we have $|f_i(x) - a_i| \leq \alpha$ (Theorem 4.10, condition 2).   □

Optimizing the above expression for α and removing the normalization factor, we find that the OnlineMW mechanism can answer each linear query to accuracy 3α except with probability β for:

$$\alpha = ||x||_1^{2/3} \left(\frac{36 \log |\mathcal{X}| \left(\log(|\mathcal{Q}|) + \log \left(\frac{32 \log |\mathcal{X}|^{1/3} ||x||_1^{2/3}}{\beta} \right) \right)}{\epsilon} \right)^{1/3}$$

which is comparable to the SmallDB mechanism.

By repeating the same argument, but instead using the utility theorem for the (ϵ, δ)-private version of Sparse Vector (Theorem 3.28), we obtain the following theorem.

Theorem 4.15. For $\delta > 0$, with probability at least $1-\beta$, for all queries f_i, OnlineMW returns an answer a_i such that $|f_i(x) - a_i| \leq 3\alpha$ for any α such that:

$$\alpha \geq \frac{(2 + 32\sqrt{2}) \cdot \sqrt{\log |\mathcal{X}| \log \frac{2}{\delta}} \left(\log |\mathcal{Q}| + \log \left(\frac{32 \log |\mathcal{X}|}{\alpha^2 \beta} \right) \right)}{\alpha \epsilon ||x||_1}$$

Again optimizing the above expression for α and removing the normalization factor, we find that the OnlineMW mechanism can answer each linear query to accuracy 3α except with probability β, for:

$$\alpha = ||x||_1^{1/2} \left(\frac{(2 + 32\sqrt{2}) \cdot \sqrt{\log |\mathcal{X}| \log \frac{2}{\delta}} \left(\log |\mathcal{Q}| + \log \left(\frac{32 ||x||_1}{\beta} \right) \right)}{\epsilon} \right)^{1/2}$$

which gives better accuracy (as a function of $||x||_1$) than the SmallDB mechanism. Intuitively, the greater accuracy comes from the iterative nature of the mechanism, which allows us to take advantage of our composition theorems for (ϵ, δ)-privacy. The SmallDB mechanism runs in just a single shot, and so there is no opportunity to take advantage of composition.

The accuracy of the private multiplicative weights algorithm has dependencies on several parameters, which are worth further discussion. In the end, the algorithm answers queries using the *sparse vector technique* paired with a *learning algorithm for linear functions*. As we proved in the last section, the sparse vector technique introduces error that scales like $O(c \log k/(\epsilon \|x\|_1))$ when a total of k sensitivity $1/\|x\|_1$ queries are made, and at most c of them can have "above threshold" answers, for any threshold T. Recall that these error terms arise because the privacy analysis for the sparse vector algorithm allows us to "pay" only for the above threshold queries, and therefore can add noise $O(c/(\epsilon \|x\|_1))$ to each query. On the other hand, since we end up adding independent Laplace noise with scale $\Omega(c/(\epsilon \|x\|_1))$ to k queries in total, we expect that the maximum error over all k queries is larger by a $\log k$ factor. But what is c, and what queries should we ask? The multiplicative weights learning algorithm gives us a query strategy and a guarantee that no more than $c = O(\log |\mathcal{X}|/\alpha^2)$ queries will be above a threshold of $T = O(\alpha)$, for any α. (The queries we ask are always: " How much does the real answer differ from the predicted answer of the current multiplicative weights hypothesis." The answers to these questions both give us the true answers to the queries, as well as instructions how to update the learning algorithm appropriately when a query is above threshold.) Together, this leads us to set the threshold to be $O(\alpha)$, where α is the expression that satisfies: $\alpha = O(\log |\mathcal{X}| \log k/(\epsilon \|x\|_1 \alpha^2))$. This minimizes the two sources of error: error from the sparse vector technique, and error from failing to update the multiplicative weights hypothesis.

4.3 Bibliographical notes

The offline query release mechanism given in this section is from Blum et al. [8], which gave bounds in terms of the VC-Dimension of the query class (Theorem 4.9). The generalization to fat shattering dimension is given in [72].

The online query release mechanism given in this section is from Hardt and Rothblum [44]. This mechanism uses the classic multiplicative weights update method, for which Arora, Hazan and Kale give an excellent survey [1]. Slightly improved bounds for the private multiplicative weights mechanism were given by Gupta et al. [39], and the analysis here follows the presentation from [39].

5

Generalizations

In this section we generalize the query release algorithms of the previous section. As a result, we get bounds for arbitrary low sensitivity queries (not just linear queries), as well as new bounds for linear queries. These generalizations also shed some light on a connection between query release and machine learning.

The SmallDB offline query release mechanism in Section 4 is a special case of what we call the *net mechanism*. We saw that both mechanisms in that section yield *synthetic databases*, which provide a convenient means for approximating the value of any query in $\mathcal{Q}$ on the private database: just evaluate the query on the synthetic database and take the result as the noisy answer. More generally, a mechanism can produce a *data structure* of arbitrary form, that, together with a fixed, public, algorithm (independent of the database) provides a method for approximating the values of queries.

The Net mechanism is a straightforward generalization of the SmallDB mechanism: First, fix, independent of the actual database, an α-net of data structures such that evaluation of any query in $\mathcal{Q}$ using the released data structure gives a good (within an additive α error) estimate of the value of the query on the private database. Next, apply the exponential mechanism to choose an element of this net, where the quality function minimizes the maximum error, over the queries in $\mathcal{Q}$, for the elements of the net.

We also generalize the online multiplicative weights algorithm so that we can instantiate it with any other *online learning algorithm* for learning a database with respect to a set of queries. We note that such a mechanism can be run either online, or offline, where the set of queries to be asked to the "online" mechanism is instead selected using a "private distinguisher," which identifies queries on which the current hypothesis of the learner differs substantially from the real database. These are queries that would have yielded an update step in the online algorithm. A "distinguisher" turns out to be equivalent to an agnostic learning algorithm, which sheds light on a source of hardness for efficient query release mechanisms.

In the following sections, we will discuss *data structures* for classes of queries $\mathcal{Q}$.

Definition 5.1. A data structure D drawn from some class of data structures $\mathcal{D}$ for a class of queries $\mathcal{Q}$ is implicitly endowed with an evaluation function $\text{Eval} : \mathcal{D} \times \mathcal{Q} \to \mathbb{R}$ with which we can evaluate any query in $\mathcal{Q}$ on D. However, to avoid being encumbered by notation, we will write simply $f(D)$ to denote $\text{Eval}(D, f)$ when the meaning is clear from context.

5.1 Mechanisms via α-nets

Given a collection of queries $\mathcal{Q}$, we define an α-net as follows:

Definition 5.2 (α-net). An α-net of data structures with respect to a class of queries $\mathcal{Q}$ is a set $\mathcal{N} \subset \mathbb{N}^{|\mathcal{X}|}$ such that for all $x \in \mathbb{N}^{|\mathcal{X}|}$, there exists an element of the α-net $y \in \mathcal{N}$ such that:

$$\max_{f \in \mathcal{Q}} |f(x) - f(y)| \le \alpha .$$

We write $\mathcal{N}_\alpha(\mathcal{Q})$ to denote an α-net of minimum cardinality among the set of all α-nets for $\mathcal{Q}$.

That is, for every possible database x, there exists a member of the α-net that "looks like" x with respect to all queries in $\mathcal{Q}$, up to an error tolerance of α.

Small α-nets will be useful for us, because when paired with the exponential mechanism, they will lead directly to mechanisms for answering queries with high accuracy. Given a class of functions $\mathcal{Q}$, we will define an instantiation of the exponential mechanism known as the *Net* mechanism. We first observe that the Net mechanism preserves ε-differential privacy.

Algorithm 7 The Net Mechanism

NetMechanism$(x, \mathcal{Q}, \varepsilon, \alpha)$

Let $\mathcal{R} \leftarrow \mathcal{N}_\alpha(\mathcal{Q})$

Let $q : \mathbb{N}^{|\mathcal{X}|} \times \mathcal{R} \to \mathbb{R}$ be defined to be:

$$q(x, y) = -\max_{f \in \mathcal{Q}} |f(x) - f(y)|$$

Sample And Output $y \in \mathcal{R}$ with the exponential mechanism $\mathcal{M}_E(x, q, \mathcal{R})$

Proposition 5.1. The Net mechanism is $(\varepsilon, 0)$ differentially private.

Proof. The Net mechanism is simply an instantiation of the exponential mechanism. Therefore, privacy follows from Theorem 3.10. $\square$

We may similarly call on our analysis of the exponential mechanism to begin understanding the utility guarantees of the Net mechanism:

Proposition 5.2. Let $\mathcal{Q}$ be any class of sensitivity $1/\|x\|_1$ queries. Let y be the database output by NetMechanism$(x, \mathcal{Q}, \varepsilon, \alpha)$. Then with probability $1 - \beta$:

$$\max_{f \in \mathcal{Q}} |f(x) - f(y)| \leq \alpha + \frac{2 \left(\log \left(|\mathcal{N}_\alpha(\mathcal{Q})| \right) + \log \left(\frac{1}{\beta} \right) \right)}{\varepsilon \|x\|_1}.$$

Proof. By applying Theorem 3.11 and noting that $S(q) = \frac{1}{\|x\|_1}$, and that $\mathrm{OPT}_q(D) \le \alpha$ by the definition of an α-net, we find:

$$\Pr\left[\max_{f \in \mathcal{Q}} |f(x) - f(y)| \ge \alpha + \frac{2}{\varepsilon\|x\|_1}\left(\log\left(|\mathcal{N}_\alpha(\mathcal{Q})|\right) + t\right)\right] \le e^{-t}.$$

Plugging in $t = \log\left(\frac{1}{\beta}\right)$ completes the proof. $\qquad\square$

We can therefore see that an upper bound on $|\mathcal{N}_\alpha(\mathcal{Q})|$ for a collection of functions $\mathcal{Q}$ immediately gives an upper bound on the accuracy that a differentially private mechanism can provide simultaneously for *all* functions in the class $\mathcal{Q}$.

This is exactly what we did in Section 4.1, where we saw that the key quantity is the VC-dimension of $\mathcal{Q}$, when $\mathcal{Q}$ is a class of linear queries.

5.2 The iterative construction mechanism

In this section, we derive an offline generalization of the private multiplicative weights algorithm, which can be instantiated with any properly defined learning algorithm. Informally, a database update algorithm maintains a sequence of data structures $D^1, D^2, \ldots$ that give increasingly good approximations to the input database x (in a sense that depends on the database update algorithm). Moreover, these mechanisms produce the next data structure in the sequence by considering only one query f that *distinguishes* the real database in the sense that $f(D^t)$ differs significantly from $f(x)$. The algorithm in this section shows that, up to small factors, solving the query-release problem in a differentially private manner is equivalent to solving the simpler *learning* or *distinguishing* problem in a differentially private manner: given a private distinguishing algorithm and a non-private database update algorithm, we get a corresponding private release algorithm. We can plug in the exponential mechanism as a canonical private distinguisher, and the multiplicative weights algorithm as a generic database update algorithm for the general linear query setting, but more efficient distinguishers are possible in special cases.

Syntactically, we will consider functions of the form $U : \mathcal{D} \times \mathcal{Q} \times \mathbb{R} \to \mathcal{D}$, where $\mathcal{D}$ represents a class of data structures on which queries in $\mathcal{Q}$ can be evaluated. The inputs to U are a data structure in $\mathcal{D}$, which represents the current data structure D^t; a query f, which represents the distinguishing query, and may be restricted to a certain set $\mathcal{Q}$; and also a real number, which estimates $f(x)$. Formally, we define a *database update sequence*, to capture the sequence of inputs to U used to generate the database sequence $D^1, D^2, \ldots$.

Definition 5.3 (Database Update Sequence). Let $x \in \mathbb{N}^{|\mathcal{X}|}$ be any database and let $\{(D^t, f_t, v_t)\}_{t=1,\ldots,L} \in (\mathcal{D} \times \mathcal{Q} \times \mathbb{R})^L$ be a sequence of tuples. We say the sequence is a $(U, x, \mathcal{Q}, \alpha, T)$-*database update sequence* if it satisfies the following properties:

1. $D^1 = U(\bot, \cdot, \cdot)$,
2. for every $t = 1, 2, \ldots, L$, $|f_t(x) - f_t(D^t)| \geq \alpha$,
3. for every $t = 1, 2, \ldots, L$, $|f_t(x) - v_t| < \alpha$,
4. and for every $t = 1, 2, \ldots, L - 1$, $D^{t+1} = U(D^t, f_t, v_t)$.

We note that for all of the database update algorithms we consider, the approximate answer v_t is used only to determine the *sign* of $f_t(x) - f_t(D^t)$, which is the motivation for requiring that the estimate of $f_t(x)$ (v_t) have error smaller than α. The main measure of efficiency we're interested in from a database update algorithm is the maximum number of updates we need to perform before the database D^t approximates x well with respect to the queries in $\mathcal{Q}$. To this end we define a database update algorithm as follows:

Definition 5.4 (Database Update Algorithm). Let $U : \mathcal{D} \times \mathcal{Q} \times \mathbb{R} \to \mathcal{D}$ be an update rule and let $T : \mathbb{R} \to \mathbb{R}$ be a function. We say U is a $T(\alpha)$-*database update algorithm for query class* $\mathcal{Q}$ if for every database $x \in \mathbb{N}^{|\mathcal{X}|}$, every $(U, x, \mathcal{Q}, \alpha, L)$-database update sequence satisfies $L \leq T(\alpha)$.

Note that the definition of a $T(\alpha)$-database update algorithm implies that if U is a $T(\alpha)$-database update algorithm, then given any maximal $(U, x, \mathcal{Q}, \alpha, U)$-database update sequence, the final database D^L must satisfy $\max_{f \in \mathcal{Q}} |f(x) - f(D^L)| \leq \alpha$ or else there would exist another query satisfying property 2 of Definition 5.3, and thus there would exist a $(U, x, \mathcal{Q}, \alpha, L+1)$-database update sequence, contradicting maximality. That is, the goal of a $T(\alpha)$ database update rule is to generate a maximal database update sequence, and the final data structure in a maximal database update sequence necessarily encodes the approximate answers to every query $f \in \mathcal{Q}$.

Now that we have defined database update algorithms, we can remark that what we really proved in Theorem 4.10 was that the Multiplicative Weights algorithm is a $T(\alpha)$-database update algorithm for $T(\alpha) = 4 \log |\mathcal{X}| / \alpha^2$.

Before we go on, let us build some intuition for what a database update algorithm is. A $T(\alpha)$-database update algorithm begins with some initial guess D^1 about what the true database x looks like. Because this guess is not based on any information, it is quite likely that D^1 and x bear little resemblance, and that there is some $f \in \mathcal{Q}$ that is able to distinguish between these two databases by at least α: that is, that $f(x)$ and $f(D^1)$ differ in value by at least α. What a database update algorithm does is to update its hypothesis D^t given evidence that its current hypothesis D^{t-1} is incorrect: at each stage, it takes as input some query in $\mathcal{Q}$ which distinguishes its current hypothesis from the true database, and then it outputs a new hypothesis. The parameter $T(\alpha)$ is an upper bound on the number of times that the database update algorithm will have to update its hypothesis: it is a promise that after at most $T(\alpha)$ distinguishing queries have been provided, the algorithm will finally have produced a hypothesis that looks like the true database with respect to $\mathcal{Q}$, at least up to error α.[1] For a database update algorithm, smaller bounds $T(\alpha)$ are more desirable.

Database Update Algorithms and Online Learning Algorithms: We remark that database update algorithms are essentially *online learning*

---

[1]Imagine that the database update algorithm is attempting to sculpt x out of a block of clay. Initially, its sculpture D^1 bears no resemblance to the true database: it is simply a block of clay. However, a helpful distinguisher points out to the sculptor places in which the clay juts out much farther than the true target database: the sculptor dutifully pats down those bumps. If the distinguisher always finds large protrusions, of magnitude at least α, the sculpture will be finished soon, and the distinguisher's time will not be wasted!

algorithms in the *mistake bound model*. In the setting of online learning, unlabeled examples arrive in some arbitrary order, and the learning algorithm must attempt to label them.

Background from Learning Theory. In the *mistake bound model of learning*, labeled examples $(x_i, y_i) \in \mathcal{X} \times \{0, 1\}$ arrive one at a time, in a potentially adversarial order. At time i, the learning algorithm A observes x_i, and must make a prediction $\hat{y}_i$ about the label for x_i. It then sees the true label y_i, and is said to *make a mistake* if its prediction was wrong: i.e., if $y_i \neq \hat{y}_i$. A learning algorithm A for a class of functions C is said to have a mistake bound of M, if for all $f \in C$, and for all adversarially selected sequences of examples $(x_1, f(x_1)), \dots, (x_i, f(x_i)), \dots$, A never makes more than M mistakes. Without loss of generality, we can think of such a learning algorithm as maintaining some hypothesis $\hat{f} : \mathcal{X} \to \{0, 1\}$ at all times, and updating it only when it makes a mistake. The adversary in this model is quite powerful — it can choose the sequence of labeled examples adaptively, knowing the current hypothesis of the learning algorithm, and its entire history of predictions. Hence, learning algorithms that have finite mistake bounds can be useful in extremely general settings.

It is not hard to see that mistake bounded online learning algorithms always exist for finite classes of functions C. Consider, for example, the *halving algorithm*. The halving algorithm initially maintains a set S of functions from C consistent with the examples that it has seen so far: Initially $S = C$. Whenever a new unlabeled example arrives, it predicts according to the majority vote of its consistent hypotheses: that is, it predicts label 1 whenever $|\{f \in S : f(x_i) = 1\}| \geq |S|/2$. Whenever it makes a mistake on an example x_i, it updates S by removing any inconsistent function: $S \leftarrow \{f \in S : f(x_i) = y_i\}$. Note that whenever it makes a mistake, the size of S is cut in half! So long as all examples are labeled by *some* function $f \in C$, there is at least one function $f \in C$ that is never removed from S. Hence, the halving algorithm has a mistake bound of $\log |C|$.

Generalizing beyond boolean labels, we can view database update algorithms as online learning algorithms in the mistake bound model:

here, examples that arrive are the queries (which may come in adversarial order). The labels are the approximate values of the queries when evaluated on the database. The database update algorithm hypothesis D^t makes a *mistake* on query f if $|f(D^t) - f(x)| \geq \alpha$, in which case we learn the label of f (that is, v_t) and allow the database update algorithm to update the hypothesis. Saying that an algorithm U is a $T(\alpha)$-database update algorithm is akin to saying that it has a mistake bound of $T(\alpha)$: no adversarially chosen sequence of queries can ever cause it to make more than $T(\alpha)$-mistakes. Indeed, the database update algorithms that we will see are taken from the online learning literature. The multiplicative weights mechanism is based on an online learning algorithm known as *Hedge*, which we have already discussed. The Median Mechanism (later in this section) is based on the *Halving Algorithm*, and the Perceptron algorithm is based (coincidentally) on an algorithm known as *Perceptron*. We won't discuss Perceptron here, but it operates by making *additive* updates, rather than the multiplicative updates used by multiplicative weights.

A database update algorithm for a class Q will be useful together with a corresponding *distinguisher*, whose job is to output a function that behaves differently on the true database x and the hypothesis D^t, that is, to point out a mistake.

Definition 5.5 (($F(\varepsilon), \gamma$)-Private Distinguisher). Let Q be a set of queries, let $\gamma \geq 0$ and let $F(\varepsilon) : \mathbb{R} \to \mathbb{R}$ be a function. An algorithm $\text{Distinguish}_\varepsilon : \mathbb{N}^{|\mathcal{X}|} \times \mathcal{D} \to Q$ is an ($F(\varepsilon), \gamma$)-Private Distinguisher for Q if for every setting of the privacy parameter ε, on every pair of inputs $x \in \mathbb{N}^{|\mathcal{X}|}$, $D \in \mathcal{D}$ it is ($\varepsilon, 0$)-differentially private with respect to x and it outputs an $f^* \in Q$ such that $|f^*(x) - f^*(D)| \geq \max_{f \in Q} |f(x) - f(D)| - F(\varepsilon)$ with probability at least $1 - \gamma$.

Remark 5.1. In machine learning, the goal is to find a function $f : \mathcal{X} \to \{0,1\}$ from a class of functions Q that *best labels* a collection of labeled examples $(x_1, y_1), \ldots, (x_m, y_m) \in \mathcal{X} \times \{0,1\}$. (Examples $(x, 0)$ are known as *negative examples*, and examples $(x, 1)$ are known as *positive examples*). Each example x_i has a *true* label y_i, and a function f correctly labels x_i if $f(x_i) = y_i$. An *agnostic learning algorithm* for a class Q is an algorithm that can find the function in Q that labels all of the data points approximately as well as the best function in $\mathcal{Q}$, even if no function in $\mathcal{Q}$ can perfectly label them. Note that equivalently, an agnostic learning algorithm is one that maximizes the number of positive examples labeled 1 minus the number of negative examples labeled 1. Phrased in this way, we can see that a *distinguisher* as defined above is just an agnostic learning algorithm: just imagine that x contains all of the "positive" examples, and that y contains all of the "negative examples." (Note that it is ok of x and y are not disjoint — in the learning problem, the same example can occur with both a positive and a negative label, since agnostic learning does not require that any function perfectly label every example.) Finally, note also that for classes of linear queries $\mathcal{Q}$, a distinguisher is simply an optimization algorithm. Because for linear queries f, $f(x) - f(y) = f(x - y)$, a distinguisher simply seeks to find $\arg\max_{f \in \mathcal{Q}} |f(x - y)|$.

Note that, *a priori*, a differentially private distinguisher is a weaker object than a differentially private release algorithm: A distinguisher merely finds a query in a set $\mathcal{Q}$ with the approximately largest value, whereas a release algorithm must find the answer to every query in $\mathcal{Q}$. In the algorithm that follows, however, we reduce release to optimization.

We will first analyze the IC algorithm, and then instantiate it with a specific distinguisher and database update algorithm. What follows is a formal analysis, but the intuition for the mechanism is simple: we simply run the iterative database construction algorithm to construct a hypothesis that approximately matches x with respect to the queries $\mathcal{Q}$. If at each round our distinguisher succeeds in finding a query that has high discrepancy between the hypothesis database and the true database, then our database update algorithm will output a database that is β-accurate with respect to $\mathcal{Q}$. If the distinguisher ever fails to find such a query, then it must be that there are no such queries, and our database update algorithm has already learned an accurate hypothesis with respect to the queries of interest! This requires at most T iterations, and so we access the data only $2T$ times using $(\varepsilon_0, 0)$-differentially private methods (running the given distinguisher, and then checking its answer with the Laplace mechanism). Privacy will therefore follow from our composition theorems.

Algorithm 8 The Iterative Construction (IC) Mechanism. It takes as input a parameter ε_0, an $(F(\varepsilon_0), \gamma)$-Private Distinguisher Distinguish for $\mathcal{Q}$, together with an $T(\alpha)$-iterative database update algorithm U for $\mathcal{Q}$.

$IC(x, \alpha, \varepsilon_0, \text{Distinguish}, U)$:

> **Let** $D^0 = U(\perp, \cdot, \cdot)$.
> **for** $t = 1$ to $T(\alpha/2)$ **do**
> > **Let** $f^{(t)} = \text{Distinguish}(x, D^{t-1})$
> > **Let** $\hat{v}^{(t)} = f^{(t)}(x) + \text{Lap}\left(\frac{1}{\|x\|_1 \varepsilon_0}\right)$.
> > **if** $|\hat{v}^{(t)} - f^{(t)}(D^{t-1})| < 3\alpha/4$ **then**
> > > **Output** $y = D^{t-1}$.
> >
> > **else**
> > > **Let** $D^t = U(D^{t-1}, f^{(t)}, \hat{v}^{(t)})$.
> >
> > **end if**
>
> **end for**
> **Output** $y = D^{T(\alpha/2)}$.

The analysis of this algorithm just involves checking the technical details of a simple intuition. Privacy will follow because the algorithm is just the composition of $2T(\alpha)$ steps, each of which is $(\varepsilon_0, 0)$-differentially private. Accuracy follows because we are always outputting the last database in a maximal database update sequence. If the algorithm has not yet formed a maximal Database Update Sequence, then the distinguishing algorithm will find a distinguishing query to add another step to the sequence.

Theorem 5.3. The IC algorithm is $(\varepsilon, 0)$-differentially private for $\varepsilon_0 \leq \varepsilon/2T(\alpha/2)$. The IC algorithm is (ε, δ)-differentially private for
$$\varepsilon_0 \leq \frac{\varepsilon}{4\sqrt{T(\alpha/2)\log(1/\delta)}}.$$

Proof. The algorithm runs at most $2T(\alpha/2)$ compositions of ε_0-differentially private algorithms. Recall from Theorem 3.20 that ε_0 differentially private algorithms are $2k\varepsilon_0$ differentially private under $2k$-fold composition, and are (ε', δ) private for $\varepsilon' = \sqrt{4k \ln(1/\delta')}\varepsilon_0 + 2k\varepsilon_0(e^{\varepsilon_0} - 1)$. Plugging in the stated values for ε_0 proves the claim. $\square$

Theorem 5.4. Given an $(F(\varepsilon), \gamma)$-private distinguisher, a parameter ε_0, and a $T(\alpha)$-Database Update Algorithm, with probability at least $1-\beta$, the IC algorithm returns a database y such that: $\max_{f \in Q} |f(x) - f(y)| \leq \alpha$ for any α such that where:

$$\alpha \geq \max \left[\frac{8 \log(2T(\alpha/2)/\beta)}{\varepsilon_0 \|x\|_1}, 8F(\varepsilon_0) \right]$$

so long as $\gamma \leq \beta/(2T(\alpha/2))$.

Proof. The analysis is straightforward.

Recall that if $Y_i \sim \text{Lap}(1/(\varepsilon\|x\|_1))$, we have: $\Pr[|Y_i| \geq t/(\varepsilon\|x\|_1)] = \exp(-t)$. By a union bound, if $Y_1, \ldots, Y_k \sim \text{Lap}(1/(\varepsilon\|x\|_1))$, then $\Pr[\max_i |Y_i| \geq t/(\varepsilon\|x\|_1)] \leq k\exp(-t)$. Therefore, because we make at most $T(\alpha/2)$ draws from $\text{Lap}(1/(\varepsilon_0\|x\|_1))$, except with probability at most $\beta/2$, for all t:

$$|\hat{v}^{(t)} - f^{(t)}(x)| \leq \frac{1}{\varepsilon_0\|x\|_1} \log \frac{2T(\alpha/2)}{\beta} \leq \frac{\alpha}{8}.$$

Note that by assumption, $\gamma \leq \beta/(2T(\alpha/2))$, so we also have that except with probability $\beta/2$:

$$|f^{(t)}(x) - f^{(t)}(D^{t-1})| \geq \max_{f \in Q} |f(x) - f(D^{t-1})| - F(\varepsilon_0)$$

$$\geq \max_{f \in Q} |f(x) - f(D^{t-1})| - \frac{\alpha}{8}.$$

For the rest of the argument, we will condition on both of these events occurring, which is the case except with probability β.

There are two cases. Either a data structure $D' = D^{T(\alpha/2)}$ is output, or data structure $D' = D^t$ for $t < T(\alpha/2)$ is output. First, suppose $D' = D^{T(\alpha/2)}$. Since for all $t < T(\alpha/2)$ it must have been the case that $|\hat{v}^{(t)} - f^{(t)}(D^{t-1})| \geq 3\alpha/4$ and by our conditioning, $|\hat{v}^{(t)} - f^{(t)}(x)| \leq \frac{\alpha}{8}$, we know for all t: $|f^{(t)}(x) - f^{(t)}(D^{t-1})| \geq \alpha/2$. Therefore, the sequence $(D^t, f^{(t)}, \hat{v}^{(t)})$, formed a maximal $(U, x, Q, \alpha/2, T(\alpha/2))$-Database Update Sequence (recall Definition 5.3), and we have that $\max_{f \in Q} |f(x) - f(x')| \leq \alpha/2$ as desired.

Next, suppose $D' = D^{t-1}$ for $t < T(\alpha/2)$. Then it must have been the case that for t, $|\hat{v}^{(t)} - f^{(t)}(D^{t-1})| < 3\alpha/4$. By our conditioning, in this case it must be that $|f^{(t)}(x) - f^{(t)}(D^{t-1})| < \frac{7\alpha}{8}$, and that therefore by the properties of an $(F(\varepsilon_0), \gamma)$-distinguisher:

$$\max_{f \in \mathcal{Q}} |f(x) - f(D')| < \frac{7\alpha}{8} + F(\varepsilon_0) \leq \alpha$$

as desired. $\square$

Note that we can use the exponential mechanism as a private distinguisher: take the domain to be $\mathcal{Q}$, and let the quality score be: $q(D, f) = |f(D) - f(D^t)|$, which has sensitivity $1/\|x\|_1$. Applying the exponential mechanism utility theorem, we get:

Theorem 5.5. The exponential mechanism is an $(F(\varepsilon), \gamma)$ distinguisher for:

$$F(\varepsilon) = \frac{2}{\|x\|_1 \varepsilon} \left(\log \frac{|\mathcal{Q}|}{\gamma} \right).$$

Therefore, using the exponential mechanism as a distinguisher, Theorem 5.4 gives:

Theorem 5.6. Given a $T(\alpha)$-Database Update Algorithm and a parameter ε_0 together with the exponential mechanism distinguisher, with probability at least $1 - \beta$, the IC algorithm returns a database y such that: $\max_{f \in \mathcal{Q}} |f(x) - f(y)| \leq \alpha$ where:

$$\alpha \leq \max \left[\frac{8 \log(2T(\alpha/2)/\beta)}{\varepsilon_0 \|x\|_1}, \frac{16}{\|x\|_1 \varepsilon_0} \left(\log \frac{|\mathcal{Q}|}{\gamma} \right) \right]$$

so long as $\gamma \leq \beta/(2T(\alpha/2))$.

Plugging in our values of ε_0:

Theorem 5.7. Given a $T(\alpha)$-Database Update Algorithm, together with the exponential mechanism distinguisher, the IC mechanism is ε-differentially private and with probability at least $1 - \beta$, the IC algorithm returns a database y such that: $\max_{f \in \mathcal{Q}} |f(x) - f(y)| \leq \alpha$ where:

$$\alpha \leq \frac{8T(\alpha/2)}{\|x\|_1 \varepsilon} \left(\log \frac{|\mathcal{Q}|}{\gamma} \right)$$

and (ε, δ)-differentially private for:

$$\alpha \leq \frac{16\sqrt{T(\alpha/2)\log(1/\delta)}}{\|x\|_1 \varepsilon}\left(\log\frac{|\mathcal{Q}|}{\gamma}\right)$$

so long as $\gamma \leq \beta/(2T(\alpha/2))$.

Note that in the language of this section, what we proved in Theorem 4.10 was exactly that the multiplicative weights algorithm is a $T(\alpha)$-Database Update Algorithm for $T(\alpha) = \frac{4\log|\mathcal{X}|}{\alpha^2}$. Plugging this bound into Theorem 5.7 recovers the bound we got for the online multiplicative weights algorithm. Note that now, however, we can plug in other database update algorithms as well.

5.2.1 Applications: other database update algorithms

Here we give several other database update algorithms. The first works directly from α-nets, and therefore can get non-trivial bounds even for nonlinear queries (unlike multiplicative weights, which only works for linear queries). The second is another database update algorithm for linear queries, but with bounds incomparable to multiplicative weights. (In general, it will yield improved bounds when the dataset has size close to the size of the data universe, whereas multiplicative weights will give better bounds when the dataset is much smaller than the data universe.)

We first discuss the median mechanism, which takes advantage of α-nets. The median mechanism does not operate on databases, but instead on median data structures:

Definition 5.6 (Median Data Structure). A median data structure $\mathbf{D}$ is a collection of databases: $\mathbf{D} \subset \mathbb{N}^{|\mathcal{X}|}$. Any query f can be evaluated on a median data structure as follows: $f(\mathbf{D}) = \text{Median}(\{f(x) : x \in \mathbf{D}\})$.

In words, a median data structure is just a set of databases. To evaluate a query on it, we just evaluate the query on every database in the set, and then return the median value. Note that the answers given by the median data structure need not be consistent with *any* database! However, it will have the useful property that whenever it makes an error, it will rule out at least half of the data sets in its collection as being inconsistent with the true data set.

The median mechanism is then very simple:

Algorithm 9 The Median Mechanism (MM) Update Rule. It inputs and outputs a median data structure. It is instantiated with an α-net $\mathcal{N}_\alpha(\mathcal{Q})$ for a query class $\mathcal{Q}$, and its initial state is $\mathbf{D} = \mathcal{N}_\alpha(\mathcal{Q})$

$MM_{\alpha,\mathcal{Q}}(\mathbf{D}^t, f_t, v_t)$:

   if $\mathbf{D}^t = \perp$ **then**

      Output $\mathbf{D}^0 \leftarrow \mathcal{N}_\alpha(\mathcal{Q})$.

   end if

   if $v_t < f_t(\mathbf{D}^t)$ **then**

      Output $\mathbf{D}^{t+1} \leftarrow \mathbf{D}^t \setminus \{x \in \mathbf{D} : f_t(x) \geq f_t(\mathbf{D}^t)\}$.

   else

      Output $\mathbf{D}^{t+1} \leftarrow \mathbf{D}^t \setminus \{x \in \mathbf{D} : f_t(x) \leq f_t(\mathbf{D}^t)\}$.

   end if

The intuition for the median mechanism is as follows. It maintains a set of databases that are consistent with the answers to the distinguishing queries it has seen so far. Whenever it receives a query and answer that differ substantially from the real database, it updates itself to remove all of the databases that are inconsistent with the new information. Because it always chooses its answer as the median database among the set of consistent databases it is maintaining, every update step removes at least half of the consistent databases! Moreover, because the set of databases that it chooses initially is an α-net with respect to $\mathcal{Q}$, there is always some database that is never removed, because it remains consistent on all queries. This limits how many update rounds the mechanism can perform. How does the median mechanism do?

Theorem 5.8. For any class of queries $\mathcal{Q}$, The Median Mechanism is a $T(\alpha)$-database update algorithm for $T(\alpha) = \log |\mathcal{N}_\alpha(\mathcal{Q})|$.

Proof. We must show that any sequence $\{(D^t, f_t, v_t)\}_{t=1,\dots,L}$ with the property that $|f^t(\mathbf{D}^t) - f^t(x)| > \alpha$ and $|v_t - f^t(x)| < \alpha$ cannot have $L > \log |\mathcal{N}_\alpha(\mathcal{Q})|$. First observe that because $\mathbf{D}^0 = \mathcal{N}_\alpha(\mathcal{Q})$ is an α-net for $\mathcal{Q}$, by definition there is at least one y such that $y \in \mathbf{D}^t$ for all t (Recall that the update rule is only invoked on queries with error at least α. Since there is guaranteed to be a database y that has error less than α on all queries, it is never removed by an update step). Thus, we can always answer queries with $\mathbf{D}^t$, and for all t, $|\mathbf{D}^t| \geq 1$. Next observe that for each t, $|\mathbf{D}^t| \leq |\mathbf{D}^{t-1}|/2$. This is because each update step removes at least half of the elements: all of the elements at least as large as, or at most as large as the median element in $\mathbf{D}^t$ with respect to query f_t. Therefore, after L update steps, $|\mathbf{D}^L| \leq 1/2^L \cdot |\mathcal{N}_\alpha(\mathcal{Q})|$. Setting $L > \log |\mathcal{N}_\alpha(\mathcal{Q})|$ gives $|\mathbf{D}^L| < 1$, a contradiction. $\square$

Remark 5.2. For classes of linear queries $\mathcal{Q}$, we may refer to the upper bound on $\mathcal{N}_\alpha(\mathcal{Q})$ given in Theorem 4.2 to see that the Median Mechanism is a $T(\alpha)$-database update algorithm for $T(\alpha) = \log |\mathcal{Q}| \log |\mathcal{X}|/\alpha^2$. This is worse than the bound we gave for the Multiplicative Weights algorithm by a factor of $\log |\mathcal{Q}|$. On the other hand, nothing about the Median Mechanism algorithm is specific to linear queries — it works just as well for any class of queries that admits a small net. We can take advantage of this fact for nonlinear low sensitivity queries.

Note that if we want a mechanism which promises (ε, δ)-privacy for $\delta > 0$, we do not even need a particularly small net. In fact, the trivial net that simply includes every database of size $\|x\|_1$ will be sufficient:

Theorem 5.9. For every class of queries $\mathcal{Q}$ and every $\alpha \geq 0$, there is an α-net for databases of size $\|x\|_1 = n$ of size $\mathcal{N}_\alpha(\mathcal{Q}) \leq |\mathcal{X}|^n$.

Proof. We can simply let $\mathcal{N}_\alpha(\mathcal{Q})$ be the set of all $|\mathcal{X}|^n$ databases y of size $\|y\|_1 = n$. Then, for every x such that $\|x\|_1 = n$, we have $x \in \mathcal{N}_\alpha(\mathcal{Q})$, and so clearly: $\min_{y \in \mathcal{N}_\alpha(\mathcal{Q})} \max_{f \in \mathcal{Q}} |f(x) - f(y)| = 0$. $\square$

We can use this fact to get query release algorithms for *arbitrary* low sensitivity queries, not just linear queries. Applying Theorem 5.7 to the above bound, we find:

Theorem 5.10. Using the median mechanism, together with the exponential mechanism distinguisher, the IC mechanism is (ε, δ)-differentially private and with probability at least $1 - \beta$, the IC algorithm returns a database y such that: $\max_{f \in \mathcal{Q}} |f(x) - f(y)| \leq \alpha$ where:

$$\alpha \leq \frac{16 \sqrt{\log |\mathcal{X}| \log \frac{1}{\delta}} \log \left(\frac{2|\mathcal{Q}|n \log |\mathcal{X}|}{\beta} \right)}{\sqrt{n}\varepsilon},$$

where $\mathcal{Q}$ can be *any* family of sensitivity $1/n$ queries, not necessarily linear.

Proof. This follows simply by combining Theorems 5.8 and 5.9 to find that the Median Mechanism is a $T(\alpha)$-Database Update Algorithm for $T(\alpha) = n \log |\mathcal{X}|$ for databases of size $\|x\|_1 = n$ for every $\alpha > 0$ and every class of queries $\mathcal{Q}$. Plugging this into Theorem 5.7 gives the desired bound. $\qquad \square$

Note that this bound is almost as good as we were able to achieve for the special case of linear queries in Theorem 4.15! However, unlike in the case of linear queries, because arbitrary queries may not have α-nets which are significantly smaller than the trivial net used here, we are not able to get nontrivial accuracy guarantees if we want $(\varepsilon, 0)$-differential privacy.

The next database update algorithm we present is again for linear queries, but achieves incomparable bounds to those of the multiplicative weights database update algorithm. It is based on the *Perceptron* algorithm from online learning (just as multiplicative weights is derived from the *hedge* algorithm from online learning). Since the algorithm is for linear queries, we treat each query $f_t \in \mathcal{Q}$ as being a vector $f_t \in [0, 1]^{|\mathcal{X}|}$. Note that rather than doing a multiplicative update,

---

Algorithm 10 The Perceptron update rule

$\textbf{Perceptron}_{\alpha, \mathcal{Q}}(x^t, f_t, v_t)$:

   If: $x^t = \perp$ then: output $x^{t+1} = 0^{|\mathcal{X}|}$

   Else if: $f_t(x^t) > v_t$ then: output $x^{t+1} = x^t - \frac{\alpha}{|\mathcal{X}|} \cdot f_t$

   Else if: $f_t(x^t) \leq v_t$ then: output $x^{t+1} = x^t + \frac{\alpha}{|\mathcal{X}|} \cdot f_t$

---

as in the MW database update algorithm, here we do an additive update. In the analysis, we will see that this database update algorithm has an exponentially worse dependence (as compared to multiplicative weights) on the size of the universe, but a superior dependence on the size of the database. Thus, it will achieve better performance for databases that are large compared to the size of the data universe, and worse performance for databases that are small compared to the size of the data universe.

Theorem 5.11. Perceptron is a $T(\alpha)$-database update algorithm for:

$$T(\alpha) = \left(\frac{\|x\|_2}{\|x\|_1}\right)^2 \cdot \frac{|\mathcal{X}|}{\alpha^2}.$$

Proof. Unlike for multiplicative weights, it will be more convenient to analyze the Perceptron algorithm without normalizing the database to be a probability distribution, and then prove that it is a $T(\alpha')$ database update algorithm for $T(\alpha') = \frac{\|x\|_2^2 |\mathcal{X}|}{\alpha'^2}$. Plugging in $\alpha' = \alpha\|x\|_1$ will then complete the proof. Recall that since each query f_t is linear, we can view $f_t \in [0,1]^{|\mathcal{X}|}$ as a vector with the evaluation of $f_t(x)$ being equal to $\langle f_t, x \rangle$.

We must show that any sequence $\{(x^t, f_t, v_t)\}_{t=1,\ldots,L}$ with the property that $|f_t(x^t) - f_t(x)| > \alpha'$ and $|v_t - f_t(x)| < \alpha'$ cannot have $L > \frac{\|x\|_2^2 |\mathcal{X}|}{\alpha'^2}$.

We use a potential argument to show that for every $t = 1, 2, \ldots, L$, x^{t+1} is significantly closer to x than x^t. Specifically, our potential function is the L_2^2 norm of the database $x - x^t$, defined as

$$\|x\|_2^2 = \sum_{i \in \mathcal{X}} x(i)^2.$$

Observe that $\|x - x^1\|_2^2 = \|x\|_2^2$ since $x^1 = 0$, and $\|x\|_2^2 \geq 0$. Thus it suffices to show that in every step, the potential decreases by $\alpha'^2/|\mathcal{X}|$. We analyze the case where $f_t(x^t) > v_t$, the analysis for the opposite case will be similar. Let $R^t = x^t - x$. Observe that in this case we have

$$f_t(R^t) = f_t(x^t) - f_t(x) \geq \alpha'.$$

Now we can analyze the drop in potential.

$$\|R^t\|_2^2 - \|R^{t+1}\|_2^2 = \|R^t\|_2^2 - \|R^t - (\alpha'/|\mathcal{X}|) \cdot f_t\|_2^2$$

$$= \sum_{i \in \mathcal{X}} ((R^t(i))^2 - (R^t(i) - (\alpha'/|\mathcal{X}|) \cdot f_t(i))^2)$$

$$= \sum_{i \in \mathcal{X}} \left(\frac{2\alpha'}{|\mathcal{X}|} \cdot R^t(i) f_t(i) - \frac{\alpha'^2}{|\mathcal{X}|^2} f_t(i)^2 \right)$$

$$= \frac{2\alpha'}{|\mathcal{X}|} f_t(R^t) - \frac{\alpha'^2}{|\mathcal{X}|^2} \sum_{i \in \mathcal{X}} f_t(i)^2$$

$$\geq \frac{2\alpha'}{|\mathcal{X}|} f_t(R^t) - \frac{\alpha'^2}{|\mathcal{X}|^2} |\mathcal{X}|$$

$$\geq \frac{2\alpha'^2}{|\mathcal{X}|} - \frac{\alpha'^2}{|\mathcal{X}|} = \frac{\alpha'^2}{|\mathcal{X}|}.$$

This bounds the number of steps by $\|x\|_2^2 |\mathcal{X}|/\alpha'^2$, and completes the proof. $\qquad\qquad\qquad\qquad\qquad\qquad\qquad\qquad\qquad\qquad\qquad\qquad\quad\Box$

We may now plug this bound into Theorem 5.7 to obtain the following bound on the iterative construction mechanism:

Theorem 5.12. Using the perceptron database update algorithm, together with the exponential mechanism distinguisher, the IC mechanism is (ε, δ)-differentially private and with probability at least $1 - \beta$, the IC algorithm returns a database y such that: $\max_{f \in \mathcal{Q}} |f(x) - f(y)| \leq \alpha$ where:

$$\alpha \leq \frac{4\sqrt{4}\sqrt{\|x\|_2} \, (4|\mathcal{X}| \ln(1/\delta))^{1/4} \sqrt{\frac{\log(2|\mathcal{Q}|\|\mathcal{X}| \cdot \|x\|_2^2)}{\beta}}}{\sqrt{\epsilon}\|x\|_1},$$

where $\mathcal{Q}$ is a class of linear queries.

If the database x represents the edge set of a graph, for example, we will have $x_i \in [0, 1]$ for all i, and so:

$$\frac{\sqrt{\|x\|_2}}{\|x\|_1} \leq \left(\frac{1}{\|x\|_1} \right)^{3/4}.$$

Therefore, the perceptron database update algorithm will outperform the multiplicative weights database update algorithm on dense graphs.

5.2.2   Iterative construction mechanisms and online algorithms

In this section, we generalize the iterative construction framework to the online setting by using the NumericSparse algorithm. The online multiplicative weights algorithm which saw in the last chapter is an instantiation of this approach. One way of viewing the online algorithm is that the NumericSparse algorithm is serving as the private distinguisher in the IC framework, but that the "hard work" of distinguishing is being foisted upon the unsuspecting user. That is: if the user asks a query that does not serve as a good distinguishing query, this is a good case. We cannot use the database update algorithm to update our hypothesis, but we don't need to! By definition, the current hypothesis is a good approximation to the private database with respect to this query. On the other hand, if the user asks a query for which our current hypothesis is not a good approximation to the true database, then by definition the user has found a good distinguishing query, and we are again in a good case — we can run the database update algorithm to update our hypothesis!

The idea of this algorithm is very simple. We will use a database update algorithm to publicly maintain a hypothesis database. Every time a query arrives, we will classify it as either a hard query, or an easy query. An easy query is one for which the answer given by the hypothesis database is approximately correct, and no update step is needed: if we know that a given query is easy, we can simply compute its answer on the publicly known hypothesis database rather than on the private database, and incur no privacy loss. If we know that a query is hard, we can compute and release its answer using the Laplace mechanism, and update our hypothesis using the database update algorithm. This way, our total privacy loss is not proportional to the number of queries asked, but instead proportional to the number of *hard* queries asked. Because the database update algorithm guarantees that there will not need to be many update steps, we can be guaranteed that the total privacy loss will be small.

Theorem 5.13. OnlineIC is (ε, δ)-differentially private.

Algorithm 11 The Online Iterative Construction Mechanism parameterized by a $T(\alpha)$-database update algorithm U. It takes as input a private database x, privacy parameters ε, δ, accuracy parameters α and β, and a stream of queries $\{f_i\}$ that may be chosen adaptively from a class of queries $\mathcal{Q}$. It outputs a stream of answers $\{a_i\}$.

OnlineIC$_U(x, \{f_i\}, \varepsilon, \delta, \alpha, \beta)$

> **Let** $c \leftarrow T(\alpha)$,
> **if** $\delta = 0$ **then**
>> **Let** $T \leftarrow \dfrac{18c(\log(2|\mathcal{Q}|) + \log(4c/\beta))}{\epsilon \|x\|_1}$
>
> **else**
>> **Let** $T \leftarrow \dfrac{(2 + 32\sqrt{2})\sqrt{c \log \frac{2}{\delta}}(\log k + \log \frac{4c}{\beta})}{\epsilon \|x\|_1}$
>
> **end if**
> **Initialize** NumericSparse$(x, \{f'_i\}, T, c, \varepsilon, \delta)$ with a stream of queries $\{f'_i\}$, outputting a stream of answers a'_i.
> **Let** $t \leftarrow 0$, $D^0 \in x$ be such that $D_i^0 = 1/|\mathcal{X}|$ for all $i \in [|\mathcal{X}|]$.
> **for** each query f_i **do**
>> **Let** $f'_{2i-1}(\cdot) = f_i(\cdot) - f_i(D^t)$.
>> **Let** $f'_{2i}(\cdot) = f_i(D^t) - f_i(\cdot)$
>> **if** $a'_{2i-1} = \bot$ and $a'_{2i} = \bot$ **then**
>>> **Let** $a_i = f_i(D^t)$
>>
>> **else**
>>> **if** $a'_{2i-1} \in \mathbb{R}$ **then**
>>>> **Let** $a_i = f_i(D^t) + a'_{2i-1}$
>>>
>>> **else**
>>>> **Let** $a_i = f_i(D^t) - a'_{2i}$
>>>
>>> **end if**
>>> **Let** $D^{t+1} = U(D^t, f_i, a_i)$
>>> **Let** $t \leftarrow t + 1$.
>>
>> **end if**
>
> **end for**

Proof. This follows directly from the privacy analysis of Numeric-Sparse, because the OnlineIC algorithm accesses the database only through NumericSparse. $\qquad\square$

Theorem 5.14. For $\delta = 0$, With probability at least $1 - \beta$, for all queries f_i, OnlineIC returns an answer a_i such that $|f_i(x) - a_i| \leq 3\alpha$ for any α such that:

$$\alpha \geq \frac{9T(\alpha)(\log(2|\mathcal{Q}|) + \log(4T(\alpha)/\beta))}{\epsilon||x||_1}.$$

Proof. Recall that by Theorem 3.28 that given k queries and a maximum number of above-threshold queries of c, Sparse Vector is (α, β)-accurate for:

$$\alpha = \frac{9c(\log k + \log(4c/\beta))}{\epsilon||x||_1}.$$

Here, we have $c = T(\alpha)$ and $k = 2|\mathcal{Q}|$. Note that we have set the threshold $T = 2\alpha$ in the algorithm. First let us assume that the sparse vector algorithm does not halt prematurely. In this case, by the utility theorem, except with probability at most β, we have for all i such that $a_i = f_i(D^t)$: $|f_i(D) - f_i(D^t)| \leq T + \alpha = 3\alpha$, as we wanted. Additionally, for all i such that $a_i = a'_{2i-1}$ or $a_i = a'_{2i}$, we have $|f_i(D) - a'_i| \leq \alpha$.

Note that we also have for all i such that $a_i = a'_{2i-1}$ or $a_i = a'_{2i}$: $|f_i(D) - f_i(D')| \geq T - \alpha = \alpha$, since $T = 2\alpha$. Therefore, f_i, a_i form a valid step in a database update sequence. Therefore, there can be at most $c = T(\alpha)$ such update steps, and so the Sparse vector algorithm does not halt prematurely. $\square$

Similarly, we can prove a corresponding bound for (ε, δ)-privacy.

Theorem 5.15. For $\delta > 0$, With probability at least $1 - \beta$, for all queries f_i, OnlineIC returns an answer a_i such that $|f_i(x) - a_i| \leq 3\alpha$ for any α such that:

$$\alpha \geq \frac{(\sqrt{512} + 1)(\ln(2|\mathcal{Q}|) + \ln\frac{4T(\alpha)}{\beta})\sqrt{T(\alpha)\ln\frac{2}{\delta}}}{\epsilon||x||_1}$$

We can recover the bounds we proved for online multiplicative weights by recalling that the MW database update algorithm is a $T(\alpha)$-database update algorithm for $T(\alpha) = \frac{4\log|\mathcal{X}|}{\alpha^2}$. More generally, we have that *any* algorithm in the iterative construction framework can be converted into an algorithm which works in the interactive setting without loss in accuracy. (i.e., we could equally well plug in the median mechanism database update algorithm or the Perceptron database update algorithm, or any other). Tantalizingly, this means that (at least in the iterative construction framework), there is no gap in the accuracy achievable in the online vs. the offline query release models, despite the fact that the online model seems like it should be more difficult.

5.3 Connections

5.3.1 Iterative construction mechanism and α-nets

The Iterative Construction mechanism is implemented differently than the Net mechanism, but at its heart, its analysis is still based on the existence of small α-nets for the queries C. This connection is explicit for the median mechanism, which is parameterized by a net, but it holds for all database update algorithms. Note that the database output by the iterative database construction algorithm is entirely determined by the at most T functions $f_1, \ldots, f_T \in \mathcal{Q}$ fed into it, as selected by the distinguisher while the algorithm is running. Each of these functions can be indexed by at most $\log|\mathcal{Q}|$ bits, and so every database output by the mechanism can be described using only $T\log|\mathcal{Q}|$ bits. In other words, the IC algorithm itself describes an α-net for $\mathcal{Q}$ of size at most $\mathcal{N}_\alpha(\mathcal{Q}) \leq |\mathcal{Q}|^T$. To obtain error α using the Multiplicative Weights algorithm as an iterative database constructor, it suffices by Theorem 4.10 to take $T = 4\log|\mathcal{X}|/\alpha^2$, which gives us $\mathcal{N}_\alpha(\mathcal{Q}) \leq |\mathcal{Q}|^{4\log|\mathcal{X}|/\alpha^2} = |\mathcal{X}|^{4\log|\mathcal{Q}|/\alpha^2}$. Note that up to the factor of 4 in the exponent, this is exactly the bound we gave using a different α-net in Theorem 4.2! There, we constructed an α-net by considering all collections of $\log|\mathcal{Q}|/\alpha^2$ data points, each of which could be indexed by $\log|\mathcal{X}|$ bits. Here, we considered all collections of $\log|\mathcal{X}|/\alpha^2$ functions in $\mathcal{Q}$, each of which could be indexed by $\log|\mathcal{Q}|$ bits. Both ways, we got α-nets of the same size! Indeed, we could just as well run the Net mechanism using the α-net defined by the IC mechanism, to obtain the same utility bounds. In some sense, one net is the "dual" of the other: one is constructed of databases, the other is constructed of queries, yet both nets are of the same size. We will see the same phenomenon in the "boosting for queries" algorithm in the next section — it too answers a large number of linear queries using a data structure that is entirely determined by a small "net" of queries.

5.3.2 Agnostic learning

One way of viewing what the IC mechanism is doing is that it is reducing the seemingly (information theoretically) more difficult problem of *query release* to the easier problem of *query distinguishing* or *learning*. Recall that the distinguishing problem is to find the query $f \in \mathcal{Q}$ which varies the most between two databases x and y. Recall that in *learning*, the learner is given a collection of labeled examples $(x_1, y_1), \ldots, (x_m, y_m) \in \mathcal{X} \times \{0, 1\}$, where $y_i \in \{0, 1\}$ is the *label* of x_i. If we view x as representing the *positive examples* in some large data set, and y as representing the *negative examples* in the same data set, then we can see that the problem of distinguishing is exactly the problem of *agnostic learning*. That is, a distinguisher finds the query that best labels the positive examples, even when there is no query in the class that is guaranteed to perfectly label them (Note that in this setting, the same example can appear with both a positive and a negative label — so the reduction still makes sense even when x and y are not disjoint). Intuitively, learning should be an information-theoretically easier problem than query release. The query release problem requires that we release the approximate value of every query f in some class $\mathcal{Q}$, evaluated on the database. In contrast, the agnostic learning problem asks only that we return the evaluation and identity of a single query: the query that best labels the dataset. It is clear that information theoretically, the learning problem is no harder than the query release problem. If we can solve the query release problem on databases x and y, then we can solve the distinguishing problem without any further access to the true private dataset, merely by checking the approximate evaluations of every query $f \in \mathcal{Q}$ on x and y that are made available to us with our query release algorithm. What we have shown in this section is that the reverse is true as well: given access to a private distinguishing or agnostic learning algorithm, we can solve the query release problem by making a small (i.e., only $\log |\mathcal{X}|/\alpha^2$) number of calls to the private distinguishing algorithm, *with no further access to the private dataset.*

What are the implications of this? It tells us that up to small factors, the information complexity of agnostic learning is equal to the information complexity of query release. Computationally, the reduction is only as efficient as our database update algorithm, which, depending on our setting and algorithm, may or may not be efficient. But it tells us that any sort of information theoretic bound we may prove for the one problem can be ported over to the other problem, and vice versa. For example, most of the algorithms that we have seen (and most of the algorithms that we know about!) ultimately access the dataset by making linear queries via the Laplace mechanism. It turns out that any such algorithm can be seen as operating within the so-called *statistical query* model of data access, defined by Kearns in the context of machine learning. But agnostic learning is very hard in the statistical query model: even ignoring computational considerations, there is no algorithm which can make only a polynomial number of queries to the dataset and agnostically learn conjunctions to subconstant error. For query release this means that, *in the statistical query model,* there is no algorithm for *releasing* conjunctions (i.e., contingency tables) that runs in time polynomial in $1/\alpha$, where α is the desired accuracy level. If there is a privacy preserving query release algorithm with this run-time guarantee, it must operate outside of the SQ model, and therefore look very different from the currently known algorithms.

Because privacy guarantees compose linearly, this also tells us that (up to the possible factor of $\log |\mathcal{X}|/\alpha^2$) we should not expect to be able to privately learn to significantly higher accuracy than we can privately perform query release, and vice versa: an accurate algorithm for the one problem automatically gives us an accurate algorithm for the other.

5.3.3 A game theoretic view of query release

In this section, we take a brief sojourn into game theory to interpret some of the query release algorithms we have (and will see). Let us consider an interaction between two adversarial players, Alice and Bob.

Alice has some set of actions she might take, $\mathcal{A}$, and Bob has a set of actions $\mathcal{B}$. The game is played as follows: simultaneously, Alice picks some action $a \in \mathcal{A}$ (possibly at random), and Bob picks some action $b \in \mathcal{B}$ (possibly at random). Alice experiences a cost $c(a, b) \in [-1, 1]$. Alice wishes to play so as to minimize this cost, and since he is adversarial, Bob wishes to play so as to *maximize* this cost. This is what is called a *zero sum game*.

So how should Alice play? First, we consider an easier question. Suppose we handicap Alice and require that she announce her randomized strategy to Bob before she play it, and allow Bob to respond optimally using this information? If Alice announces that she will draw some action $a \in \mathcal{A}$ according to a probability distribution $\mathcal{D}_A$, then Bob will respond optimally so as to maximize Alice's expected cost. That is, Bob will play:

$$b^* = \arg \max_{b \in \mathcal{B}} \mathbb{E}_{a \sim \mathcal{D}_A}[c(a, b)].$$

Hence, once Alice announces her strategy, she knows what her cost will be, since Bob will be able to respond optimally. Therefore, Alice will wish to play a distribution over actions which *minimizes her cost once Bob responds*. That is, Alice will wish to play the distribution $\mathcal{D}_A$ defined as:

$$\mathcal{D}_A = \arg \min_{\mathcal{D} \in \Delta \mathcal{A}} \max_{b \in \mathcal{B}} \mathbb{E}_{a \sim \mathcal{D}}[c(a, b)].$$

If she plays $\mathcal{D}_A$ (and Bob responds optimally), Alice will experience the lowest possible cost that she can guarantee, with the handicap that she must announce her strategy ahead of time. Such a strategy for Alice is called a *min-max* strategy. Let us call the cost that Alice achieves when playing a min-max strategy Alice's *value* for the game, denoted v^A:

$$v^A = \min_{\mathcal{D} \in \Delta \mathcal{A}} \max_{b \in \mathcal{B}} \mathbb{E}_{a \sim \mathcal{D}}[c(a, b)].$$

We can similarly ask what Bob should play if we instead place *him* at the disadvantage and force him to announce his strategy first to Alice. If he does this, he will play the distribution $\mathcal{D}_B$ over actions $b \in \mathcal{B}$ that *maximizes* Alice's expected cost when Alice responds optimally. We call such a strategy $\mathcal{D}_B$ for Bob a *max-min* strategy. We can define

Bob's value for the game, v^B, as the maximum cost he can ensure by any strategy he might announce:

$$v^B = \max_{\mathcal{D} \in \Delta \mathcal{B}} \min_{a \in \mathcal{A}} \mathbb{E}_{b \sim \mathcal{D}}[c(a, b)].$$

Clearly, $v^B \leq v^A$, since announcing one's strategy is only a handicap.

One of the foundational results of game theory is Von-Neumann's min-max Theorem, which states that in any zero sum game, $v^A = v^B$.[2] In other words, there is no disadvantage to "going first" in a zero sum game, and if players play optimally, we can predict exactly Alice's cost: it will be $v^A = v^b \equiv v$, which we refer to as the value of the game.

Definition 5.7. In a zero sum game defined by action sets $\mathcal{A}, \mathcal{B}$ and a cost function $c : \mathcal{A} \times \mathcal{B} \to [-1, 1]$, let v be the value of the game. An α-approximate min-max strategy is a distribution $\mathcal{D}_A$ such that:

$$\max_{b \in \mathcal{B}} \mathbb{E}_{a \sim \mathcal{D}_A}[c(a, b)] \leq v + \alpha$$

Similarly, an α-approximate max-min strategy is a distribution $\mathcal{D}_B$ such that:

$$\min_{a \in \mathcal{A}} \mathbb{E}_{b \sim \mathcal{D}_B}[c(a, b)] \geq v - \alpha$$

If $\mathcal{D}_A$ and $\mathcal{D}_B$ are both α-approximate min-max and max-min strategies respectively, then we say that the pair $(\mathcal{D}_A, \mathcal{D}_B)$ is an α-approximate Nash equilibrium of the zero sum game.

So how does this relate to query release?

Consider a particular zero sum-game tailored to the problem of releasing a set of linear queries $\mathcal{Q}$ over a data universe $\mathcal{X}$. First, assume without loss of generality that for every $f \in \mathcal{Q}$, there is a query $\hat{f} \in \mathcal{Q}$ such that $\hat{f} = 1 - f$ (i.e., for each $\chi \in \mathcal{X}$, $\hat{f}(\chi) = 1 - f(\chi)$). Define Alice's action set to be $\mathcal{A} = \mathcal{X}$ and define Bob's action set to be $\mathcal{B} = \mathcal{Q}$. We will refer to Alice as the *database player*, and to Bob as the *query player*. Finally, fixing a true private database x normalized to be a probability distribution (i.e., $\|x\|_1 = 1$), define the cost function $c : \mathcal{A} \times \mathcal{B} \to [-1, 1]$

---

[2]Von Neumann is quoted as saying "As far as I can see, there could be no theory of games ... without that theorem ... I thought there was nothing worth publishing until the Minimax Theorem was proved" [10].

to be: $c(\chi, f) = f(\chi) - f(x)$. Let us call this game the "Query Release Game."

We begin with a simple observation:

Proposition 5.16. The value of the query release game is $v = 0$.

Proof. We first show that $v^A = v \leq 0$. Consider what happens if we let the database player's strategy correspond to the true database: $\mathcal{D}_A = x$. Then we have:

$$v^A \leq \max_{f \in \mathcal{B}} \mathbb{E}_{\chi \sim \mathcal{D}_A}[c(\chi, f)]$$

$$= \max_{f \in \mathcal{B}} \sum_{i=1}^{|\mathcal{X}|} f(\chi_i) \cdot x_i - f(x)$$

$$= f(x) - f(x)$$

$$= 0.$$

Next we observe that $v = v^B \geq 0$. For point of contradiction, assume that $v < 0$. In other words, that there exists a distribution $\mathcal{D}_A$ such that *for all* $f \in \mathcal{Q}$

$$\mathbb{E}_{\chi \sim \mathcal{D}_A} c(\chi, f) < 0.$$

Here, we simply note that by definition, if $\mathbb{E}_{\chi \sim \mathcal{D}_A} c(\chi, f) = c < 0$ then $\mathbb{E}_{\chi \sim \mathcal{D}_A} c(\chi, \hat{f}) = -c > 0$, which is a contradiction since $\hat{f} \in \mathcal{Q}$. $\qquad \square$

What we have established implies that for any distribution $\mathcal{D}_A$ that is an α-approximate min-max strategy for the database player, we have that for all queries $f \in \mathcal{Q}$: $|\mathbb{E}_{\chi \sim \mathcal{D}_A} f(\chi) - f(x)| \leq \alpha$. In other words, the distribution $\mathcal{D}_A$ can be viewed as a synthetic database that answers every query in $\mathcal{Q}$ with α-accuracy.

How about for nonlinear queries? We can repeat the same argument above if we change the query release game slightly. Rather than letting the database player have strategies corresponding to universe elements $\chi \in \mathcal{X}$, we let the database player have strategies corresponding to *databases* themselves! Then, $c(f, y) = |f(x) - f(y)|$. Its not hard to see that this game still has value 0 and that α-approximate min-max strategies correspond to synthetic data which give α-accurate answers to queries in $\mathcal{Q}$.

So how do we compute approximate min-max strategies in zero sum games? There are many ways! It is well known that if Alice plays the game repeatedly, updating her distribution on actions using an online-learning algorithm with a no-regret guarantee (defined in Section 11.2), and Bob responds at each round with an approximately-cost-maximizing response, then Alice's distribution will quickly converge to an approximate min-max strategy. Multiplicative weights is such an algorithm, and one way of understanding the multiplicative weights mechanism is as a strategy for Alice to play in the query release game defined in this section. (The private distinguisher is playing the role of Bob here, picking at each round the query that corresponds to approximately maximizing Alice's cost). The median mechanism is another such algorithm, for the game in which Alice's strategies correspond to databases, rather than universe elements, and so is also computing an approximate min-max solution to the query release game.

However, there are other ways to compute approximate equilibria as well! For example, *Bob*, the query player, could play the game using a no-regret learning algorithm (such as multiplicative weights), and *Alice* could repeatedly respond at each round with an approximately-cost-minimizing database! In this case, the *average* over the databases that Alice plays over the course of this experiment will converge to an approximate min-max solution as well. This is exactly what is being done in Section 6, in which the private base-sanitizer plays the role of Alice, at each round playing an approximately cost-minimizing database given Bob's distribution over queries.

In fact, a third way of computing an approximate equilibrium of a zero-sum game is to have *both* Alice and Bob play according to no-regret learning algorithms. We won't cover this approach here, but this approach has applications in guaranteeing privacy not just to the database, but also to the set of queries being asked, and to privately solving certain types of linear programs.

5.4   Bibliographical notes

The Iterative Construction Mechanism abstraction (together with the perception based database update algorithm) was formalized by

Gupta et al. [39], generalizing the median mechanism of Roth and Roughgarden [74] (initially presented as an online algorithm), the online private multiplicative weights mechanism of Hardt and Rothblum [44], and its offline variant of Gupta et al. [38]; see also Hardt et al. [41]. All these algorithm can be seen to be instantiations. The connection between query release and agnostic learning was observed in [38]. The observation that the median mechanism, when analyzed using the composition theorems of Dwork et al. [32] for (ε, δ) privacy, can be used to answer arbitrary low sensitivity queries is due to Hardt and Rothblum. The game theoretic view of query release, along with its applications to analyst privacy, is due to Hardt, Roth, and Ullman [48].

6

Boosting for Queries

In the previous sections, we have focused on the problem of private query release in which we insist on bounding the worst-case error over all queries. Would our problem be easier if we instead asked only for low error on average, given some distribution over the queries? In this section, we see that the answer is no: given a mechanism which is able to solve the query release problem with low average error given any distribution on queries, we can "boost" it into a mechanism which solves the query release problem to worst-case error. This both sheds light on the difficulty of private query release, and gives us a new tool for designing private query release algorithms.

Boosting is a general and widely used method for improving the accuracy of learning algorithms. Given a set of labeled training examples

$$\{(x_1, y_1), (x_2, y_2), \ldots, (x_m, y_m)\},$$

where each x_i is drawn from an underlying distribution $\mathcal{D}$ on a universe $\mathcal{U}$, and each $y_i \in \{+1, -1\}$, a learning algorithm produces a hypothesis $h : \mathcal{U} \to \{+1, -1\}$. Ideally, h will not just "describe" the labeling on the given samples, but will also *generalize*, providing a reasonably accurate method of classifying other elements drawn from the underlying distribution. The goal of boosting is to convert a weak *base* learner, which produces a hypothesis that may do just a little better than random guessing, into a strong learner, which yields a very accurate predictor for samples drawn according to $\mathcal{D}$. Many boosting algorithms share the following basic structure. First, an initial (typically uniform) probability distribution is imposed on the sample set. Computation then proceeds in rounds. In each round t:

1. The base learner is run on the current distribution, denoted $\mathcal{D}_t$, producing a classification hypothesis h_t; and

2. The hypotheses $h_1, \ldots, h_t$ are used to re-weight the samples, defining a new distribution $\mathcal{D}_{t+1}$.

The process halts either after a predetermined number of rounds or when an appropriate combining of the hypotheses is determined to be sufficiently accurate. Thus, given a base learner, the design decisions for a boosting algorithm are (1) are how to modify the probability distribution from one round to the next, and (2) how to combine the hypotheses $\{h_t\}_{t=1,\ldots,T}$ to form a final output hypothesis.

In this section we will use boosting on queries — that is, for the purposes of the boosting algorithm the universe $\mathcal{U}$ is a set of queries $\mathcal{Q}$ — to obtain an offline algorithm for answering large numbers of arbitrary low-sensitivity queries. This algorithm requires less space than the median mechanism, and, depending on the base learner, is potentially more time efficient as well.

The algorithm revolves around a somewhat magical fact (Lemma 6.5): if we can find a synopsis that provides accurate answers on a few selected queries, then in fact this synopsis provides accurate answers on *most* queries! We apply this fact to the base learner, which samples from a distribution on $\mathcal{Q}$ and produces as output a "weak" synopsis that yields "good" answers for a majority of the weight in $\mathcal{Q}$, boosting, in a differentially private fashion, to obtain a synopsis that is good for all of $\mathcal{Q}$.

Although the boosting is performed over the queries, the privacy is still for the rows of the database. The privacy challenge in boosting for queries comes from the fact that each row in the database affects the answers to all the queries. This will manifest in the reweighting of the queries: adjacent databases could cause radically different reweightings, which will be observable in the generated h_t that, collectively, will form the synopsis.

The running time of the boosting procedure depends quasi-linearly on the number $|Q|$ of queries and on the running time of the base synopsis generator, independent of the data universe size $|\mathcal{X}|$. This yields a new avenue for constructing efficient and accurate privacy-preserving mechanisms, analogous to the approach enabled by boosting in the machine learning literature: an algorithm designer can tackle the (potentially much easier) task of constructing a weak privacy-preserving base synopsis generator, and automatically obtain a stronger mechanism.

6.1 The boosting for queries algorithm

We will use the *row representation* for databases, outlined in Section 2, where we think of the database as a multiset of rows, or elements of $\mathcal{X}$. Fix a database size n, a data universe $\mathcal{X}$, and a query set $Q = \{q : \mathcal{X}^* \to \mathbb{R}\}$ of real-valued queries of sensitivity at most ρ.

We assume the existence of a *base synopsis generator* (in Section 6.2 we will see how to construct these). The property we will need of the base generator, formulated next, is that, for any distribution $\mathcal{D}$ on the query set Q, the output of base generator can be used for computing accurate answers for a *large fraction* of the queries, where the "large fraction" is defined in terms of the weights given by $\mathcal{D}$. The base generator is parameterized by k, the number of queries to be sampled; λ, an accuracy requirement for its outputs; η, a measurement of "large" describing what we mean by a large fraction of the queries, and β, a failure probability.

Definition 6.1 $((k, \lambda, \eta, \beta)$-base synopsis generator). For a fixed database size n, data universe $\mathcal{X}$ and query set Q, consider a synopsis generator $\mathcal{M}$, that samples k queries independently from a distribution $\mathcal{D}$ on Q and outputs a synopsis. We say that $\mathcal{M}$ is a $(k, \lambda, \eta, \beta)$-*base synopsis generator* if for any distribution $\mathcal{D}$ on Q, with all but β probability over the coin flips of $\mathcal{M}$, the synopsis $\mathcal{S}$ that $\mathcal{M}$ outputs is λ-accurate for a $(1/2 + \eta)$-fraction of the mass of $\mathcal{Q}$ as weighted by $\mathcal{D}$:

$$\Pr_{q \sim \mathcal{D}}[|q(\mathcal{S}) - q(x)| \leq \lambda] \geq 1/2 + \eta. \qquad (6.1)$$

The query-boosting algorithm can be used for any class of queries and any differentially private base synopsis generator. The running time is inherited from the base synopsis generator. The booster invests additional time that is quasi-linear in $|\mathcal{Q}|$, and in particular its running time does not depend directly on the size of the data universe.

To specify the boosting algorithm we will need to specify a stopping condition, an aggregation mechanism, and an algorithm for updating the current distribution on $\mathcal{Q}$.

Stopping Condition.   We will run the algorithm for a fixed number T of rounds — this will be our stopping condition. T will be selected so as to ensure sufficient accuracy (with very high probability); as we will see, $\log|\mathcal{Q}|/\eta^2$ rounds will suffice.

Updating the Distribution.   Although the distributions are never directly revealed in the outputs, the base synopses $\mathcal{A}_1, \mathcal{A}_2, \ldots, \mathcal{A}_T$ are revealed, and each $\mathcal{A}_i$ can in principle leak information about the queries chosen, from $\mathcal{D}_i$, in constructing $\mathcal{A}_i$. We therefore need to constrain the max-divergence between the probability distributions obtained on neighboring databases. This is technically challenging because, given $\mathcal{A}_i$, the database is very heavily involved in constructing $\mathcal{D}_{i+1}$.

The initial distribution, $\mathcal{D}_1$, will be uniform over $\mathcal{Q}$. A standard method for updating $\mathcal{D}_t$ is to increase the weight of poorly handled elements, in our case, queries for which $|q(x) - q(\mathcal{A}_t)| > \lambda$, by a fixed factor, say, e, and decrease the weight of well-handled elements by the same factor. (The weights are then normalized so as to sum to 1.) To get a feel for the difficulty, let $x = y \cup \{\xi\}$, and suppose that all queries q are handled well by $\mathcal{A}_t$ when the database is y, but the addition of ξ causes this to fail for, say, a $1/10$ fraction of the queries; that is, $|q(y) - q(\mathcal{A}_t)| \leq \lambda$ for all queries q, but $|q(x) - q(\mathcal{A}_t)| > \lambda$ for some $|\mathcal{Q}|/10$ queries. Note that, since $\mathcal{A}_t$ "does well" on $9/10$ of the queries even when the database is x, it could be returned from the base sanitizer no matter which of x, y is the true data set. Our concern is with the effects of the updating: when the database is y all queries are well handled and there is no reweighting (after normalization), but when the database is x there is a reweighting: one tenth of the queries have their weights increased, the remaining nine tenths have their weights decreased. This difference in reweighting may be detected in the next iteration via $\mathcal{A}_{t+1}$, which is observable, and which will be built from samples drawn from rather different distributions depending on whether the database is x or y.

For example, suppose we start from the uniform distribution $\mathcal{D}_1$. Then $\mathcal{D}_2^{(y)} = \mathcal{D}_1^{(y)}$, where by $\mathcal{D}_i^{(z)}$ we mean the distribution at round i when the database is z. This is because the weight of every query is decreased by a factor of e, which disappears in the normalization. So each $q \in \mathcal{Q}$ is assigned weight $1/|\mathcal{Q}|$ in $\mathcal{D}_2^{(y)}$. In contrast, when the database is x the "unhappy" queries have normalized weight

$$\frac{\frac{e}{|\mathcal{Q}|}}{\frac{9}{10}\frac{1}{|\mathcal{Q}|}\frac{1}{e} + \frac{1}{10}\frac{e}{|\mathcal{Q}|}}.$$

Consider any such unhappy query q. The *ratio* $\mathcal{D}_2^{(x)}(q)/\mathcal{D}_2^{(y)}(q)$ is given by

$$\frac{\mathcal{D}_2^{(x)}(q)}{\mathcal{D}_2^{(y)}(q)} = \frac{\frac{\frac{e}{|\mathcal{Q}|}}{\frac{9}{10}\frac{1}{|\mathcal{Q}|}\frac{1}{e} + \frac{1}{10}\frac{e}{|\mathcal{Q}|}}}{\frac{1}{|\mathcal{Q}|}}$$

$$= \frac{10}{1 + \frac{9}{e^2}} \stackrel{\text{def}}{=} F \approx 4.5085.$$

Now, $\ln F \approx 1.506$, and even though the choice of queries used in round 2 by the base generator are not explicitly made public, they may be detectable from the resulting $\mathcal{A}_2$, which is made public. Thus, there is a potential privacy loss of up to 1.506 per query (of course, we expect cancellations; we are simply trying to explain the source of the difficulty). This is partially addressed by ensuring that the number of samples used by the base generator is relatively small, although we still have the problem that, over multiple iterations, the distributions $\mathcal{D}_t$ may evolve very differently even on neighboring databases.

The solution will be to attenuate the re-weighting procedure. Instead of always using a fixed ratio either for increasing the weight (when the answer is "accurate") or decreasing it (when it is not), we set separate thresholds for "accuracy" (λ) and "inaccuracy" ($\lambda + \mu$, for an appropriately chosen μ that scales with the *bit size* of the output of the base generator; see Lemma 6.5 below). Queries for which the error is below or above these thresholds have their weight decreased or increased, respectively, by a factor of e. For queries whose error lies between these two thresholds, we scale the natural logarithm of the weight change linearly: $1 - 2(|q(x) - q(A_t)| - \lambda)/\mu$, so queries with errors of magnitude exceeding $\lambda + \mu/2$ increase in weight, and those with errors of magnitude less than $\lambda + \mu/2$ decrease in weight.

The attenuated scaling reduces the effect of any individual on the re-weighting of any query. This is because an individual can only affect the true answer to a query — and thus also the accuracy of the base synopsis generator's output $q(A_t)$ — by a small amount, and the attenuation divides this amount by a parameter μ which will be chosen to compensate for the kT samples chosen (total) from the T distributions obtained over the course of the execution of the boosting algorithm. This helps to ensure privacy. Intuitively, we view each of these kT samples as a "mini-mechanism." We first bound the privacy loss of sampling at any round (Claim 6.4) and then bound the cumulative loss via the composition theorem.

The larger the gap (μ) between the thresholds for "accurate" and "inaccurate," the smaller the effect of each individual on a query's weight can be. This means that larger gaps are better for privacy. For accuracy, however, large gaps are bad. If the inaccuracy threshold is large, we can only guarantee that queries for which the base synopsis generator is very inaccurate have their weight substantially increased during re-weighting. This degrades the accuracy guarantee of the boosting algorithm: the errors are roughly equal to the "inaccuracy" threshold ($\lambda + \mu$).

Aggregation. For $t \in [T]$ we will run the base generator to obtain a synopsis A_t. The synopses will be aggregated by taking the median: given $A_1, \ldots, A_T$, the quantity $q(x)$ is estimated by taking the T

approximate values for $q(x)$ computed using each of the $\mathcal{A}_i$, and then computing their median. With this aggregation method we can show accuracy for query q by arguing that a majority of the $\mathcal{A}_i$, $1 \leq i \leq T$ provide $\lambda + \mu$ accuracy (or better) for q. This implies that the median value of the T approximations to $q(x)$ will be within $\lambda + \mu$ of the true value.

Notation.

1. Throughout the algorithm's operation, we keep track of several variables (explicitly or implicitly). Variables indexed by $q \in \mathcal{Q}$ hold information pertaining to query q in the query set. Variables indexed by $t \in [T]$, usually computed in round t, will be used to construct the distribution $\mathcal{D}_{t+1}$ used for sampling in time period $t + 1$.

2. For a predicate P we use $[[P]]$ to denote 1 if the predicate is true and 0 if it is false.

3. There is a final tuning parameter α used in the algorithm. It will be chosen (see Corollary 6.3 below) to have value

$$\alpha = \alpha(\eta) = (1/2) \ln \left(\frac{1 + 2\eta}{1 - 2\eta} \right).$$

The algorithm appears in Figure 6.1. The quantity $u_{t,q}$ in Step 2(2b) is the new, un-normalized, weight of the query. For the moment, let us set $\alpha = 1$ (just so that we can ignore any α factors). Letting $a_{j,q}$ be the natural logarithm of the weight change in round j, $1 \leq j \leq t$, the new weight is given by:

$$u_{t,q} \leftarrow \exp \left(-\sum_{j=1}^{t} a_{j,q} \right).$$

Thus, at the end of the previous step the un-normalized weight was $u_{t-1,q} = \exp(-\sum_{j=1}^{t-1} a_{j,q})$ and the update corresponds to multiplication by $e^{-a_{j,t}}$. When the sum $\sum_{j=1}^{t} a_{j,q}$ is large, the weight is small. Every time a synopsis gives a very good approximation to $q(x)$, we add 1 to this sum; if the approximation is only moderately good (between λ and

---

Boosting for Queries$(k, \lambda, \eta, \rho, \mu, T)$
Given: database $x \in \mathcal{X}^n$, query set $\mathcal{Q}$, where each $q \in \mathcal{Q}$ is a function $q : X^n \to \mathbb{R}$ with sensitivity at most ρ.
Initialize $\mathcal{D}_1$ to be the uniform distribution over $\mathcal{Q}$.
For $t = 1, \ldots, T$:

1. Sample a sequence $S_t \subseteq \mathcal{Q}$ of k samples chosen independently and at random from $\mathcal{D}_t$.
   Run the base synopsis generator to compute a synopsis $\mathcal{A}_t : \mathcal{Q} \to \mathbb{R}$ that is w.h.p. accurate for at least $1/2 + \eta$ of the mass of $\mathcal{D}_t$.

2. Reweight the queries. For each $q \in \mathcal{Q}$:

   (a) If $\mathcal{A}_t$ is λ-accurate, then $a_{t,q} \leftarrow 1$
       If $\mathcal{A}_t$ is $(\lambda + \mu)$-inaccurate, then $a_{t,q} \leftarrow -1$
       Otherwise, let $d_{q,t} = |q(x) - \mathcal{A}_t(q)|$ be the error of $\mathcal{A}_t$ (between λ and $\lambda + \mu$) on q:

   $$a_{t,q} \leftarrow 1 - 2(d_{t,q} - \lambda)/\mu$$

   (b) $u_{t,q} \leftarrow \exp(-\alpha \cdot \sum_{j=1}^{t} a_{j,q})$, where $\alpha = (1/2)\ln((1 + 2\eta)/(1 - 2\eta))$.

3. Renormalize:

$$Z_t \leftarrow \sum_{q \in \mathcal{Q}} u_{t,q}$$
$$D_{t+1}[q] = u_{t,q}/Z_t$$

Output the final answer data structure $\mathcal{A} = (\mathcal{A}_1, \ldots, \mathcal{A}_T)$. For $q \in \mathcal{Q}$:

$$\mathcal{A}(q) = median\{\mathcal{A}_1(q), \ldots, \mathcal{A}_T(q)\}$$

Figure 6.1: Boosting for queries.

$\lambda + \mu/2$), we add a positive amount, but less than 1. Conversely, when the synopsis is very bad (worse than $\lambda + \mu$ accuracy), we subtract 1; when it is barely acceptable (between $\lambda + \mu/2$ and $\lambda + \mu$), we subtract a smaller amount.

In the theorem below we see an inverse relationship between privacy loss due to sampling, captured by $\varepsilon_{\text{sample}}$, and the gap μ between the thresholds for accurate and inaccurate.

Theorem 6.1. Let $\mathcal{Q}$ be a query family with sensitivity at most ρ. For an appropriate setting of parameters, and with $T = \log|\mathcal{Q}|/\eta^2$ rounds, the algorithm of Figure 6.1 is an accurate and differentially private query-boosting algorithm:

1. When instantiated with a $(k, \lambda, \eta, \beta)$-base synopsis generator, the output of the boosting algorithm gives $(\lambda + \mu)$-accurate answers to *all* the queries in $\mathcal{Q}$ with probability at least $1 - T\beta$, where

$$\mu \in O(((\log^{3/2}|\mathcal{Q}|)\sqrt{k}\sqrt{\log(1/\beta)}\rho)/(\varepsilon_{\text{sample}} \cdot \eta^3)). \qquad (6.2)$$

2. If the base synopsis generator is $(\varepsilon_{\text{base}}, \delta_{\text{base}})$-differentially private, then the boosting algorithm is $(\varepsilon_{\text{sample}} + T \cdot \varepsilon_{\text{base}}, \delta_{\text{sample}} + T\delta_{\text{base}})$-differentially private.

Allowing the constant η to be swallowed up into the big-O notation, and taking $\rho = 1$ for simplicity, we get $\mu = O(((\log^{3/2}|Q|)\sqrt{k} \sqrt{\log(1/\beta)})/\varepsilon_{\text{sample}})$. Thus we see that reducing the number k of input queries needed by the base sanitizer improves the quality of the output. Similarly, from the full statement of the theorem, we see that improving the generalization power of the base sanitizer, which corresponds to having a larger value of η (a bigger "strong majority"), also improves the accuracy.

Proof of Theorem 6.1. We first prove accuracy, then privacy.

We introduce the notation $a_{t,q}^-$ and $a_{t,q}^+$, satisfying

1. $a_{t,q}^-, a_{t,q}^+ \in \{-1, 1\}$; and
2. $a_{t,q}^- \leq a_{t,q} \leq a_{t,q}^+$.

Recall that a larger $a_{t,q}$ indicates a higher quality of the approximation of the synopsis $\mathcal{A}_t$ for $q(x)$.

1. $a_{t,q}^-$ is 1 if $\mathcal{A}_t$ is λ-accurate on q, and -1 otherwise. To check that $a_{t,q}^- \leq a_{t,q}$, note that if $a_{t,q}^- = 1$ then $\mathcal{A}_t$ is λ-accurate for q, and so by definition $a_{t,q} = 1$ as well. If instead we have $a_{t,q}^- = -1$ then since we always have $a_{t,q} \in [-1, 1]$, we are done.

   We will use the $a_{t,q}^-$ to lower bound a measure of the quality of the output of the base generator. By the promise of the base generator, $\mathcal{A}_t$ is λ-accurate for at least a $1/2 + \eta$ fraction of the mass of $\mathcal{D}_t$. Thus,

   $$r_t \triangleq \sum_{q \in Q} \mathcal{D}_t[q] \cdot a_{t,q}^- \geq (1/2 + \eta) - (1/2 - \eta) = 2\eta. \qquad (6.3)$$

2. $a_{t,q}^+$ is -1 if $\mathcal{A}_t$ is $(\lambda + \mu)$-*inaccurate* for q, and 1 otherwise. To check that $a_{t,q} \leq a_{t,q}^+$, note that if $a_{t,q}^+ = -1$ then $\mathcal{A}_t$ is $(\lambda + \mu)$-*inaccurate* for q, so by definition $a_{t,q} = -1$ as well. If instead $a_{t,q}^+ = 1$ then since we always have $a_{t,q} \in [-1, 1]$, we are done.

   Thus $a_{t,q}^+$ is positive if and only if $\mathcal{A}_t$ is at least minimally adequately accurate for q. We will use the $a_{t,q}^+$ to prove accuracy of the aggregation. When we sum the values $a_{t,q}^+$, we get a positive number if and only if the majority of the $\mathcal{A}_t$ are providing passable — that is, within $\lambda + \mu$ — approximations to $q(x)$. In this case the median value will be within $\lambda + \mu$.

Lemma 6.2. After T rounds of boosting, with all but $T\beta$ probability, the answers to all but an $\exp(-\eta^2 T)$-fraction of the queries are $(\lambda+\mu)$-accurate.

Proof. In the last round of boosting, we have:

$$\mathcal{D}_{T+1}[q] = \frac{u_{T,q}}{Z_T}. \tag{6.4}$$

Since $a_{t,q} \leq a_{t,q}^+$ we have:

$$u_{T,q}^+ \triangleq e^{-\alpha \sum_{t=1}^T a_{t,q}^+} \leq e^{-\alpha \sum_{t=1}^T a_{t,q}} = u_{T,q}. \tag{6.5}$$

(The superscript "+" reminds us that this unweighted value was computed using the terms $a_{t,q}^+$.) Note that we always have $u_{T,q}^+ \geq 0$. Combining Equations (6.4) and (6.5), for all $q \in \mathcal{Q}$:

$$\mathcal{D}_{T+1}[q] \geq \frac{u_{T,q}^+}{Z_T}. \tag{6.6}$$

Recalling that $[[P]]$ denotes the boolean variable that has value 1 if and only if the predicate P is true, we turn to examining the value $[[\mathcal{A}$ is $(\lambda+\mu)$-inaccurate for $q]]$. If this predicate is 1, then it must be the case that the majority of $\{\mathcal{A}_j\}_{j=1}^T$ are $(\lambda + \mu)$-inaccurate, as otherwise their median would be $(\lambda + \mu)$-accurate.

From our discussion of the significance of the sign of $\sum_{t=1}^T a_{t,q}^+$, we have:

$$\mathcal{A} \text{ is } (\lambda + \mu)\text{-inaccurate for } q \Rightarrow \sum_{t=1}^T a_{t,q}^+ \leq 0$$

$$\Leftrightarrow e^{-\alpha \sum_{t=1}^T a_{t,q}^+} \geq 1$$

$$\Leftrightarrow u_{T,q}^+ \geq 1$$

Since $u_{T,q}^+ \geq 0$, We conclude that:

$$[[\mathcal{A} \text{ is } (\lambda + \mu)\text{-inaccurate for } q]] \leq u_{T,q}^+$$

Using this together with Equation (6.6) yields:

$$\frac{1}{|\mathcal{Q}|} \cdot \sum_{q \in \mathcal{Q}} [[\mathcal{A} \text{ is } (\lambda + \mu)\text{-inaccurate for } q]] \leq \frac{1}{|\mathcal{Q}|} \cdot \sum_{q \in \mathcal{Q}} u_{T,q}^+$$

$$\leq \frac{1}{|\mathcal{Q}|} \cdot \sum_{q \in \mathcal{Q}} \mathcal{D}_{T+1}[q] \cdot Z_T$$

$$= \frac{Z_T}{|\mathcal{Q}|}.$$

Thus the following claim completes the proof:

Claim 6.3. In round t of boosting, with all but $t\beta$ probability:

$$Z_t \leq \exp(-\eta^2 \cdot t) \cdot |\mathcal{Q}|$$

Proof. By definition of a base synopsis generator, with all but β probability, the synopsis generated is λ-accurate for at least a $(1/2 + \eta)$-fraction of the mass of the distribution $\mathcal{D}_t$. Recall that $a_{t,q}^- \in \{-1, 1\}$ is 1 if and only if $\mathcal{A}_t$ is λ-accurate on q, and that $a_{t,q}^- \leq a_{t,q}$ and recall further the quantity $r_t \triangleq \sum_{q \in \mathcal{Q}} \mathcal{D}_t[q] \cdot a_{t,q}^-$ defined in Equation (6.3). As discussed above, r_t measures the "success" of the base synopsis generator in round t, where by "success" we mean the stricter notion of λ-accuracy. As summarized in Equation (6.3), if a $(1/2 + \eta)$-fraction of the mass of $\mathcal{D}_t$ is computed with λ-accuracy, then $r_t \geq 2\eta$. Now observe also that for $t \in [T]$, assuming the base sanitizer did not fail in round t:

$$Z_t = \sum_{q \in \mathcal{Q}} u_{t,q}$$

$$= \sum_{q \in \mathcal{Q}} u_{t-1,q} \cdot e^{-\alpha \cdot a_{t,q}}$$

$$= \sum_{q \in \mathcal{Q}} Z_{t-1} \cdot \mathcal{D}_t[q] \cdot e^{-\alpha \cdot a_{t,q}}$$

$$\leq \sum_{q \in \mathcal{Q}} Z_{t-1} \cdot \mathcal{D}_t[q] \cdot e^{-\alpha \cdot a_{t,q}^-}$$

$$= Z_{t-1} \cdot \sum_{q \in \mathcal{Q}} \mathcal{D}_t[q] \cdot \left(\left(\frac{1 + a_{t,q}^-}{2} \right) \cdot e^{-\alpha} + \left(\frac{1 - a_{t,q}^-}{2} \right) \cdot e^{\alpha} \right)$$

(case analysis)

$$= \frac{Z_{t-1}}{2}\left[(e^\alpha + e^{-\alpha}) + r_t(e^{-\alpha} - e^\alpha)\right]$$

$$\leq \frac{Z_{t-1}}{2}\left[(e^\alpha + e^{-\alpha}) + 2\eta(e^{-\alpha} - e^\alpha)\right] \quad (r_t \geq 2\eta \text{ and } (e^{-\alpha} - e^\alpha) \leq 0)$$

By simple calculus we see that $(e^\alpha + e^{-\alpha}) + 2\eta(e^{-\alpha} - e^\alpha)$ is minimized when

$$\alpha = (1/2)\ln\left(\frac{1 + 2\eta}{1 - 2\eta}\right).$$

Plugging this into the recurrence, we get

$$Z_t \leq (\sqrt{1 - 4\eta^2})^t |\mathcal{Q}| \leq \exp(-2\eta^2 t)|\mathcal{Q}|. \qquad \square$$

This completes the proof of Lemma 6.2. $\qquad \square$

The lemma implies that accuracy for *all* queries simultaneously can be achieved by setting

$$T > \frac{\ln|\mathcal{Q}|}{\eta^2}.$$

Privacy. We will show that the entire sequence $(S_1, \mathcal{A}_1, \ldots, S_T, \mathcal{A}_T)$ can be output while preserving differential privacy. Note that this is stronger than we need — we do not actually output the sets $S_1, \ldots, S_T$. By our adaptive composition theorems, the privacy of each $\mathcal{A}_i$ will be guaranteed by the privacy guarantees of the base synopsis generator, together with the fact that S_{i-1} was computed in a differentially private way. Therefore, it suffices to prove that given that $(S_1, \mathcal{A}_1, \ldots, S_i, \mathcal{A}_i)$ is differentially private, S_{i+1} is as well. We can then combine the privacy parameters using our composition theorems to compute a final guarantee.

Lemma 6.4. Let $\varepsilon^* = \frac{4\alpha T\rho}{\mu}$. For all $i \in [T]$, once $(S_1, \mathcal{A}_1, \ldots, S_i, \mathcal{A}_i)$ is fixed, the computation of each element of S_{i+1} is $(\varepsilon^*, 0)$-differentially private.

Proof. Fixing $\mathcal{A}_1, \ldots, \mathcal{A}_i$, for every $j \leq i$, the quantity $d_{q,j}$ has sensitivity ρ, since $\mathcal{A}_j(q)$ is database independent (because $\mathcal{A}_j$ is fixed), and every $q \in \mathcal{Q}$ has sensitivity bounded by ρ. Therefore, for every $j \leq i$, $a_{j,q}$ is $2\rho/\mu$ sensitive by construction, and so

$$g_i(q) \stackrel{\text{def}}{=} \sum_{j=1}^{i} a_{j,q}$$

has sensitivity at most $2i\rho/\mu \leq 2T\rho/\mu$. Then $\Delta g_i \stackrel{\text{def}}{=} 2T\rho/\mu$ is an upper bound on the sensitivity of g_i.

To argue privacy, we will show that the selection of queries for S_{i+1} is an instance of the exponential mechanism. Think of $-g_i(q)$ as the utility of a query q during the selection process at round $i + 1$. The exponential mechanism says that to achieve $(\varepsilon^*, 0)$-differential privacy we should choose q with probability proportional to

$$\exp\left(-g_i(q)\frac{\varepsilon^*}{2\Delta g_i}\right).$$

Since $\varepsilon^*/2\Delta g_i = \alpha$ and the algorithm selects q with probability proportional to $e^{-\alpha g_i(q)}$, we see that this is exactly what the algorithm does! $\qquad\square$

We bound the privacy loss of releasing the S_is by treating each selection of a query as a "mini-mechanism" that, over the course of T rounds of boosting, is invoked kT times. By Lemma 6.4 each mini-mechanism is $(4\alpha T\rho/\mu, 0)$-differentially private. By Theorem 3.20, for all $\beta > 0$ the composition of kT mechanisms, each of which is $(\alpha 4T\rho/\mu, 0)$-differentially private, is $(\varepsilon_{\text{sample}}, \delta_{\text{sample}})$-differentially private, where

$$\varepsilon_{\text{sample}} \stackrel{\text{def}}{=} \sqrt{2kT\log(1/\delta_{\text{sample}})}(\alpha 4T\rho/\mu) + kT\left(\frac{\alpha 4T\rho}{\mu}\right)^2. \qquad (6.7)$$

Our total privacy loss comes from the composition of T calls to the base sanitizer and the cumulative loss from the kT samples. We conclude that the boosting algorithm in its entirety is: $(\varepsilon_{\text{boost}}, \delta_{\text{boost}})$-differentially private, where

$$\varepsilon_{\text{boost}} = T\varepsilon_{\text{base}} + \varepsilon_{\text{sample}}$$
$$\delta_{\text{boost}} = T\delta_{\text{base}} + \delta_{\text{sample}}$$

To get the parameters claimed in the statement of the theorem, we can take:

$$\mu \in O((T^{3/2}\sqrt{k}\sqrt{\log(1/\beta)}\alpha\rho)/\varepsilon_{\text{sample}}). \qquad (6.8)$$

$\square$

6.2   Base synopsis generators

Algorithm SmallDB (Section 4) is based on the insight that a small randomly selected subset of database rows provides good answers to large sets of fractional counting queries. The base synopsis generators described in the current section have an analogous insight: a small synopsis that gives good approximations to the answers to a small subset of queries also yields good approximations to most queries. Both of these are instances of *generalization bounds.* In the remainder of this section we firs prove a generalization bound and then use it to construct differentially base synopsis generators.

6.2.1   A generalization bound

We have a distribution $\mathcal{D}$ over a large set $\mathcal{Q}$ of queries to be approximated. The lemma below says that a sufficiently small synopsis that gives sufficiently good approximations to the answers of a *randomly selected* subset $S \subset \mathcal{Q}$ of queries, sampled according to the distribution $\mathcal{D}$ on $\mathcal{Q}$, will, with high probability over the choice of S, also give good approximations to the answers to *most* queries in $\mathcal{Q}$ (that is, to most of the mass of $\mathcal{Q}$, weighted by $\mathcal{D}$). Of course, to make any sense the synopsis must include a method of providing an answer to all queries in $\mathcal{Q}$, not just the subset $S \subseteq \mathcal{Q}$ received as input. Our particular generators, described in Sections 6.2.2 and Theorem 6.6 will produce synthetic databases; to answer any query one can simply apply the query to the synthetic database, but the lemma will be stated in full generality.

Let $R(y, q)$ denote the answer given by the synopsis y (when used as input for the reconstruction procedure) on query q. A synopsis y λ-*fits* a database x w.r.t a set S of queries if $\max_{q \in S} |R(y, q) - q(x)| \leq \lambda$. Let $|y|$

denote the number of bits needed to represent y. Since our synopses will be synthetic databases, $|y| = N \log_2 |\mathcal{X}|$ for some appropriately chosen number N of universe elements. The generalization bound shows that if y λ-fits x with respect to a large enough (larger than $|y|$) randomly chosen set S of queries sampled from a distribution $\mathcal{D}$, then with high probability y λ-fits x for *most* of the mass of $\mathcal{D}$.

Lemma 6.5. Let $\mathcal{D}$ be an arbitrary distribution on a query set $\mathcal{Q} = \{q : \mathcal{X}^* \to \mathbb{R}\}$. For all $m \in \mathcal{N}$, $\gamma \in (0,1)$, $\eta \in [0, 1/2)$, let $a = 2(\log(1/\gamma) + m)/(m(1 - 2\eta))$. Then with probability at least $1 - \gamma$ over the choice of $S \sim \mathcal{D}^{a \cdot m}$, every synopsis y of size at most m bits that λ-fits x with respect to the query set S, also λ-fits x with respect to at least a $(1/2 + \eta)$-fraction of $\mathcal{D}$.

Before proving the lemma we observe that a is a compression factor: we are squeezing the answers to am queries into an m-bit output, so larger a corresponds to more compression. Typically, this means better generalization, and indeed we see that if a is larger then, keeping m and γ fixed, we would be able to have larger η. The lemma also says that, for any given output size m, the number of queries needed as input to obtain an output that does well on a majority ($1/2 + \eta$ fraction) of $\mathcal{D}$ is only $O(\log(1/\gamma) + m)$. This is interesting because a smaller number of queries k needed by the base generator leads, via the privacy loss $\varepsilon_{\text{sample}}$ due to sampling of kT queries and its inverse relationship to the slackness μ (Equation 6.7), to improved accuracy of the output of the boosting algorithm.

Proof of Lemma 6.5. Fix a set of queries $S \subset \mathcal{Q}$ chosen independently according to $\mathcal{D}^{a \cdot m}$. Examine an arbitrary m-bit synopsis y. Note that y is described by an m-bit string. Let us say y is *bad* if $|R(y, q) - q(x)| > \lambda$ for at least a $(\log(1/\gamma) + m)/(a \cdot m)$ fraction of $\mathcal{D}$, meaning that $\Pr_{q \sim \mathcal{D}}[|R(y, q) - q(x)| > \lambda] \geq (\log(1/\gamma) + m)/(a \cdot m)$.

In other words, y is bad if there exists a set $Q_y \subset \mathcal{Q}$ of fractional weight at least $(\log(1/\gamma) + m)/(a \cdot m)$ such that $|R(y, q) - q(x)| > \lambda$ for $q \in Q_y$. For such a y, what is the probability that y gives λ-accurate answers for *every* $q \in S$? This is exactly the probability that none of the queries in S is in Q_y, or

$$(1 - (\log(1/\gamma) + m)/(a \cdot m))^{a \cdot m} \leq e^{-(\log(1/\gamma)+m)} \leq \gamma \cdot 2^{-m}$$

Taking a union bound over all 2^m possible choices for y, the probability that there exists an m-bit synopsis y that is accurate on all the queries in S but inaccurate on a set of fractional weight $(\log(1/\beta) + m)/(a \cdot m)$ is at most γ. Letting $k = am = |S|$ we see that it is sufficient to have

$$a > \frac{2(\log(1/\gamma) + m)}{m \cdot (1 - 2\eta)}. \tag{6.9}$$

□

This simple lemma is extremely powerful. It tells us that when constructing a base generator at round t, we only need to worry about ensuring good answers for the small set of random queries sampled from $\mathcal{D}_t$; doing well for most of $\mathcal{D}_t$ will happen automatically!

6.2.2 The base generator

Our first generator works by brute force. After sampling a set S of k queries independently according to a distribution $\mathcal{D}$, the base generator will produce noisy answers for all queries in S via the Laplace mechanism. Then, making no further use of the actual database, the algorithm searches for *any* database of size n for which these noisy answers are sufficiently close, and outputs this database. Privacy will be immediate because everything after the k invocations of the Laplace mechanism is in post-processing. Thus the only source of privacy loss is the cumulative loss from these k invocations of the Laplace mechanism, which we know how to analyze via the composition theorem. Utility will follow from the utility of the Laplace mechanism — which says that we are unlikely to have "very large" error on even one query — coupled with the fact that the true database x is an n-element database that fits these noisy responses.[1]

---

[1]This argument assumes the size n of the database is known. Alternatively we can include a noisy query of the form "How many rows are in the database?" and exhaustively search all databases of size close to the response to this query.

Theorem 6.6 (Base Synopsis Generator for Arbitrary Queries). For any data universe $\mathcal{X}$, database size n, and class $\mathcal{Q} : \{\mathcal{X}^* \to \mathbb{R}\}$ of queries of sensitivity at most ρ, for any $\varepsilon_{\text{base}}, \delta_{\text{base}} > 0$, there exists an $(\varepsilon_{\text{base}}, \delta_{\text{base}})$-differentially private $(k, \lambda, \eta = 1/3, \beta)$-base synopsis generator for $\mathcal{Q}$, where $k = am > 6(m + \log(2/\beta)) = 6(n \log |\mathcal{X}| + \log(2/\beta))$ and $\lambda > 2b(\log k + log(2/\beta))$, where $b = \rho\sqrt{am \log(1/\delta_{\text{base}})}/\varepsilon_{\text{base}}$.

The running time of the generator is

$$|\mathcal{X}|^n \cdot \text{poly}(n, \log(1/\beta), \log(1/\varepsilon_{\text{base}}), \log(1/\delta_{\text{base}})).$$

Proof. We first describe the base generator at a high level, then determine the values for k and λ. The synopsis y produced by the base generator will be a synthetic database of size n. Thus $m = |y| = n \cdot \log |\mathcal{X}|$. The generator begins by choosing a set S of k queries, sampled independently according to $\mathcal{D}$. It computes a noisy answer for each query $q \in S$ using the Laplace mechanism, adding to each true answer an independent draw from $\text{Lap}(b)$ for an appropriate b to be determined later. Let $\{\widehat{q(x)}\}_{q \in \mathcal{Q}}$ be the collection of noisy answers. The generator enumerates over all $|\mathcal{X}|^n$ databases of size n, and outputs the lexicographically first database y such that for every $q \in S$ we have $|q(y) - \widehat{q(x)}| \leq \lambda/2$. If no such database is found, it outputs $\bot$ instead, and we say it *fails*. Note that if $|\widehat{q(x)} - q(x)| < \lambda/2$ and $|q(y) - \widehat{q(x)}| < \lambda/2$, then $|q(y) - q(x)| < \lambda$.

There are two potential sources of failure for our particular generator. One possibility is that y fails to generalize, or is *bad* as defined in the proof of Lemma 6.5. A second possibility is that one of the samples from the Laplace distribution is of excessively large magnitude, which might cause the generator to fail. We will choose our parameters so as to bound the probability of each of these events individually by at most $\beta/2$.

Substituting $\eta = 1/3$ and $m = n \log |X|$ into Equation 6.9 shows that taking $a > 6(1 + \log(2/\beta)/m)$ suffices in order for the probability of failure due to the choice of S to be bounded by $\beta/2$. Thus, taking $k = am > 6(m + \log(2/\beta)) = 6(n \log |\mathcal{X}| + \log(2/\beta))$ suffices.

We have k queries of sensitivity at most ρ. Using the Laplace mechanism with parameter $b = 2\sqrt{2k \log(1/\delta_{\text{base}})}\rho/\varepsilon_{\text{base}}$, ensures that each query incurs privacy loss at most $\varepsilon_{\text{base}}/\sqrt{2k \ln(1/\delta_{\text{base}})}$, which by

Corollary 3.21 ensures that the entire procedure will be $(\varepsilon_{\mathrm{base}}, \delta_{\mathrm{base}})$-differentially private.

We will choose λ so that the probability that any draw from $\mathrm{Lap}(b)$ has magnitude exceeding $\lambda/2$ is at most $\beta/2$. Conditioned on the event that all k draws have magnitude at most λ we know that the input database itself will λ-fit our noisy answers, so the procedure will not fail.

Recall that the concentration properties of the Laplace distribution ensure that with probability at least $1 - e^t$ a draw from $\mathrm{Lap}(b)$ will have magnitude bounded by tb. Setting $\lambda/2 = tb$, the probability that a given draw will have magnitude exceeding $\lambda/2$ is bounded by $e^{-t} = e^{-\lambda/2b}$. To ensure that none of the k draws has magnitude exceeding $\lambda/2$ it suffices, by a union bound, to have

$$ke^{-\lambda/2b} < \beta/2$$

$$\Leftrightarrow e^{\lambda/2b} > k\frac{2}{\beta}$$

$$\Leftrightarrow \lambda/2 > b(\log k + \log(2/\beta))$$

$$\Leftrightarrow \lambda > 2b(\log k + \log(2/\beta)). \qquad \square$$

The Special Case of Linear Queries. For the special case of linear queries it is possible to avoid the brute force search for a small database. The technique requires time that is polynomial in $(|\mathcal{Q}|, |\mathcal{X}|, n, \log(1/\beta))$. We will focus on the case of counting queries and sketch the construction.

As in the case of the base generator for arbitrary queries, the base generator begins by selecting a set S of $k = am$ queries according to $\mathcal{D}$ and computing noisy answers using Laplace noise. The generator for linear queries then runs a *syntheticizer* on S which, roughly speaking, transforms any synopsis giving good approximations to *any* set R of queries into a synthetic database yielding approximations of similar quality on the set R. The input to the syntheticizer will be the noisy values for the queries in S, that is, $R = S$. (Recall that when we modify the size of the database we always think in terms of the fractional version of the counting queries: "What fraction of the database rows satisfies property P?")

The resulting database may be quite large, meaning it may have many rows. The base generator then subsamples only $n' = (\log k \log(1/\beta))/\alpha^2$ of the rows of the synthetic database, creating a smaller synthetic database that with probability at least $1 - \beta$ has α-accuracy with respect to the answers given by the large synthetic database. This yields an $m = ((\log k \log(1/\beta))/\alpha^2) \log |\mathcal{X}|$-bit synopsis that, by the generalization lemma, with probability $(1 - \log(1/\beta))$ over the choice of the k queries, answers well on a $(1/2 + \eta)$ fraction of $\mathcal{Q}$ (as weighted by $\mathcal{D}$).

As in the case of the base generator for arbitrary queries, we require $k = am > 6\log(1/\beta) + 6m$. Taking $\alpha^2 = (\log \mathcal{Q})/n$ we get that

$$k > 6\log(1/\beta) + 6\frac{\log k \log(1/\beta) \log |\mathcal{X}|}{\alpha^2}$$

$$= 6\log(1/\beta) + 6n \log k \log(1/\beta)\frac{\log |\mathcal{X}|}{\log |\mathcal{Q}|}.$$

The syntheticizer is nontrivial. Its properties are summarized by the following theorem.

Theorem 6.7. Let $\mathcal{X}$ be a data universe, $\mathcal{Q}$ a set of fractional counting queries, and A an (ε, δ)-differentially private synopsis generator with utility $(\alpha, \beta, 0)$ and arbitrary output. Then there exists a syntheticizer A' that is (ε, δ)-differentially private and has utility $(3\alpha, \beta, 0)$. A' outputs a (potentially large) synthetic database. Its running time is polynomial in the running time of A and $(|\mathcal{X}|, |\mathcal{Q}|, 1/\alpha, \log(1/\beta))$.

In our case, A is the Laplace mechanism, and the synopsis is simply the set of noisy answers. The composition theorem says that for A to be $(\varepsilon_{\text{base}}, \delta_{\text{base}})$-differentially private the parameter to the Laplace mechanism should be $\rho/(\varepsilon_{\text{base}}/\sqrt{2k \log(1/\delta_{\text{base}})})$. For fractional counting queries the sensitivity is $\rho = 1/n$.

Thus, when we apply the Theorem we will have an α of order $(\sqrt{k \log(1/\beta)}/\varepsilon_{\text{base}})\rho$. Here, ρ is the sensitivity. For counting queries it is 1, but we will shift to fractional counting queries, so $\rho = 1/n$.

Proof Sketch for Theorem 6.7. Run A to get (differentially private) (fractional) counts on all the queries in R. We will then use linear programming to find a low-weight fractional database that approximates these fractional counts, as explained below. Finally, we transform this fractional database into a standard synthetic database by rounding the fractional counts.

The output of A yields a fractional count for each query $q \in \mathcal{Q}$. The input database x is never accessed again and so A' is (ε, δ)-differentially private. Let v be the resulting vector of counts, i.e., v_q is the fractional count that A's output gives on query q. With probability $1 - \beta$, all of the entries in v are α-accurate.

A "fractional" database z that approximates these counts is obtained as follows. Recall the histogram representation of a database, where for each element in the universe $\mathcal{X}$ the histogram contains the number of instances of this element in the database. Now, for every $i \in \mathcal{X}$, we introduce a variable $a_i \geq 0$ that will "count" the (fractional) number of occurrences of i in the fractional database z. We will impose the constraint

$$\sum_{i \in \mathcal{X}} a_i = 1.$$

We represent the count of query q in z as the sum of the count of items i that satisfy q:

$$\sum_{i \in \mathcal{X} \text{ s.t. } q(i)=1} a_i$$

We want all of these counts to be within a an additive α accuracy of the respective counts in v_q. Writing this as a linear inequality we get:

$$(v_q - \alpha) \sum_{i \in \mathcal{X}} a_i \leq \sum_{i \in \mathcal{X} \text{ s.t. } q(i)=1} a_i \leq (v_q + \alpha) \sum_{i \in \mathcal{X}} a_i.$$

When the counts are all α-accurate with respect to the counts in v_c, it is also the case that (with probability $1 - \beta$) they are all 2α-accurate with respect to the true counts on the original database x.

We write a linear program with two such constraints for each query (a total of $2|\mathcal{Q}|$ constraints). A' tries to find a fractional solution to this linear program. To see that such a solution exists, observe that the database x itself is α-close to the vector of counts v, and so there *exists* a solution to the linear program (in fact even an integer solution), and hence A' will find *some* fractional solution.

We conclude that A' can generate a fractional database with $(2\alpha, \beta, 0)$-utility, but we really want a synthetic (integer) database. To transform the fractional database into an integer one, we round down each a_i, for $i \in \mathcal{X}$, to the closest multiple of $\alpha/|\mathcal{X}|$, this changes each fractional count by at most a $\alpha/|\mathcal{X}|$ additive factor, and so the rounded counts have $(3\alpha, \beta, 0)$ utility. Now we can treat the rounded fractional database (which has total weight 1), as an integer synthetic database of (polynomial) size at most $|\mathcal{X}|/\alpha$. $\qquad\square$

Recall that in our application of Theorem 6.7 we defined A to be the mechanism that adds Laplace noise with parameter $\rho/(\varepsilon_{\text{base}}/\sqrt{2k \log(1/\delta_{\text{base}})})$. We have k draws, so by taking

$$\alpha' = \rho\sqrt{2k \log(1/\delta_{\text{base}})}(\log k + \log(1/\beta))$$

we have that A is $(\alpha', \beta, 0)$-accurate. For the base generator we chose error $\alpha^2 = (\log |\mathcal{Q}|)/n$. If the output of the syntheticizer is too large, we subsample

$$n' = \frac{\log |\mathcal{Q}| \log(1/\beta)}{\alpha^2} = \frac{\log k \log(1/\beta)}{\alpha^2}$$

rows. With probability $1 - \beta$ the resulting database maintains $O(\rho\sqrt{(\log |\mathcal{Q}|)/n} + (\sqrt{2k \log(1/\delta_{\text{base}})}/\varepsilon_{\text{base}})(\log k + \log(1/\beta))$-accuracy on all of the concepts simultaneously.

Finally, the base generator can fail if the choice of queries $S \in \mathcal{D}^k$ does not lead to good generalization. With the parameters we have chosen this occurs with probability at most β, leading to a total failure probability of the entire generator of 3β.

Theorem 6.8 (Base Generator for Fractional Linear Queries). For any data universe $\mathcal{X}$, database size n, and class $\mathcal{Q} : \{\mathcal{X}^n \to \mathbb{R}\}$ of fractional linear queries (with sensitivity at most $1/n$), for any $\varepsilon_{\text{base}}, \delta_{\text{base}} > 0$, there exists an $(\varepsilon_{\text{base}}, \delta_{\text{base}})$-differentially private $(k, \lambda, 1/3, 3\beta)$-base synopsis generator for $\mathcal{Q}$, where

$$k = O\left(\frac{n \log(|\mathcal{X}|) \log(1/\beta)}{\log |\mathcal{Q}|}\right)$$

$$\lambda = O\left(\frac{\log(1/\beta)}{\sqrt{n}}\left(\sqrt{\log |\mathcal{Q}|} + \sqrt{\frac{log|\mathcal{X}|}{log|\mathcal{Q}|}} \cdot \frac{1}{\varepsilon_{\text{base}}}\right)\right).$$

The running time of the base generator is $\mathrm{poly}(|\mathcal{X}|, n, \log(1/\beta),$ $\log(1/\varepsilon_{\mathrm{base}}))$.

The sampling bound used here is the same as that used in the construction of the SmallDB mechanism, but with different parameters. Here we are using these bounds for a base generator in a complicated boosting algorithm with a very small query set; there we are using them for a single-shot generation of a synthetic database with an enormous query set.

6.2.3   Assembling the ingredients

The total error comes from the choice of μ (see Equation 6.2) and λ, the accuracy parameter for the based generator.

Let us recall Theorem 6.1:

Theorem 6.9 (Theorem 6.1). Let $\mathcal{Q}$ be a query family with sensitivity at most ρ. For an appropriate setting of parameters, and with $T = \log|\mathcal{Q}|/\eta^2$ rounds, the algorithm of Figure 6.1 is an accurate and differentially private query-boosting algorithm:

1. When instantiated with a $(k, \lambda, \eta, \beta)$-base synopsis generator, the output of the boosting algorithm gives $(\lambda + \mu)$-accurate answers to *all* the queries in $\mathcal{Q}$ with probability at least $1 - T\beta$, where

$$\mu \in O(((\log^{3/2}|\mathcal{Q}|)\sqrt{k}\sqrt{\log(1/\beta)}\rho)/(\varepsilon_{\mathrm{sample}} \cdot \eta^3)). \quad (6.10)$$

2. If the base synopsis generator is $(\varepsilon_{\mathrm{base}}, \delta_{\mathrm{base}})$-differentially private, then the boosting algorithm is $((\varepsilon_{\mathrm{sample}} + T \cdot \varepsilon_{\mathrm{base}}), T(\beta + \delta_{\mathrm{base}}))$-differentially private.

By Equation 6.7,

$$\varepsilon_{\mathrm{sample}} \stackrel{\mathrm{def}}{=} \sqrt{2kT\log(1/\beta)}(\alpha 4T\rho/\mu) + kT\left(\frac{\alpha 4T\rho}{\mu}\right)^2,$$

where $\alpha = (1/2)(\ln(1 + 2\eta)(1 - 2\eta)) \in O(1)$. We always have $T = (\log|\mathcal{Q}|)/\eta^2$, so substituting in this value into the above equation we see that the bound

$$\mu \in O(((\log^{3/2}|\mathcal{Q}|)\sqrt{k}\sqrt{\log(1/\beta)}\rho)/(\varepsilon_{\mathrm{sample}} \cdot \eta^3))$$

in the statement of the theorem is acceptable.

For the case of arbitrary queries, with η a constant, we have

$$\lambda \in O\left(\frac{\rho}{\varepsilon_{\text{base}}}(\sqrt{n \log |\mathcal{X}| \log(1/\delta_{\text{base}})})(\log(n \log |\mathcal{X}|) + \log(2/\beta)))\right).$$

Now, $\varepsilon_{\text{boost}} = T\varepsilon_{\text{base}} + \varepsilon_{\text{sample}}$. Set these two terms equal, so $T\varepsilon_{\text{base}} = \varepsilon_{\text{boost}}/2 = \varepsilon_{\text{sample}}$, whence we can replace the $1/\varepsilon_{\text{base}}$ term with $2T/\varepsilon_{\text{boost}} = (\log |\mathcal{Q}|/\eta^2)/2\varepsilon_{\text{boost}}$. Now our terms for λ and μ have similar denominators, since η is constant. We may therefore conclude that the total error is bounded by:

$$\lambda + \mu \in \tilde{O}\left(\frac{\sqrt{n \log |\mathcal{X}|}\rho \log^{3/2} |\mathcal{Q}|(\log(1/\beta))^{3/2}}{\varepsilon_{\text{boost}}}\right).$$

With similar reasoning, for the case of fractional counting queries we get

$$\lambda + \mu \in \tilde{O}\left(\frac{\sqrt{\log |\mathcal{X}|} \log |\mathcal{Q}| \log(1/\beta)^{3/2}}{\varepsilon_{\text{boost}} \sqrt{n}}\right).$$

To convert to a bound for ordinary, non-fractional, counting queries we multiply by n to obtain

$$\lambda + \mu \in \tilde{O}\left(\frac{\sqrt{n \log |\mathcal{X}|} \log |\mathcal{Q}| \log(1/\beta)^{3/2}}{\varepsilon_{\text{boost}}}\right).$$

6.3 Bibliographical notes

The boosting algorithm (Figure 6.1) is a variant of AdaBoost algorithm of Schapire and Singer [78]. See Schapire [77] for an excellent survey of boosting, and the textbook "Boosting" by Freund and Schapire [79] for a thorough treatment. The private boosting algorithm covered in this section is due to Dwork et al. [32], which also contains the base generator for linear queries. This base generator, in turn, relies on the syntheticizer of Dwork et al. [28]. In particular, Theorem 6.7 comes from [28]. Dwork, Rothblum, and Vadhan also addressed differentially private boosting in the usual sense.

7

When Worst-Case Sensitivity is Atypical

In this section, we briefly describe two general techniques, both enjoying unconditional privacy guarantees, that can often make life easier for the data analyst, especially when dealing with a function that has arbitrary, or difficult to analyze, worst-case sensitivity. These algorithms are most useful in computing functions that, for some exogenous reason, the analyst has reason to believe are "usually" insensitive in practice.

7.1 Subsample and aggregate

The Subsample and Aggregate technique yields a method for "forcing" the computation of a function $f(x)$ to be insensitive, even for an *arbitrary* function f. Proving privacy will be trivial. Accuracy depends on properties of the function f and the specific data set x; in particular, if $f(x)$ can be accurately estimated, with high probability, on $f(S)$, where S is a random subset of the elements in x, then accuracy should be good. Many maximum likelihood statistical estimators enjoy this property on "typical" data sets — this is why these estimators are employed in practice.

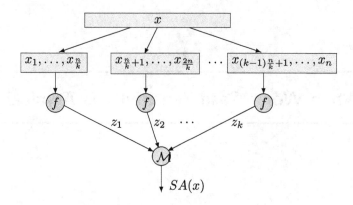

Figure 7.1: Subsample and Aggregate with a generic differentially private aggregation algorithm $\mathcal{M}$.

In Subsample and Aggregate, the n rows of the database x are randomly partitioned into m blocks $B_1, \ldots, B_m$, each of size n/m. The function f is computed *exactly, without noise,* independently on each block. The intermediate outcomes $f(B_1), \ldots, f(B_m)$ are then combined via a differentially private aggregation mechanism — typical examples include standard aggregations, such as the α-trimmed mean,[1] the Winsorized mean,[2] and the median, but there are no restrictions — and then adding Laplace noise scaled to the sensitivity of the aggregation function in question; see Figure 7.1.

The key observation in Subsample and Aggregate is that any single element can affect at most one block, and therefore the value of just a single $f(B_i)$. Thus, changing the data of any individual can change at most a single input to the aggregation function. Even if f is arbitrary, the analyst chooses the aggregation function, and so is free to choose one that is insensitive, *provided that choice is independent of the database!* Privacy is therefore immediate: For any $\delta \geq 0$ and any function f, if the aggregation mechanism $\mathcal{M}$ is (ε, δ)-differentially private

---

[1]The α-trimmed mean is the mean after the top and bottom α fraction of the inputs have been discarded.

[2]The Winsorized mean is similar to the α-trimmed mean except that, rather than being discarded, the top and bottom α fraction are replaced with the most extreme remaining values.

then so is the Subsample and Aggregate technique when instantiated with f and $\mathcal{M}$.[3]

Utility is a different story, and it is frustratingly difficult to argue even for the case in which data are plentiful and large random subsets are very likely to give similar results. For example, the data may be labeled training points in high dimensional space and the function is logistic regression, which produces a vector v and labels a point p with $+1$ if and only if $p \cdot v \geq T$ for some (say, fixed) threshold T. Intuitively, if the samples are sufficiently plentiful and typical then all blocks should yield similar vectors v. The difficulty comes in getting a good bound on the worst-case sensitivity of the aggregation function — we may need to use the size of the range as a fallback. Nonetheless, some nice applications are known, especially in the realm of statistical estimators, where, for example, it can be shown that, under the assumption of "generic normality," privacy can be achieved at *no* additional cost in statistical efficiency (roughly, accuracy as the number of samples grows). We do not define generic normality here, but note that estimators fitting these assumptions include the maximum likelihood estimator for "nice" parametric families of distributions such as gaussians, and maximum-likelihood estimators for linear regression and logistic regression.

Suppose the function f has a *discrete* range of cardinality m, say, $[m]$. In this case Subsample and Aggregate will need to aggregate a set of b elements drawn from $[m]$, and we can use Report Noisy Arg-Max to find the most popular outcome. This approach to aggregation requires $b \geq \log m$ to obtain meaningful results even when the intermediate outcomes are unanimous. We will see an alternative below with no such requirement.

Example 7.1 (Choosing a Model). Much work in statistics and machine learning addresses the problem of *model selection*: Given a data set and a discrete collection of "models," each of which is a family of probability distributions, the goal is to determine the model that best "fits"

---

[3]The choice of aggregation function can even depend on the database, but the selection must be made in a differentially private fashion. The privacy cost is then the cost of composing the choice operation with the aggregation function.

the data. For example, given a set of labeled d-dimensional data, the collection of models might be all subsets of at most $s \ll d$ features, and the goal is to find the set of features that best permits prediction of the labels. The function f might be choosing the best model from the given set of of m models, a process known as *model fitting*, via an arbitrary learning algorithm. Aggregation to find the most popular value could be done via Report Noisy Max, which also yields an estimate of its popularity.

Example 7.2 (Significant Features). This is a special case of model fitting. The data are a collection of points in $\mathbb{R}^d$ and the function is the very popular LASSO, which yields as output a list $L \in [d]^s$ of at most $s \ll d$ significant features. We can aggregate the output in two ways: feature by feature — equivalent to running d executions of Subsample and Aggregate, one for each feature, each with a range of size 2 — or on the set as a whole, in which case the cardinality of the range is $\binom{d}{s}$.

7.2   Propose-test-Release

At this point one might ask: what is the meaning of the aggregation if there is not substantial agreement among the blocks? More generally, for any reasonably large-scale statistical analysis in real life, we expect the results to be fairly stable, independent of the presence or absence of any single individual. Indeed, this is the entire intuition behind the significance of a statistic and underlying the utility of differential privacy. We can even go further, and argue that if a statistic is not stable, we should have no interest in computing it. Often, our database will in fact be a sample from a larger population, and our true goal is not to compute the value of the statistic on the database itself, but rather estimate it for the underlying population. Implicitly, therefore, when computing a statistic we are already assuming that the statistic is stable under subsampling!

Everything we have seen so far has provided privacy even on very "idiosyncratic" datasets, for which "typically" stable algorithms my be highly unstable. In this section we introduce a methodology, Propose-Test-Release, which is motivated by the philosophy that if there is insufficient stability then the analysis can be abandoned because the results are not in fact meaningful. That is, the methodology allows the analyst to check that, *on the given dataset*, the function satisfies some "robustness" or "stability" criterion and, if it does not, to halt the analysis.

The goal of our first application of Propose-Test-Release is to come up with a variant of the Laplace mechanism that adds noise scaled to something strictly smaller than the sensitivity of a function. This leads to the notion of *local sensitivity*, which is defined for a (function, database) pair, say, (f, x). Quite simply, the local sensitivity of f with respect to x is the amount by which the $f(y)$ can differ from $f(x)$ for any y adjacent to x.

Definition 7.1 (Local Sensitivity). The local sensitivity of a function $f : \mathcal{X}^n \to \mathbb{R}^k$ with respect to a database x is:

$$\max_{y \text{ adjacent to } x} \|f(x) - f(y)\|_1.$$

The Propose-Test-Release approach is to first *propose* a bound, say b, on local sensitivity — typically the data analyst has some idea of what this should be — and then run a differentially private *test* to ensure that the database is "far" from any database for which this bound fails to hold. If the test is passed, then the sensitivity is assumed to be bounded by b, and a differentially private mechanism such as, for example, the Laplace mechanism with parameter b/ϵ, is used to *release* the (slightly) noisy response to the query.

Note that we can view this approach as a two-party algorithm where one party plays an honest data analyst and the other is the Laplace mechanism. There is an interplay between the honest analyst and the mechanism in which the algorithm asks for an estimate of the sensitivity and then "instructs" the mechanism to use this estimated sensitivity in responding to subsequent queries. Why does it need to be so complicated? Why can't the mechanism simply add noise scaled to the local sensitivity without playing this private estimation game? The reason is that the local sensitivity may *itself* be sensitive. This fact, combined with some auxiliary information about the database, can lead to privacy problems: the adversary may know that the database is one of x, which has very low local sensitivity for the computation in question, and a neighboring y, for which the function has very high local sensitivity. In this case the adversary may be able to guess rather accurately which of x and y is the true database. For example, if $f(x) = f(y) = s$ and the reponse is far from s, then the adversary would guess y.

This is captured by the math of differential privacy. There are neighboring instances of the median function which have the same median, say, m, but arbitrarily large gaps in the local sensitivity. Suppose the response R to the median query is computed via the Laplace mechanism with noise scaled to the local sensitivity. When the database is x the probability mass is close to m, because the sensitivity is small, but when the database is y the mass is far flung, because the sensitivity is large. As an extreme case, suppose the local sensitivity on x is exactly zero, for example, $\mathcal{X} = \{0, 10^6\}$, n is even, and x, which has size $n + 1$, contains $1 + n/2$ zeros. Then the median of x is zero and the local sensitivity of the median, when the database is x, is 0. In contrast, the neighboring database y has size n, contains $n/2$ zeros, has median zero (we have defined median to break ties in favor of the smaller value), and the local sensitivity of the median, when the database is y, is 10^6. On x all the mass of the Laplace mechanism (with parameter $0/\varepsilon = 0$) is concentrated on the single point 0; but on y the probability distribution has standard deviation $\sqrt{2} \cdot 10^6$. This destroys all hope of differential privacy.

To test that the database is "far" from one with local sensitivity greater than the proposed bound b, we may pose the query: "What is the distance of the true database to the closest one with local sensitivity exceeding b?" Distance to a fixed set of databases is a (global) sensitivity 1 query, so this test can be run in a differentially private fashion by adding noise $\mathrm{Lap}(1/\varepsilon)$ to the true answer. To err on the side of privacy, the algorithm can compare this noisy distance to a conservative threshold — one that is only negligibly likely to be exceeded due to a freak event of very large magnitude Laplace noise. For example, if the threshold used is, say, $\ln^2 n$, the probability of a false positive (passing the test when the local sensitivity in fact exceeds b) is at most $O(n^{-\varepsilon \ln n})$, by the properties of the Laplace distribution. Because of the negligible probability of a false positive, the technique cannot yield $(\varepsilon, 0)$-differential privacy for any ε.

To apply this methodology to consensus on blocks, as in our discussion of Subsample and Aggregate, view the intermediate results $f(B_1), \ldots, f(B_m)$ as a data set and consider some measure of the concentration of these values. Intuitively, if the values are tightly concentrated then we have consensus among the blocks. Of course, we still need to find the correct notion of concentration, one that is meaningful and that has a differentially private instantiation. In a later section we will define and weave together two notions of stability that seem relevant to Subsample and Aggregate: insensitivity (to the removal or addition of a few data points) and stability under subsampling, capturing the notion that a subsample should yield similar results to the full data set.

7.2.1 Example: the scale of a dataset

Given a dataset, a natural question to ask is, "What is the scale, or dispersion, of the dataset?" This is a different question from *data location*, which might be captured by the median or the mean. The data scale is more often captured by the variance or an interquantile range. We will focus on the *interquartile range (IQR)*, a well-known robust estimator for the scale of the data. We begin with some rough intuition. Suppose the data are *i.i.d.* samples drawn from a distribution with cumulative distribution function F. Then IQR(F), defined as $F^{-1}(3/4) - F^{-1}(1/4)$, is a constant, depending only on F. It might be very large, or very tiny, but either way, if the density of F is sufficiently high at the two quartiles, then, given enough samples from F, the empirical (that is, sample) interquartile distance should be close to IQR(F).

Our Propose-Test-Release algorithm for the interquartile distance first tests how many database points need to be changed to obtain a data set with a "sufficiently different" interquartile distance. Only if the (noisy) reply is "sufficiently large" will the algorithm release an approximation to the interquartile range of the dataset.

The definition of "sufficiently different" is multiplicative, as an additive notion for difference of scale makes no sense — what would be the right scale for the additive amount? The algorithm therefore works with the logarithm of the scale, which leads to a multiplicative noise on the IQR. To see this, suppose that, as in what might be the typical case, the sample interquartile distance cannot change by a factor of 2 by modifying a single point. Then the logarithm (base 2) of the sample interquartile has local sensitivity bounded by 1. This lets us privately release an approximation to *the logarithm of* the sample interquartile range by adding to this value a random draw from $\mathrm{Lap}(1/\varepsilon)$.

Let $\mathrm{IQR}(x)$ denote the sample interquartile range when the the data set is x. The algorithm is (implicitly) *proposing* to add noise drawn from $\mathrm{Lap}(1/\varepsilon)$ to the value $\log_2(\mathrm{IQR}(x))$. To *test* whether this magnitude of noise is sufficient for differential privacy, we discretize $\mathbb{R}$ into disjoint bins $\{[k \ln 2, (k+1) \ln 2)\}_{k \in \mathbf{Z}}$ and ask how many data points must be modified in order to obtain a new database, the logarithm (base 2) of whose interquartile range is in a different bin than that of $\log_2(\mathrm{IQR}(x))$. If the answer is at least two then the local sensitivity (of the logarithm of the interquartile range) is bounded by the bin width. We now give more details.

To understand the choice of bin size, we write

$$\log_2(\mathrm{IQR}(x)) = \frac{\ln \mathrm{IQR}(x)}{\ln 2} = \frac{c \ln 2}{\ln 2},$$

whence we find that looking at $\ln(\mathrm{IQR}(x))$ on the scale of $\ln 2$ is equivalent to looking at $\log_2(\mathrm{IQR}(x))$ on the scale of 1. Thus we have scaled bins which are intervals whose endpoints are a pair of adjacent integers: $B_k = [k, k+1)$, $k \in \mathbf{Z}$, and we let $k_1 = \lfloor \log_2(\mathrm{IQR}(x)) \rfloor$, so $\log_2(\mathrm{IQR}(x)) \in [k_1, k_1 + 1)$ and we say informally that the logarithm of the IQR is in bin k_1. Consider the following testing query:

> $\mathbf{Q_0}$: How many data points need to change in order to get
> a new database z such that $\log_2(\mathrm{IQR}(z)) \notin B_{k_1}$?

Let $A_0(x)$ be the true answer to $\mathbf{Q_0}$ when the database is x. If $A_0(x) \geq 2$, then neighbors y of x satisfy $|\log_2(\mathrm{IQR}(y)) - \log_2(\mathrm{IQR}(x))| \leq 1$. That is, they are close to each other. This is not equivalent to being in the same interval in the discretization: $\log_2(\mathrm{IQR}(x))$ may lie close to one of the endpoints of the interval $[k_1, k_1 + 1)$ and $\log_2(\mathrm{IQR}(y))$ may lie just on the other side of the endpoint. Letting $R_0 = A_0(x) + \mathrm{Lap}(1/\varepsilon)$, a small R_0, even when the draw from the Laplace distribution has small magnitude, might not actually indicate high sensitivity of the interquartile range. To cope with the case that the local sensitivity is very small, but $\log_2(\mathrm{IQR}(x))$ is very close to the boundary, we consider a second discretization $\{B_k^{(2)} = [k-0.5, k+0.5)\}_{k\in\mathbf{Z}}$. We denote the two discretizations by $B^{(1)}$ and $B^{(2)}$ respectively. The value $\log_2(\mathrm{IQR}(x))$ — indeed, any value — cannot be close to a boundary in both discretizations. The test is passed if R_0 is large in at least one discretization.

The **Scale** algorithm (Algorithm 12) below for computing database scale assumes that n, the size of the database, is known, and the distance query ("How far to a database whose interquartile range has sensitivity exceeding b?") is asking how many points must be *moved* to reach a database with high sensitivity of the IQR. We can avoid this assumption by having the algorithm first ask the (sensitivity 1) query: "How many data points are in x?" We remark that, for technical reasons, to cope with the case $IQR(x) = 0$, we define $\log 0 = -\infty$, $\lfloor -\infty \rfloor = -\infty$, and let $[-\infty, -\infty) = \{-\infty\}$.

Algorithm 12 The **Scale** Algorithm (releasing the interquartile range)

Require: dataset: $x \in \mathcal{X}^*$, privacy parameters: $\epsilon, \delta > 0$
1: **for** the jth discretization $(j = 1, 2)$ **do**
2:     Compute $R_0(x) = A_0(x) + z_0$, where $z_0 \in_R \mathrm{Lap}(1/\varepsilon)$.
3:     **if** $R_0 \leq 1 + \ln(1/\delta)$ **then**
4:         Let $s^{(j)} = \perp$.
5:     **else**
6:         Let $s^{(j)} = IQR(x) \times 2^{z_s^{(j)}}$, where $z_s^{(j)} \sim \mathrm{Lap}(1/\varepsilon)$.
7:     **end if**
8: **end for**
9: **if** $s^{(1)} \neq \perp$ **then**
10:     Return $s^{(1)}$.
11: **else**
12:     Return $s^{(2)}$.
13: **end if**

Note that the algorithm is efficient: let $x_{(1)}, x_{(2)}, \ldots, x_{(n)}$ denote the n database points *after sorting*, and let $x(m)$ denote the median, so $m = \lfloor (n+1)/2 \rfloor$. Then the local sensitivity of the median is $\max\{x(m) - x(m-1), x(m+1) - x(m)\}$ and, more importantly, one can compute $A_0(x)$ by considering $O(n)$ sliding intervals with width 2^{k_1} and 2^{k_1+1}, each having one endpoint in x. The computational cost for each interval is constant.

We will not prove convergence bounds for this algorithm because, for the sake of simplicity, we have used a base for the logarithm that is far from optimal (a better base is $1 + 1/\ln n$). We briefly outline the steps in the proof of privacy.

Theorem 7.1. Algorithm **Scale** (Algorithm 12) is $(4\varepsilon, \delta)$-differentially private.

Proof. (Sketch.) Letting s be shorthand for the result obtained with a single discretization, and defining $\mathcal{D}_0 = \{x : A_0(x) \geq 2\}$, the proof shows:

1. The worst-case sensitivity of query $\mathbf{Q_0}$ is at most 1.
2. Neighboring databases are almost equally likely to result in $\perp$: For all neighboring database x, y:

$$\Pr[s = \perp | x] \leq e^\varepsilon \Pr[s = \perp | y].$$

3. Databases not in $\mathcal{D}_0$ are unlikely to pass the test:

$$\forall x \notin \mathcal{D}_0 : \Pr[s \neq \perp | x] \leq \frac{\delta}{2}.$$

4. $\forall C \in \mathbb{R}^+, x \in \mathcal{D}_0$ and all neighbors y of x:

$$\Pr[s \in C | x] \leq e^{2\varepsilon} \Pr[s \in C | y].$$

Thus, we get $(2\varepsilon, \delta/2)$-differential privacy for each discretization. Applying Theorem 3.16 (Appendix B), which says that "the epsilons and the deltas add up," yields $(4\varepsilon, \delta)$-differential privacy. $\square$

7.3   Stability and privacy

7.3.1   Two notions of stability

We begin by making a distinction between the two notions of stability intertwined in this section: stability under subsampling, which yields similar results under random subsamples of the data, and perturbation stability, or low local sensitivity, for a given dataset. In this section we will define and make use of extreme versions of both of these.

- *Subsampling stability*: We say f is q-subsampling stable on x if $f(\hat{x}) = f(x)$ with probability at least $3/4$ when $\hat{x}$ is a random subsample from x which includes each entry independently with probability q. We will use this notion in Algorithm $\mathcal{A}_{\text{samp}}$, a variant of Sample and Aggregate.

- *Perturbation Stability*: We say that f is *stable* on x if f takes the value $f(x)$ on all of the neighbors of x (and *unstable* otherwise). In other words, f is stable on x if the local sensitivity of f on x is zero. We will use this notion (implemented in Algorithm $\mathcal{A}_{\text{dist}}$ below) for the aggregation step of $\mathcal{A}_{\text{samp}}$.

At the heart of Algorithm $\mathcal{A}_{\text{samp}}$ is a relaxed version of perturbation stability, where instead of requiring that the value be unchanged on neighboring databases — a notion that makes sense for arbitrary ranges, including arbitrary discrete ranges — we required only that the value be "close" on neighboring databases — a notion that requires a metric on the range.

Functions f with arbitrary ranges, and in particular the problem of aggregating outputs in Subsample and Aggregate, motivate the next algorithm, $\mathcal{A}_{\text{dist}}$. On input f, x, $\mathcal{A}_{\text{dist}}$ outputs $f(x)$ with high probability if x is at distance at least $\frac{2\log(1/\delta)}{\varepsilon}$ from the nearest *unstable* data set. The algorithm is conceptually trivial: compute the distance to the nearest unstable data set, add Laplace noise $\text{Lap}(1/\varepsilon)$, and check that this noisy distance is at least $\frac{2\log(1/\delta)}{\varepsilon}$. If so, release $f(x)$, otherwise output $\bot$. We now make this a little more formal.

We begin by defining a quantitative measure of perturbation stability.

Definition 7.2. A function $f : \mathcal{X}^* \to \mathcal{R}$ is *k-stable on input* x if adding or removing any k elements from x does not change the value of f, that is, $f(x) = f(y)$ for all y such that $|x \triangle y| \leq k$. We say f is *stable* on x if it is (at least) 1-stable on x, and *unstable* otherwise.

Definition 7.3. The *distance to instability* of a data set $x \in \mathcal{X}^*$ with respect to a function f is the number of elements that must be added to or removed from y to reach a data set that is not stable under f.

Note that f is k-stable on x if and only if the distance of x to instability is at least k.

Algorithm $\mathcal{A}_{\text{dist}}$, an instantiation of Propose-Test-Release for discrete-valued functions g, appears in Figure 13.

Algorithm 13 $\mathcal{A}_{\text{dist}}$ (releasing $g(x)$ based on distance to instability)

Require: dataset: $x \in \mathcal{X}^*$, privacy parameters: $\epsilon, \delta > 0$, function g : $\mathcal{X}^* \to \mathbb{R}$

1: $d \leftarrow$ distance from x to nearest unstable instance
2: $\hat{d} \leftarrow d + \text{Lap}(1/\varepsilon)$
3: **if** $\hat{d} > \frac{\log(1/\delta)}{\varepsilon}$ **then**
4:    Output $g(x)$
5: **else**
6:    Output $\perp$
7: **end if**

The proof of the following propostion is immediate from the properties of the Laplace distribution.

Proposition 7.2. For every function g:

1. $\mathcal{A}_{\text{dist}}$ is (ε, δ)-differentially private.
2. For all $\beta > 0$: if g is $\frac{\ln(1/\delta) + \ln(1/\beta)}{\varepsilon}$-stable on x, then $\mathcal{A}_{\text{dist}}(x) = g(x)$ with probability at least $1 - \beta$, where the probability space is the coin flips of $\mathcal{A}_{\text{dist}}$.

This distance-based result is the best possible, in the following sense: if there are two data sets x and y for which $\mathcal{A}_{\text{dist}}$ outputs different values $g(x)$ and $g(y)$, respectively, with at least constant probability, then the distance from x to y must be $\Omega(\log(1/\delta)/\varepsilon)$.

Distance to instability can be difficult to compute, or even to lower bound, so this is not in general a practical solution. Two examples where distance to instability turns out to be easy to bound are the median and the mode (most frequently occurring value).

$\mathcal{A}_{\text{dist}}$ may also be unsatisfactory if the function, say f, is not stable on the specific datasets of interest. For example, suppose f is not stable because of the presence of a few outliers in x. Instances of the average behave this way, although for this function there are well know robust alternatives such as the winsorized mean, the trimmed mean, and the median. By what about for general functions f? Is there a method of "forcing" an arbitrary f to be stable on a database x?

This will be the goal of $\mathcal{A}_{\text{samp}}$, a variant of Subsample and Aggregate that outputs $f(x)$ with high probability (over its own random choices) whenever f is subsampling stable on x.

7.3.2 Algorithm $\mathcal{A}_{\text{samp}}$

In $\mathcal{A}_{\text{samp}}$, the blocks $B_1, \ldots, B_m$ are chosen *with replacement*, so that each block has the same distribution as the inputs (although now an element of x may appear in multiple blocks). We will call these subsampled datasets $\hat{x}_1, \ldots, \hat{x}_m$. The intermediate outputs $z = \{f(\hat{x}_1), \ldots, f(\hat{x}_m)\}$ are then aggregated via $\mathcal{A}_{\text{dist}}$ with function $g = \text{mode}$. The distance measure used to estimate the stability of the mode on z is a scaled version of the difference between the popularity of the mode and that of the second most frequent value. Algorithm $\mathcal{A}_{\text{samp}}$, appears in Figure 14. Its running time is dominated by running f about $1/q^2$ times; hence it is efficient whenever f is.

The key property of Algorithm $\mathcal{A}_{\text{samp}}$ is that, on input f, x, it outputs $f(x)$ with high probability, over its own random choices, whenever f is q-subsampling stable on x for $q = \frac{\varepsilon}{64 \log(1/\delta)}$. This result has an important statistical interpretation. Recall the discussion of model selection from Example 7.1. Given a collection of models, the *sample complexity* of model selection is the number of samples from a distribution in one of the models necessary to select the correct model with probability at least 2/3. The result says that *differentially private* model selection increases the sample complexity of (non-private) model selection by a problem-independent (and range-independent) factor of $O(\log(1/\delta)/\varepsilon)$.

Algorithm 14 $\mathcal{A}_{\text{samp}}$: Bootstrapping for Subsampling-Stable f

---

Require: dataset: x, function $f : \mathcal{X}^* \to \mathbb{R}$, privacy parameters $\epsilon, \delta > 0$.

1: $q \leftarrow \frac{\epsilon}{64 \ln(1/\delta)}$, $m \leftarrow \frac{\log(n/\delta)}{q^2}$.

2: Subsample m data sets $\hat{x}_1, ..., \hat{x}_m$ from x, where $\hat{x}_i$ includes each position of x independently with probability q.

3: **if** some element of x appears in more than $2mq$ sets $\hat{x}_i$ **then**

4:     Halt and output $\perp$.

5: **else**

6:     $z \leftarrow \{f(\hat{x}_1), \cdots, f(\hat{x}_m)\}$.

7:     For each $r \in \mathbb{R}$, let $count(r) = \#\{i : f(\hat{x}_i) = r\}$.

8:     Let $count_{(i)}$ denote the the ith largest count, $i = 1, 2$.

9:     $d \leftarrow (count_{(1)} - count_{(2)})/(4mq) - 1$

10:     **Comment** Now run $\mathcal{A}_{\text{dist}}(g, z)$ using d to estimate distance to instability:

11:     $\hat{d} \leftarrow d + \text{Lap}(\frac{1}{\epsilon})$.

12:     **if** $\hat{d} > \ln(1/\delta)/\varepsilon$ **then**

13:         Output $g(z) = mode(z)$.

14:     **else**

15:         Output $\perp$.

16:     **end if**

17: **end if**

Theorem 7.3.

1. Algorithm $\mathcal{A}_{\text{samp}}$ is (ε, δ)-differentially private.

2. If f is q-subsampling stable on input x where $q = \frac{\epsilon}{64 \ln(1/\delta)}$, then algorithm $\mathcal{A}_{\text{samp}}(x)$ outputs $f(x)$ with probability at least $1 - 3\delta$.

3. If f can be computed in time $T(n)$ on inputs of length n, then $\mathcal{A}_{\text{samp}}$ runs in expected time $O(\frac{\log n}{q^2})(T(qn) + n)$.

Note that the utility statement here is an input-by-input guarantee; f need not be q-subsampling stable on all inputs. Importantly, there is no dependence on the size of the range $\mathcal{R}$. In the context of model selection, this means that one can efficiently satisfy differential privacy with a modest blowup in sample complexity (about $\log(1/\delta)/\varepsilon$) whenever there is a particular model that gets selected with reasonable probability.

The proof of privacy comes from the insensitivity of the computation of d, the privacy of the Propose-Test-Release technique, and the privacy of Subsample and Aggregate, modified slightly to allow for the fact that this algorithm performs sampling with replacement and thus the aggregator has higher sensitivity, since any individual might affect up to $2mq$ blocks. The main observation for analyzing the utility of this approach is that the stability of the *mode* is a function of the difference between the frequency of the mode and that of the next most popular element. The next lemma says that if f is subsampling stable on x, then x is far from unstable with respect to the mode $g(z) = g(f(\hat{x}_1), \ldots, f(\hat{x}_m))$ (but not necessarily with respect to f), and moreover one can estimate the distance to instability of x *efficiently* and *privately*.

Lemma 7.4. Fix $q \in (0,1)$. Given $f : \mathcal{X}^* \rightarrow \mathcal{R}$, let $\hat{f} : \mathcal{X}^* \rightarrow \mathcal{R}$ be the function $\hat{f} = \mathrm{mode}(f(\hat{x}_1), \ldots, f(\hat{x}_m))$ where each $\hat{x}_i$ includes each element of x independently with probability q and $m = \ln(n/\delta)/q^2$. Let $d(z) = (\mathrm{count}_{(1)} - \mathrm{count}_{(2)})/(4mq) - 1$; that is, given a "database" z of values, $d(z) + 1$ is a scaled difference between the number of occurrences of the two most popular values. Fix a data set x. Let E be the event that no position of x is included in more than $2mq$ of the subsets $\hat{x}_i$. Then, when $q \le \varepsilon/64\ln(1/\delta)$ we have:

1. E occurs with probability at least $1 - \delta$.

2. Conditioned on E, d lower bounds the stability of $\hat{f}$ on x, and d has global sensitivity 1.

3. If f is q-subsampling stable on x, then with probability at least $1 - \delta$ over the choice of subsamples, we have $\hat{f}(x) = f(x)$, and, conditioned on this event, the final test will be passed with

probability at least $1 - \delta$, where the probability is over the draw from $\mathrm{Lap}(1/\varepsilon)$.

The events in Parts 2 and 3 occur simultaenously with probability at least $1 - 2\delta$.

Proof. Part 1 follows from the Chernoff bound. To prove Part 2, notice that, conditioned on the event E, adding or removing one entry in the original data set changes any of the counts $count_{(r)}$ by at most $2mq$. Therefore, $count_{(1)} - count_{(2)}$ changes by at most $4mq$. This in turn means that $d(f(\hat{x}_1), \ldots, f(\hat{x}_m))$ changes by at most one for any x and hence has global sensitivity of one. This also implies that d lower bounds the stability of $\hat{f}$ on x.

We now turn to part 3. We want to argue two facts:

1. If f is q-subsampling stable on x, then there is likely to be a large gap between the counts of the two most popular bins. Specifically, we want to show that with high probability $count_{(1)} - count_{(2)} \geq m/4$. Note that if the most popular bin has count at least $5m/8$ then the second most popular bin can have count at most $3m/8$, with a difference of $m/4$. By definition of subsampling stability the most popular bin has an expected count of at least $3m/4$ and hence, by the Chernoff bound, taking $\alpha = 1/8$, has probability at most $e^{-2m\alpha^2} = e^{-m/32}$ of having a count less than $5m/8$. (All the probabilities are over the subsampling.)

2. When the gap between the counts of the two most popular bins is large, then the algorithm is unlikely to fail; that is, the test is likely to succeed. The worry is that the draw from $\mathrm{Lap}(\frac{1}{\varepsilon})$ will be negative and have large absolute value, so that $\hat{d}$ falls below the threshold $(\ln(1/\delta)/\varepsilon)$ even when d is large. To ensure this happens with probability at most δ it suffices that $d > 2\ln(1/\delta)/\varepsilon$.

   By definition, $d = (count_{(1)} - count_{(2)})/(4mq) - 1$, and, assuming we are in the high probability case just described, this implies

$$d \geq \frac{m/4}{4mq} - 1 = \frac{1}{16q} - 1$$

so it is enough to have

$$\frac{1}{16q} > 2\ln(1/\delta)/\varepsilon.$$

Taking $q \leq \varepsilon/64\ln(1/\delta)$ suffices.

Finally, note that with these values of q and m we have $e^{-m/32} < \delta$. ☐

Example 7.3. [The Raw Data Problem] Suppose we have an analyst whom we can trust to follow instructions and only publish information obtained according to these instructions. Better yet, suppose we have b such analysts, and we can trust them not to communicate among themselves. The analysts do not need to be identical, but they do need to be considering a common set of *options*. For example, these options might be different statistics in a fixed set S of possible statistics, and in this first step the analyst's goal is to choose, for eventual publication, the most significant statistic in S. Later, the chosen statistic will be recomputed in a differentially private fashion, and the result can be published.

As described the procedure is not private at all: the *choice* of statistic made in the first step may depend on the data of a single individual! Nonetheless, we can use the Subsample-and-Aggregate framework to carry out the first step, with the ith analyst receiving a subsample of the data points and applying to this smaller database the function f_i to obtain an option. The options are then aggregated as in algorithm $\mathcal{A}_{\text{samp}}$; if there is a clear winner this is overwhelmingly likely to be the selected statistic. This was *chosen* in a differentially private manner, and in the second step it will be *computed* with differential privacy.

Bibliographic Notes

Subsample and Aggregate was invented by Nissim, Raskhodnikova, and Smith [68], who were the first to define and exploit low local sensitivity. Propose-Test-Release is due to Dwork and Lei [22], as is the algorithm for releasing the interquartile range. The discussion of stability and privacy, and Algorithm $\mathcal{A}_{samp}$ which blends these two techniques, is due to Smith and Thakurta [80]. This paper demonstrates the power of

$\mathcal{A}_{samp}$ by analyzing the subsampling stability conditions of the famous LASSO algorithm and showing that differential privacy can be obtained "for free," via (a generalization of $\mathcal{A}_{samp}$), precisely under the (fixed data as well as distributional) conditions for which LASSO is known to have good explanatory power.

8

Lower Bounds and Separation Results

In this section, we investigate various lower bounds and tradeoffs:

1. How *inaccurate* must responses be in order not to completely destroy any reasonable notion of privacy?

2. How does the answer to the previous question depend on the number of queries?

3. Can we separate $(\varepsilon, 0)$-differential privacy from (ε, δ)-differential privacy in terms of the accuracy each permits?

4. Is there an intrinsic difference between what can be achieved for linear queries and for arbitrary low-sensitivity queries while maintaining $(\varepsilon, 0)$-differential privacy?

A different flavor of separation result distinguishes the computational complexity of generating a *data structure* handling all the queries in a given class from that of generating a *synthetic database* that achieves the same goal. We postpone a discussion of this result to Section 9.

8.1   Reconstruction attacks

We argued in Section 1 that any non-trivial mechanism must be randomized. It follows that, at least for some database, query, and choice of random bits, the response produced by the mechanism is not perfectly accurate. The question of how *inaccurate* answers must be in order to protect privacy makes sense in all computational models: interactive, non-interactive, and the models discussed in Section 12.

For the lower bounds on distortion, we assume for simplicity that the database consists of a single — but very sensitive — bit per person, so we can think of the database as an n-bit Boolean vector $d = (d_1, \ldots, d_n)$. This is an abstraction of a setting in which the database rows are quite complex, for example, they may be medical records, but the attacker is interested in one specific field, such as the presence or absence of the sickle cell trait. The abstracted attack consists of issuing a string of queries, each described by a subset S of the database rows. The query is asking how many 1's are in the selected rows. Representing the query as the n-bit characteristic vector $\mathbf{S}$ of the set S, with 1s in all the positions corresponding to rows in S and 0s everywhere else, the true answer to the query is the inner product $A(S) = \sum_{i=1}^{n} d_i \mathbf{S}_i$.

Fix an arbitrary privacy mechanism. We will let $r(S)$ denote the response to the query S. This may be obtained explicitly, say, if the mechanism is interactive and the query S is issued, or if the mechanism is given all the queries in advance and produces a list of answers, or implicitly, which occurs if the mechanism produces a synopsis from which the analysts extracts $r(S)$. Note that $r(S)$ may depend on random choices made by the mechanism and the history of queries. Let $E(S, r(S))$ denote the *error*, also called *noise* or *distortion*, of the response $r(S)$, so $E(S, r(S)) = |A(S) - r(S)|$.

The question we want to ask is, "How much noise is needed in order to preserve privacy?" Differential privacy is a specific privacy guarantee, but one might also consider weaker notions, so rather than guaranteeing privacy the modest goal in the lower bound arguments will simply be to prevent privacy catastrophes.

Definition 8.1. A mechanism is *blatantly non-private* if an adversary can construct a candidate database c that agrees with the real database d in all but $o(n)$ entries, i.e., $\|c - d\|_0 \in o(n)$.

In other words, a mechanism is blatantly non-private if it permits a reconstruction attack that allows the adversary to correctly guess the secret bit of all but $o(n)$ members of the database. (There is no requirement that the adversary know on which answers it is correct.)

Theorem 8.1. Let $\mathcal{M}$ be a mechanism with distortion of magnitude bounded by E. Then there exists an adversary that can reconstruct the database to within $4E$ positions.

An easy consequence of the theorem is that a privacy mechanism adding noise with magnitude always bounded by, say, $n/401$, permits an adversary to correctly reconstruct 99% of the entries.

Proof. Let d be the true database. The adversary attacks in two phases:

1. **Estimate the number of 1s in all possible sets:** Query $\mathcal{M}$ on all subsets $S \subseteq [n]$.

2. **Rule out "distant" databases:** For every candidate database $c \in \{0,1\}^n$, if $\exists S \subseteq [n]$ such that $|\sum_{i \in S} c_i - \mathcal{M}(S)| > E$, then rule out c. If c is not ruled out, then output c and halt.

Since $\mathcal{M}(S)$ never errs by more than E, the real database will not be ruled out, so this simple (but inefficient!) algorithm will output *some* candidate database c. We will argue that the number of positions in which c and d differ is at most $4 \cdot E$.

Let I_0 be the indices in which $d_i = 0$, that is, $I_0 = \{i \mid d_i = 0\}$. Similarly, define $I_1 = \{i \mid d_i = 1\}$. Since c was not ruled out, $|\mathcal{M}(I_0) - \sum_{i \in I_0} c_i| \leq E$. However, by assumption $|\mathcal{M}(I_0) - \sum_{i \in I_0} d_i| \leq E$. It follows from the triangle inequality that c and d differ in at most $2E$ positions in I_0; the same argument shows that they differ in at most $2E$ positions in I_1. Thus, c and d agree on all but at most $4E$ positions. $\square$

What if we consider more realistic bounds on the number of queries? We think of $\sqrt{n}$ as an interesting threshold on noise, for the following reason: if the database contains n people drawn uniformly at random from a population of size $N \gg n$, and the fraction of the population satisfying a given condition is p, then we expect the number of rows in the database satisfying the property to be roughly $np \pm \Theta(\sqrt{n})$, by the properties of the binomial distribution. That is, the sampling error is on the order of $\sqrt{n}$. We would like that the noise introduced for privacy is smaller than the sampling error, ideally $o(\sqrt{n})$. The next result investigates the feasibility of such small error when the number of queries is linear in n. The result is negative.

Ignoring computational complexity, to see why there might exist a query-efficient attack we modify the problem slightly, looking at databases $d \in \{-1,1\}^n$ and query vectors $v \in \{-1,1\}^n$. The true answer is again defined to be $d \cdot v$, and the response is a noisy version of the true answer. Now, consider a candidate database c that is far from d, say, $\|c-d\|_0 \in \Omega(n)$. For a random $v \in_R \{-1,1\}^n$, with constant probability we have $(c - d) \cdot v \in \Omega(\sqrt{n})$. To see this, fix $x \in \{-1,1\}^n$ and choose $v \in_R \{-1,1\}^n$. Then $x \cdot v$ is a sum of independent random variables $x_i v_i \in_R \{-1,1\}$, which has expectation 0 and variance n, and is distributed according to a scaled and shifted binomial distribuiton. For the same reason, if c and d differ in at least αn rows, and v is chosen at random, then $(c - d) \cdot v$ is binomially distributed with mean 0 and variance at least αn. Thus, we expect $c \cdot v$ and $d \cdot v$ to differ by at least $\alpha \sqrt{n}$ with constant probability, by the properties of the binomial distribution. Note that we are using the *anti*-concentration property of the distribution, rather than the usual appeal to concentration.

This opens an attack for ruling out c when the noise is constrained to be $o(\sqrt{n})$: compute the difference between $c \cdot v$ and the noisy response $r(v)$. If the magnitude of this difference exceeds $\sqrt{n}$ — which will occur with constant probability over the choice of v — then rule out c. The next theorem formalizes this argument and further shows that the attack is resilient even to a large fraction of completely arbitrary responses: Using a linear number of ± 1 questions, an attacker can reconstruct almost the whole database if the curator is constrained to answer at least $\frac{1}{2}+\eta$ of the questions within an absolute error of $o(\sqrt{n})$.

Theorem 8.2. For any $\eta > 0$ and any function $\alpha = \alpha(n)$, there is constant b and an attack using bn ± 1 questions that reconstructs a database that agrees with the real database in all but at most $(\frac{2\alpha}{\eta})^2$ entries, if the curator answers at least $\frac{1}{2} + \eta$ of the questions within an absolute error of α.

Proof. We begin with a simple lemma.

Lemma 8.3. Let $Y = \sum_{i=1}^{k} X_i$ where each X_i is a ± 2 independent Bernoulli random variable with mean zero. Then for any y and any $\ell \in \mathbb{N}$, $Pr[Y \in [2y, 2(y + \ell)]] \leq \frac{\ell+1}{\sqrt{k}}$.

Proof. Note that Y is always even and that $Pr[Y = 2y] = \binom{k}{(k+y)/2}(\frac{1}{2})^k$. This expression is at most $\binom{k}{\lceil k/2 \rceil}(\frac{1}{2})^k$. Using Stirling's approximation, which says that $n!$ can be approximated by $\sqrt{2n\pi}(n/e)^n$, this is bounded by $\sqrt{\frac{2}{\pi k}}$. The claim follows by a union bound over the $\ell + 1$ possible values for Y in $[2y, 2(y + \ell)]$. $\qquad\square$

The adversary's attack is to choose bn random vectors $v \in \{-1, 1\}^n$, obtain responses $(y_1, \ldots, y_{bn})$, and then output any database c such that $|y_i - (Ac)_i| \leq \alpha$ for at least $\frac{1}{2} + \eta$ of the indices i, where A is the $bn \times n$ matrix whose rows are the random query vectors v.

Let the true database be d and let c be the reconstructed database. By assumption on the behavior of the mechanism, $|(Ad)_i - y_i| \leq \alpha$ for a $1/2 + \eta$ fraction of $i \in [bn]$. Since c was not ruled out, we also have that $|(Ac)_i - y_i| \leq \alpha$ for a $1/2 + \eta$ fraction of $i \in [bn]$. Since any two such sets of indices agree on at least a 2η fraction of $i \in [bn]$, we have from the triangle inequality that for at least $2\eta bn$ values of i, $|[(c - d)A]_i| \leq 2\alpha$.

We wish to argue that c agrees with d in all but $(\frac{2\alpha}{\eta})^2$ entries. We will show that if the reconstructed c is far from d, disagreeing on at least $(2\alpha/\eta)^2$ entries, the probability that a randomly chosen A will satisfy $|[A(c-d)]_i| \leq 2\alpha$ for at least $2\eta bn$ values of i will be extremely small — so small that, for a random A, it is extremely unlikely that there even exists a c far from d that is not eliminated by the queries in A.

Assume the vector $z = (c - d) \in \{-2, 0, 2\}^n$ has Hamming weight at least $(\frac{2\alpha}{\eta})^2$, so c is far from d. We have argued that, since c is produced by the attacker, $|(Az)_i| \leq 2\alpha$ for at least $2\eta bn$ values of i. We shall call such a z *bad with respect to* A. We will show that, with high probability over the choice of A, no z is bad with respect to A.

For any i, $v_i z$ is the sum of at least $(\frac{2\alpha}{\eta})^2 \pm 2$ random values. Letting $k = (2\alpha/\eta)^2$ and $\ell = 2\alpha$, we have by Lemma 8.3 that the probability that $v_i z$ lies in an interval of size 4α is at most η, so the expected number of queries for which $|v_i z| \leq 2\alpha$ is at most ηbn. Chernoff bounds now imply that the probability that this number exceeds $2\eta bn$ is at most $\exp(-\frac{\eta bn}{4})$. Thus the probability of a particular $z = c - d$ being bad with respect to A is at most $\exp(-\frac{\eta bn}{4})$.

Taking a union bound over the atmost 3^n possible zs, we get that with probability at least $1 - \exp(-n(\frac{\eta b}{4} - \ln 3))$, no bad z exists. Taking $b > 4\ln 3/\eta$, the probability that such a bad z exists is exponentially small in n.   □

Preventing blatant non-privacy is a very low bar for a privacy mechanism, so if differential privacy is meaningful then lower bounds for preventing blatant non-privacy will also apply to any mechanism ensuring differential privacy. Although for the most part we ignore computational issues in this monograph, there is also the question of the efficiency of the attack. Suppose we were able to prove that (perhaps under some computational assumption) there exist low-distortion mechanisms that are "hard" to break; for example, mechanisms for which producing a candidate database c close to the original database is hard? Then, although a low-distortion mechanism might fail to be differentially private in theory, it could conceivably provide privacy against bounded adversaries. Unfortunately, this is not the case. In particular, when the noise is always in $o(\sqrt{n})$, there is an efficient attack using exactly n fixed queries; moreover, there is even a computationally efficient attack requiring a linear number of queries in which a 0.239 fraction may be answered with wild noise.

In the case of "internet scale" data sets, obtaining responses to n queries is infeasible, as n is extremely large, say, $n \geq 10^8$. What happens if the curator permits only a sublinear number of questions? This inquiry led to the first algorithmic results in (what has evolved to be) (ε, δ)-differential privacy, in which it was shown how to maintain privacy against a sublinear number of counting queries by adding binomial noise of order $o(\sqrt{n})$ — less than the sampling error! — to each true answer. Using the tools of differential privacy we can do this either using either (1) the Gaussian mechanism or (2) the Laplace mechanism and advanced composition.

8.2 Lower bounds for differential privacy

The results of the previous section yielded lower bounds on distortion needed to ensure any reasonable notion of privacy. In contrast, the result in this section is specific to differential privacy. Although some of the details in the proof are quite technical, the main idea is elegant: suppose (somehow) the adversary has narrowed down the set of possible databases to a relatively small set S of 2^s vectors, where the L_1 distance between each pair of vectors is some large number Δ. Suppose further that we can find a k-dimensional query F, 1-Lipschitz in each of its output coordinates, with the property that the true answers to the query look very different (in L_∞ norm) on the different vectors in our set; for example, the distance on any two elements in the set may be $\Omega(k)$. It is helpful to think geometrically about the "answer space" $\mathbb{R}^k$. Each element x in the set S gives rise to a vector $F(x)$ in answer space. The actual response will be a perturbation of this point in answer space. Then a volume-based pigeon hole argument (in answer space) shows that, if with even moderate probability the (noisy) responses are "reasonably" close to the true answers, then ϵ cannot be very small.

This stems from the fact that for $(\varepsilon, 0)$-differentially private mechanisms $\mathcal{M}$, for *arbitrarily different* databases x, y, any response in the support of $\mathcal{M}(x)$ is also in the support of $\mathcal{M}(y)$. Taken together with the construction of an appropriate collection of vectors and a (contrived, non-counting) query, the result yields a lower bound on distortion that is linear k/ε. The argument appeals to Theorem 2.2, which discusses group privacy. In our case the group in question corresponds to the indices contributing to the (L_1) distance between a pair of vectors in S.

8.2.1 Lower bound by packing arguments

We begin with an observation which says, intuitively, that if the "likely" response regions, when the query is F, are disjoint, then we can bound

ϵ from below, showing that privacy can't be too good. When $\|F(x_i) - F(x_j)\|_\infty$ is large, this says that to get very good privacy, even when restricted to databases that differ in many places, we must get very erroneous responses on some coordinate of F.

The argument uses the histogram representation of databases. In the sequel, $d = |\mathcal{X}|$ denotes the size of the universe from which database elements are drawn.

Lemma 8.4. Assume the existence of a set $S = \{x_1, \ldots, x_{2^s}\}$, where each $x_i \in \mathbb{N}^d$, such that for $i \neq j$, $\|x_i - x_j\|_1 \leq \Delta$. Further, let $F : \mathbb{N}^d \to \mathbb{R}^k$ be a k-dimensional query. For $1 \leq i \leq 2^s$, let B_i denote a region in $\mathbb{R}^k$, the answer space, and assume that the B_i are mutually disjoint. If $\mathcal{M}$ is an $(\varepsilon, 0)$-differentially private mechanism for F such that, $\forall 1 \leq i \leq 2^s$, $\Pr[\mathcal{M}(x_i) \in B_i] \geq 1/2$, then $\varepsilon \geq \frac{\ln(2)(s-1)}{\Delta}$.

Proof. By assumption $\Pr[\mathcal{M}(x_j) \in B_j] \geq 2^{-1}$. Since the regions $B_1, \ldots, B_{2^s}$ are disjoint, $\exists j \neq i \in [2^s]$ such that $\Pr[\mathcal{M}(x_i) \in B_j] \leq 2^{-s}$. That is, for at least one of the $2^s - 1$ regions B_j, the probability that $\mathcal{M}(x_i)$ is mapped to this B_j is at most 2^{-s}. Combining this with differential privacy, we have

$$\frac{2^{-1}}{2^{-s}} \leq \frac{\Pr_\mathcal{M}[B_j | x_j]}{\Pr_\mathcal{M}[B_j | x_i]} \leq \exp(\varepsilon\Delta). \qquad \square$$

Corollary 8.5. Let $S = \{x_1, \ldots, x_{2^s}\}$ be as in Lemma 8.4, and assume that for any $i \neq j$, $\|F(x_i) - F(x_j)\|_\infty \geq \eta$. Let B_i denote the L_∞ ball in $\mathbb{R}^k$ of radius $\eta/2$ centered at x_i. Let $\mathcal{M}$ be any ε-differentially private mechansim for F satisfying

$$\forall 1 \leq i \leq 2^s : \Pr[\mathcal{M}(x_i) \in B_i] \geq 1/2.$$

Then $\varepsilon \geq \frac{(\ln 2)(s-1)}{\Delta}$.

Proof. The regions $B_1, \ldots, B_{2^s}$ are disjoint, so the conditions of Lemma 8.4 are satisfied. The corollary follows by applying the lemma and taking logarithms. $\qquad \square$

In Theorem 8.8 below we will look at queries F that are simply k independently and randomly generated (nonlinear!) queries. For suitable S and F (we will work to find these) the corollary says that if with probability at least $1/2$ *all* responses simultaneously have small error, then privacy can't be too good. In other words,

Claim 8.6 (Informal Restatement of Corollary 8.5). To obtain $(\varepsilon, 0)$-differential privacy for $\varepsilon \leq \frac{\ln(2)(s-1)}{\Delta}$, the mechanism must add noise with L_∞ norm greater than $\eta/2$ with probability exceeding $1/2$.

As a warm-up exercise, we prove an easier theorem that requires a large data universe.

Theorem 8.7. Let $\mathcal{X} = \{0, 1\}^k$. Let $\mathcal{M} : \mathcal{X}^n \to \mathbb{R}^k$ be an $(\varepsilon, 0)$-differentially private mechanism such that for every database $x \in \mathcal{X}^n$ with probability at least $1/2$ $\mathcal{M}(x)$ outputs all of the 1-way marginals of x with error smaller than $n/2$. That is, for each $j \in [k]$, the jth component of $\mathcal{M}(x)$ should approximately equal the number of rows of x whose jth bit is 1, up to an error smaller than $n/2$. Then $n \in \Omega(k/\varepsilon)$.

Note that this bound is tight to within a constant factor, by the simple composition theorem, and that it separates $(\varepsilon, 0)$-differential privacy from (ε, δ)-differential privacy, for $\delta \in 2^{-o(n)}$, since, by the advanced composition theorem (Theorem 3.20), Laplace noise with parameter $b = \sqrt{k \ln(1/\delta)}/\varepsilon$ suffices for the former, in contrast to $\Omega(k/\varepsilon)$ needed for the latter. Taking $k \in \Theta(n)$ and, say, $\delta = 2^{-\log^2 n}$, yields the separation.

Proof. For every string $w \in \{0, 1\}^k$, consider the database x_w consisting of n identical rows, all of which equal w. Let $B_w \in \mathbb{R}^k$ consist of all tuples of numbers that provide answers to the 1-way marginals on x with error less than $n/2$. That is,

$$B_w = \{(a_1, \dots, a_k)\} \in \mathbb{R}^k : \forall i \in [k] \, |a_i - nw_i| < n/2\}.$$

Put differently, B_w is the open ℓ_∞ of radius $n/2$ around $nw \in \{0, n\}^k$. Notice that the sets B_w are mutually disjoint.

If M is an accurate mechanism for answering 1-way marginals, then for every w the probability of landing in B_w when the database is x_w should be at least $1/2$: $\Pr[\mathcal{M}(x_w) \in B_w] \geq 1/2$. Thus, setting $\Delta = n$ and $s = k$ in Corollary 8.5 we have $\varepsilon \geq \frac{(\ln 2)(s-1)}{\Delta}$. $\square$

Theorem 8.8. For any $k, d, n \in \mathbb{N}$ and $\varepsilon \in (0, 1/40]$, where $n \geq \min\{k/\varepsilon, d/\varepsilon\}$, there is a query $F : \mathbb{N}^d \to \mathbb{R}^k$ with per-coordinate sensitivity at most 1 such that any $(\varepsilon, 0)$-differentially private mechanism adds noise of L_∞ norm $\Omega(\min\{k/\varepsilon, d/\varepsilon\})$ with probability at least $1/2$ on some databases of weight at most n.

Note that $d = |\mathcal{X}|$ need not be large here, in contrast to the requirement in Theorem 8.7.

Proof. Let $\ell = \min\{k, d\}$. Using error-correcting codes we can construct a set $S = \{x_1, \ldots, x_{2^s}\}$, where $s = \ell/400$, such that each $x_i \in \mathbb{N}^d$ and in addition

1. $\forall i : \|x_i\|_1 \leq w = \ell/(1280\varepsilon)$
2. $\forall i \neq j, \|x_i - x_j\|_1 \geq w/10$

We do not give details here, but we note that the databases in S are of size at most $w < n$, and so $\|x_i - x_j\|_1 \leq 2w$. Taking $\Delta = 2w$ the set S satisfies the conditions of Corollary 8.5. The remainder of our effort is to obtain the queries F to which we will apply Corollary 8.5. Given $S = \{x_1, \ldots, x_{2^s}\}$, where each $x_i \in \mathbb{N}^d$, the first step is to define a mapping from the space of histograms to vectors in $\mathbb{R}^{2^s}$, $\mathcal{L}_S : \mathbb{N}^d \to \mathbb{R}^{2^s}$. Intuitively (and imprecisely!), given a histogram x, the mapping lists, for each $x_i \in S$, the L_1 distance from x to x_i. More precisely, letting w be an upper bound on the weight of any x_i in our collection we define the mapping as follows.

- For every $x_i \in S$, there is a coordinate i in the mapping.
- The ith coordinate of $\mathcal{L}_S(x)$ is $\max\{w/30 - \|x_i - z\|_1, 0\}$.

Claim 8.9. If $x_1, \ldots, x_{2^s}$ satisfy the conditions

1. $\forall i \|x_i\|_1 \leq w$; and
2. $\forall i \neq j \|x_i - x_j\|_1 \geq w/10$

then the map $\mathcal{L}_S$ is 1-Lipschitz; in particular, if $\|z_1 - z_2\|_1 = 1$, then $\|\mathcal{L}_S(z_1) - \mathcal{L}_S(z_2)\|_1 \leq 1$, assuming $w \geq 31$.

Proof. Since we assume $w \geq 31$ we have that if $z \in \mathbb{N}^d$ is close to some $x_i \in S$, meaning $w/30 > \|x_i - z\|_1$, then z cannot be close to any other $x_j \in S$, and the same is true for all $\|z' - z\|_1 \leq 1$. Thus, for any z_1, z_2 such that $\|z_1 - z_2\| \leq 1$, if A denotes the set of coordinates where at least one of $\mathcal{L}_S(z_1)$ or $\mathcal{L}_S(z_2)$ is non-zero, then A is either empty or is a singleton set. Given this, the statement in the claim is immediate from the fact that the mapping corresponding to any particular coordinate is clearly 1-Lipschitz. □

We can finally describe the queries F. Corresponding to any $r \in \{-1,1\}^{2^s}$, we define $f_r : \mathbb{N}^d \to \mathbb{R}$, as

$$f_r(x) = \sum_{i=1}^{d} \mathcal{L}_S(x)_i \cdot r_i \, ,$$

which is simply the inner product $\mathcal{L}_S \cdot r$. F will be a random map $F : \mathbb{N}^d \to \mathbb{R}^k$: Pick $r_1, \ldots, r_k \in \{-1,1\}^{2^s}$ independently and uniformly at random and define

$$F(x) = (f_{r_1}(x), \ldots, f_{r_k}(x)) \, .$$

That is, $F(x)$ is simply the result of the inner product of $\mathcal{L}_S(x)$ with k randomly chosen ± 1 vectors.

Note that for any $x \in S$ $\mathcal{L}_S(x)$ has one coordinate with value $w/30$ (and the others are all zero), so $\forall r_i \in \{-1,1\}^{2^s}$ and $x \in S$ we have $|f_{r_i}(x)| = w/30$. Now consider any $x_h, x_j \in S$, where $h \neq j$. It follows that for any $r_i \in \{-1,1\}^{2^s}$,

$$\Pr_{r_i}[|f_{r_i}(x_h) - f_{r_i}(x_j)| \geq w/15] \geq 1/2$$

(this event occurs when $(r_i)_h = -(r_i)_j$). A basic application of the Chernoff bound implies that

$$\Pr_{r_1,\ldots,r_k}[\text{For at least } 1/10 \text{ of the } r_i\text{s,}$$
$$|f_{r_i}(x_h) - f_{r_i}(x_j)| \geq w/15] \geq 1 - 2^{-k/30} \, .$$

Now, the total number of pairs (x_i, x_j) of databases such that $x_i, x_j \in S$ is at most $2^{2s} \leq 2^{k/200}$. Taking a union bound this implies

$$\Pr_{r_1,\ldots,r_k}[\forall h \neq j, \quad \text{For at least } 1/10 \text{ of the } r_i\text{s,}$$
$$|f_{r_i}(x_h) - f_{r_i}(x_j)| \geq w/15] \geq 1 - 2^{-k/40}$$

This implies that we can fix $r_1, \ldots, r_k$ such that the following is true.

$\forall h \neq j$,   For at least $1/10$ of the r_is, $|f_{r_i}(x_h) - f_{r_i}(x_j)| \geq w/15$

Thus, for any $x_h \neq x_j \in S$, $\|F(x_h) - F(x_j)\|_\infty \geq w/15$.

Setting $\Delta = 2w$ and $s = \ell/400 > 3\varepsilon w$ (as we did above), and $\eta = w/15$, we satisfy the conditions of Corollary 8.5 and conclude $\Delta \leq (s-1)/\varepsilon$, proving the theorem (via Claim 8.6). $\square$

The theorem is almost tight: if $k \leq d$ then we can apply the Laplace mechanism to each of the k sensitivity 1 component queries in F with parameter k/ε, and we expect the maximum distortion to be $\Theta(k \ln k/\varepsilon)$. On the other hand, if $d \leq k$ then we can apply the Laplace mechanism to the d-dimensional histogram representing the database, and we expect the maximum distortion to be $\Theta(d \ln d/\varepsilon)$.

The theorem actually shows that, given knowledge of the set S and knowledge that the actual database is an element $x \in S$, the adversary can completely determine x if the L_∞ norm of the distortion is too small. How in real life might the adversary obtain a set S of the type used in the attack? This can occur when a *non-private* database system has been running on a dataset, say, x. For example, x could be a vector in $\{0,1\}^n$ and the adversary may have learned, through a sequence of linear queries, that $x \in C$, a linear code of distance, say $n^{2/3}$. Of course, if the database system is not promising privacy there is no problem. The problem arises if the administrator decides to replace the existing system with a differentially private mechanism — after several queries have received noise-free responses. In particular, if the administrator chooses to use (ε, δ)-differential privacy for subsequent k queries then the distortion might fall below the $\Omega(k/\varepsilon)$ lower bound, permitting the attack described in the proof of Theorem 8.8.

The theorem also emphasizes that there is a fundamental difference between auxiliary information about (sets of) members of the database and information about the database *as a whole*. Of course, we already knew this: being told that the number of secret bits sums to exactly $5,000$ completely destroys differential privacy, and an adversary that already knew the secret bit of every member of the database except one individual could then conclude the secret bit of the remaining individual.

Additional Consequences. Suppose $k \leq d$, so $\ell = k$ in Theorem 8.8. The linear in k/ε lower bound on noise for k queries sketched in the previous section immediately yields a separation between counting queries and arbitrary 1-sensitivity queries, as the SmallDB construction answers (more than) n queries with noise roughly $n^{2/3}$ while maintaining differential privacy. Indeed, this result also permits us to conclude that there is no small α-net for large sets of arbitrary low sensitivity queries, for $\alpha \in o(n)$ (as otherwise the net mechanism would yield an $(\varepsilon, 0)$ algorithm of desired accuracy).

8.3 Bibliographic notes

The first reconstruction attacks, including Theorem 8.1, are due to Dinur and Nissim [18], who also gave an attack requiring only polynomial time computation and $O(n \log^2 n)$ queries, provided the noise is always $o(\sqrt{n})$. Realizing that attacks requiring n random linear queries, when n is "internet scale," are infeasible, Dinur, Dwork, and Nissim gave the first positive results, showing that for a sublinear number of subset sum queries, a form of privacy (now known to imply (ε, δ)-differential privacy) can be achieved by adding noise scaled to $o(\sqrt{n})$ [18]. This was exciting because it suggested that, if we think of the database as drawn from an underlying population, then, even for a relatively large number of counting queries, privacy could be achieved with distortion smaller than the sampling error. This eventulaly lead, via more general queries [31, 6], to differential privacy. The view of these queries as a privacy-preserving programming primitive [6] inspired McSherry's Privacy Integrated Queries programming platform [59].

The reconstruction attack of Theorem 8.2 appears in [24], where Dwork, McSherry, and Talwar showed that polynomial time reconstruction is possible even if a 0.239 fraction of the responses have wild, arbitrary, noise, provided the others have noise $o(\sqrt{n})$.

The geometric approach, and in particular Lemma 8.4, is due to Hardt and Talwar [45], who also gave a geometry-based algorithm proving these bounds tight for small numbers $k \leq n$ of queries, under a commonly believed conjecture. Dependence on the conjecture was later removed by Bhaskara et al. [5]. The geometric approach was extended to arbitrary numbers of queries by Nikolov et al. [66], who gave an algorithm with instance-optimal mean squared error. For the few queries case this leads, via a boosting argument, to low expected worst-case error. Theorem 8.8 is due to De [17].

9

Differential Privacy
and Computational Complexity

Our discussion of differential privacy has so far ignored issues of computational complexity, permitting both the curator and the adversary to be computationally unbounded. In reality, both curator and adversary may be computationally bounded.

Confining ourselves to a computationally bounded curator restricts what the curator can do, making it harder to achieve differential privacy. And indeed, we will show an example of a class of counting queries that, under standard complexity theoretic assumptions, does not permit *efficient* generation of a synthetic database, even though inefficient algorithms, such as SmallDB and Private Multiplicative Weights, are known. Very roughly, the database rows are digital signatures, signed with keys to which the curator does not have access. The intuition will be that any row in a synthetic database must either be copied from the original — violating privacy — or must be a signature on a *new* message, i.e., a forgery — violating the unforgeability property of a digital signature scheme. Unfortuately, this state of affairs is not limited to (potentially contrived) examples based on digital signatures: it is even difficult to create a synthetic database that maintains relatively accurate two-way marginals.[1] On the positive side, given a set $\mathcal{Q}$ of queries and an n-row database with rows drawn from a universe $\mathcal{X}$, a synthetic database can be generated in time polynomial in n, $|\mathcal{X}|$, and $|\mathcal{Q}|$.

If we abandon the goal of a synthetic database and content ourselves with a data structure from which we can obtain a relatively accurate approximation to the answer to each query, the situation is much more interesting. It turns out that the problem is intimately related to the *tracing traitors* problem, in which the goal is to discourage piracy while distributing digital content to paying customers.

If the adversary is restricted to polynomial time, then it becomes easier to achieve differential privacy. In fact, the immensely powerful concept of *secure function evaluation* yields a natural way avoid the trusted curator (while giving better accuracy than randomized response), as well as a natural way to allow multiple trusted curators, who for legal reasons cannot share their data sets, to respond to queries on what is effectively a merged data set. Briefly put, secure function evaluation is a cryptographic primitive that permits a collection of n parties $p_1, p_2, \ldots, p_n$, of which fewer than some fixed fraction are faulty (the fraction varies according to the type of faults; for "honest-but-curious" faults the fraction is 1), to cooperatively compute any function $f(x_1, \ldots, x_n)$, where x_i is the input, or *value*, of party p_i, in such a way that no coalition of faulty parties can either disrupt the computation or learn more about the values of the non-faulty parties than can be deduced from the function output and the values of the members of the coalition. These two properties are traditionally called *correctness* and *privacy*. This privacy notion, let us call it *SFE privacy*, is very different from differential privacy. Let V be the set of values held by the faulty parties, and let p_i be a non-faulty party.[2] SFE privacy permits the faulty parties to learn x_i if x_i can be deduced from $V \cup \{f(x_1, \ldots, x_n)\}$; differential privacy would therefore not permit exact release of $f(x_1, \ldots, x_n)$. However, secure function evaluation

---

[1]Recall that the two-way marginals are the counts, for every pair of attribute values, of the number of rows in the database having this pair of values.

[2]In the honest but curious case we can let $V = \{x_j\}$ for any party P_j.

protocols for computing a function f can easily be modified to obtain differentially private protocols for f, simply by defining a new function, g, to be the result of adding Laplace noise $\text{Lap}(\Delta f/\varepsilon)$ to the value of f. In principle, secure function evaluation permits evaluation of g. Since g is differentially private and the SFE privacy property, applied to g, says that nothing can be learned about the inputs that is not learnable from the value of $g(x_1, \ldots, x_n)$ together with V, differential privacy is ensured, provided the faulty players are restricted to polynomial time. Thus, secure function evaluation allows a computational notion of differential privacy to be achieved, even without a trusted curator, at no loss in accuracy when compared to what can be achieved with a trusted curator. In particular, counting queries can be answered with constant expected error while ensuring computational differential privacy, with no trusted curator. We will see that, without cryptography, the error must be $\Omega(n^{1/2})$, proving that computational assumptions provably buy accuracy, in the multiparty case.

9.1 Polynomial time curators

In this section we show that, under standard cryptographic assumptions, it is computationally difficult to create a synthetic database that will yield accurate answers to an appropriately chosen class of counting queries, while ensuring even a minimal notion of privacy.

This result has several extensions; for example, to the case in which the set of queries is small (but the data universe remains large), and the case in which the data universe is small (but the set of queries is large). In addition, similar negative results have been obtained for certain natural families of queries, such as those corresponding to conjunctions.

We will use the term *syntheticize* to denote the process of generating a synthetic database in a privacy-preserving fashion[3]. Thus, the results in this section concern the computational hardness of syntheticizing. Our notion of privacy will be far weaker than differential privacy, so hardness of syntheticizing will imply hardness of generating a synthetic

---

[3]In Section 6 a syntheticizer took as input a synopsis; here we are starting with a database, which is a trivial synopsis.

database in a differentially private fashion. Specifically, we will say that syntheticizing is hard if it is hard even to avoid leaking input items in their entirety. That is, some item is always completely exposed.

Note that if, in contrast, leaking a few input items is not considered a privacy breach, then syntheticizing is easily achieved by releasing a randomly chosen subset of the input items. Utility for this "synthetic database" comes from sampling bounds: with high probability this subset will preserve utility even with respect to a large set of counting queries.

When introducing complexity assumptions, we require a *security parameter* in order to express sizes; for example, sizes of sets, lengths of messages, number of bits in a decryption key, and so on, as well as to express computational difficulty. The security parameter, denoted κ, represents "reasonable" sizes and effort. For example, it is assumed that it is feasible to exhaustively search a set whose size is (any fixed) polynomial in the security parameter.

Computational complexity is an asymptotic notion — we are concerned with how the difficulty of a task increases as the sizes of the objects (data universe, database, query family) grow. Thus, for example, we therefore need to think not just of a distribution on databases of a single size (what we have been calling n in the rest of this monograph), but of an ensemble of distributions, indexed by the security parameter. In a related vein, when we introduce complexity we tend to "soften" claims: forging a signature is not impossible — one might be lucky! Rather, we assume that no efficient algorithm succeeds with non-negligible probability, where "efficient" and "non-negligible" are defined in terms of the security parameter. We will ignore these fine points in our intuitive discussion, but will keep them in the formal theorem statements.

Speaking informally, a distribution of databases is *hard to syntheticize* (with respect to some family $\mathcal{Q}$ of queries) if for any efficient (alleged) syntheticizer, with high probability over a database drawn from the distribution, at least one of the database items can be extracted from the alleged syntheticizer's output. Of course, to avoid triviality, we will also require that when this leaked item is excluded from the input database (and, say, replaced by a random different item), the probability that it can be extracted from the output is very small. This means that any efficient (alleged) syntheticizer indeed compromises the privacy of input items in a strong sense.

Definition 9.1 below will formalize our utility requirements for a syntheticizer. There are three parameters: α describes the accuracy requirement (being within α is considered accurate); γ describes the fraction of the queries on which a successful synthesis is allowed to be inaccurate, and β will be the probability of failure.

For an algorithm A producing synthetic databases, we say that an output $A(x)$ is (α, γ)-*accurate for a query set* $\mathcal{Q}$ if $|q(A(x)) - q(x)| \leq \alpha$ for a $1 - \gamma$ fraction of the queries $q \in \mathcal{Q}$.

Definition 9.1 $((\alpha, \beta, \gamma)$-Utility$)$. Let $\mathcal{Q}$ be a set of queries and $\mathcal{X}$ a data universe. A syntheticizer A has (α, β, γ)-utility for n-item databases with respect to $\mathcal{Q}$ and $\mathcal{X}$ if for any n-item database x:

$$\Pr\left[A(x) \text{ is } (\alpha, \gamma)\text{-accurate for } \mathcal{Q}\right] \geq 1 - \beta$$

where the probability is over the coins of A.

Let $\mathcal{Q} = \{\mathcal{Q}_n\}_{n=1,2,\dots}$ be a query family ensemble, $\mathcal{X} = \{\mathcal{X}_n\}_{n=1,2,\dots}$ be a data universe ensemble. An algorithm is said to be *efficient* if its running time is $\text{poly}(n, \log(|\mathcal{Q}_n|), \log(|\mathcal{X}_n|))$.

In the next definition we describe what it means for a family of distributions to be hard to syntheticize. A little more specifically we will say what it means to be hard to generate synthetic databases that provide (α, γ)-accuracy. As usual, we have to make this an asymptotic statement.

Definition 9.2 $((\mu, \alpha, \beta, \gamma, \mathcal{Q})$-Hard-to-Syntheticize Database Distribution$)$. Let $\mathcal{Q} = \{\mathcal{Q}_n\}_{n=1,2,\dots}$ be a query family ensemble, $\mathcal{X} = \{\mathcal{X}_n\}_{n=1,2,\dots}$ be a data universe ensemble, and let $\mu, \alpha, \beta, \gamma \in [0, 1]$. Let n be a database size and $\mathcal{D}$ an ensemble of distributions, where $\mathcal{D}_n$ is over collections of $n + 1$ items from X_n.

We denote by $(x, i, x_i') \sim \mathcal{D}_n$ the experiment of choosing an n-element database, an index i chosen uniformly from $[n]$, and an additional element x_i' from $\mathcal{X}_n$. A sample from $\mathcal{D}_n$ gives us a pair of databases: x and the result of replacing the ith element of x (under a canonical ordering) with x_i'. Thus, we think of $\mathcal{D}_n$ as specifying a distribution on n-item databases (and their neighbors).

We say that $\mathcal{D}$ is $(\mu, \alpha, \beta, \gamma, \mathcal{Q})$-*hard-to Syntheticize* if there exists an efficient algorithm T such that for any alleged efficient syntheticizer A the following two conditions hold:

1. With probability $1 - \mu$ over the choice of database $x \sim \mathcal{D}$ and the coins of A and T, if $A(x)$ maintains α-utility for a $1 - \gamma$ fraction of queries, then T can recover one of the rows of x from $A(x)$:

$$\Pr_{\substack{(x,i,x_i') \sim D_n \\ \text{coin flips of } A,T}} [(A(x) \text{ maintains } (\alpha, \beta, \gamma)\text{-utility}) \text{ and } (x \cap T(A(x)) = \emptyset)] \leq \mu$$

2. For *every* efficient algorithm A, and for every $i \in [n]$, if we draw (x, i, x_i') from D, and replace x_i with x_i' to form x', T cannot extract x_i from $A(x')$ except with small probability:

$$\Pr_{\substack{(x,i,x_i') \sim D_n \\ \text{coin flips of } A, T}} [x_i \in T(A(x'))] \leq \mu.$$

Later, we will be interested in offline mechanisms that produce arbitrary synopses, not necessarily synthetic databases. In this case we will be interested in the related notion of *hard to sanitize* (rather than hard to Syntheticize), for which we simply drop the requirement that A produce a synthetic database.

9.2   Some hard-to-Syntheticize distributions

We now construct three distributions that are hard to syntheticize.

A *signature scheme* is given by a triple of (possibly randomized) algorithms (Gen, Sign, Verify):

- Gen : $1^{\mathbb{N}} \to \{(\text{SK}, \text{VK})_n\}_{n=1,2,\ldots}$ is used to generate a pair consisting of a (secret) *signing* key and a (public) *verification* key. It takes only the security parameter $\kappa \in \mathbb{N}$, written in unary, as input, and produces a pair drawn from $(\text{SK}, \text{VK})_\kappa$, the distribution on (signature,verification) key pairs indexed by κ; we let

$p_s(\kappa), p_v(\kappa), \ell s(\kappa)$ denote the lengths of the signing key, verification key, and signature, respectively.

- Sign : $SK_\kappa \times \{0,1\}^{\ell(\kappa)} \to \{0,1\}^{\ell s(\kappa)}$ takes as input a signing key from a pair drawn from $(SK, VK)_\kappa$ and a message m of length $\ell(\kappa)$, and produces a signature on m;
- Verify : $VK_\kappa \times \{0,1\}^* \times \{0,1\}^{\ell(\kappa)} \to \{0,1\}$ takes as input a verification key, a string σ, and a message m of length $\ell(\kappa)$, and checks that σ is indeed a valid signature of m under the given verification key.

Keys, message lengths, and signature lengths are all polynomial in κ.

The notion of security required is that, given any polynomial (in κ) number of valid (message, signature) pairs, it is hard to forge *any* new signature, even a new signature of a previously signed message (recall that the signing algorithm may be randomized, so there may exist multiple valid signatures of the same message under the same signing key). Such a signature scheme can be constructed from any one-way function. Speaking informally, these are functions that are easy to compute — $f(x)$ can be computed in time polynomial in the length (number of bits) of x, but hard to invert: for every probabilistic polynomial time algorithm, running in time polyomial in the security parameter κ, the probability, over a randomly chosen x in the domain of f, of finding *any* valid pre-image of $f(x)$, grows more slowly than the inverse of any polynomial in κ.

Hard to Syntheticize Distribution I: Fix an arbitrary signature scheme. The set $\mathcal{Q}_\kappa$ of counting queries contains one counting query q_{vk} for each verification key $vk \in VK_\kappa$. The data universe $\mathcal{X}_\kappa$ consists of the set of all possible (message, signature) pairs of the form for messages of length $\ell(\kappa)$ signed with keys in VK_κ.

The distribution $\mathcal{D}_\kappa$ on databases is defined by the following sampling procedure. Run the signature scheme generator $\mathrm{Gen}(1^\kappa)$ to obtain (sk, vk). Randomly choose $n = \kappa$ messages in $\{0,1\}^{\ell(\kappa)}$ and run the signing procedure for each one, obtaining a set of n (message, signature) pairs all signed with key sk. This is the database x. Note that all the messages in the database are signed with the *same* signing key.

A data universe item (m, σ) satisfies the predicate q_{vk} if and only if Verify$(vk, m, \sigma) = 1$, i.e., σ is a valid signature for m according to verification key vk.

Let $x \in_R \mathcal{D}_\kappa$ be a database, and let sk be the signing key used, with corresponding verification key vk. Assuming that the syntheticizer has produced y, it must be the case that almost all rows of y are valid signatures under vk (because the fractional count of x for the query vk is 1). By the unforgeability properties of the signature scheme, all of these must come from the input database x — the polynomial time bounded curator, running in time poly(κ), cannot generate generate a *new* valid (message, signature) pair. (Only slightly) more formally, the probability that an efficient algorithm could produce a (message, signature) pair that is verifiable with key vk, but is not in x, is negligible, so with overwhelming probability any y that is produced by an efficient syntheticizer will only contain rows of x.[4] This contradicts (any reasonable notion of) privacy.

In this construction, both $\mathcal{Q}_\kappa$ (the set of verification keys) and $\mathcal{X}_\kappa$ (the set of (message, signature) pairs) are large (superpolynomial in κ). When both sets are small, efficient differentially private generation of synthetic datasets is possible. That is, there is a differentially private syntheticizer whose running time is polynomial in $n = \kappa$, $|\mathcal{Q}_\kappa|$ and $|\mathcal{X}_\kappa|$: compute noisy counts using the Laplace mechanism to obtain a synopsis and then run the syntheticizer from Section 6. Thus, when both of these have size polynomial in κ the running time of the syntheticizer is polynomial in κ.

We now briefly discuss generalizations of the first hardness result to the cases in which one of these sets is small (but the other remains large).

Hard to Syntheticize Distribution II: In the database distribution above, we chose a single (sk, vk) key pair and generated a database of

---

[4]The quantification order is important, as otherwise the syntheticizer could have the signing key hardwired in. We first fix the syntheticizer, then run the generator and build the database. The probability is over all the randomness in the experiment: choice of key pair, construction of the database, and randomness used by the syntheticizer.

messages, all signed using sk; hardness was obtained by requiring the syntheticizer to generate a new signature under sk, in order for the syntheticized database to provide an accurate answer to the query q_{vk}. To obtain hardness for syntheticizing when the size of the set of queries is only polynomial in the security parameter, we again use digital signatures, signed with a unique key, but we cannot afford to have a query for each possible verification key vk, as these are too numerous.

To address this, we make two changes:

1. Database rows now have the form (verification key, message, signature). more precisely, the data universe consists of (key,message,signature) triples $\mathcal{X} = \{(vk, m, s) : vk \in VK_\kappa, m \in \{0, 1\}^{\ell(\kappa)}, s \in \{0, 1\}^{\ell s(\kappa)}\}$.

2. We add to the query class exactly $2p_v(\kappa)$ queries, where $p_v(\kappa)$ is the length of the verification keys produced by running the generation algorithm $\mathrm{Gen}(1^\kappa)$. The queries have the form (i, b) where $1 \le i \le p_v(\kappa)$ and $b \in \{0, 1\}$. The meaning of the query "(i, b)" is, "What fraction of the database rows are of the form (vk, m, s) where $\mathrm{Verify}(vk, m, s) = 1$ and the ith bit of vk is b?" By populating a database with messages signed according to a single key vk, we ensure that the responses to these queries should be close to one for all $1 \le i \le p(\kappa)$ when $vk_i = b$, and close to zero when $vk_i = 1 - b$.

With this in mind, the hard to syntheticize distribution on databases is constructed by the following sampling procedure: Generate a signature-verification key pair $(sk, vk) \leftarrow \mathrm{Gen}(1^\kappa)$, and choose $n = \kappa$ messages $m_1, \ldots, m_n$ uniformly from $\{0, 1\}^{\ell(\kappa)}$. The database x will have n, rows; for $j \in [n]$ the jth row is the verification key, the jth message and its valid signature, i.e., the tuple $(vk, m_j, \mathrm{Sign}(m_j, sk))$. Next, choose i uniformly from $[n]$. To generate the $(n + 1)$st item x'_i, just generate a new message-signature pair (using the same key sk).

Hard to Syntheticize Distribution III: To prove hardness for the case of a polynomial (in κ) sized message space (but superpolynomial sized query set) we use a *pseudorandom function*. Roughly speaking, these are polynomial time computable functions with small descriptions that cannot efficiently be distinguished, based only on their input-output behavior, from truly random functions (whose descriptions are long). This result only gives hardness of syntheticizing if we insist on maintaining utility for *all* queries. Indeed, if we are interested only in ensuring on-average utility, then the base generator for counting queries described in Section 6 yields an efficient algorithm for syntheticizing when the universe $\mathcal{X}$ is of polynomial size, even when $\mathcal{Q}$ is exponentially large.

Let $\{f_s\}_{s \in \{0,1\}^\kappa}$ be a family of pseudo-random functions from $[\ell]$ to $[\ell]$, where $\ell \in \text{poly}(\kappa)$. More specifically, we need that the set of all pairs of elements in $[\ell]$ is "small," but larger than κ; this way the κ-bit string describing a function in the family is shorter than the $\ell \log_2 \ell$ bits needed to describe a random function mapping $[\ell]$ to $[\ell]$. Such a family of pseudorandom functions can be constructed from any one-way function.

Our data universe will be the set of all pairs of elements in $[\ell]$: $\mathcal{X} = \{(a,b) : a, b \in [\ell]\}$. $\mathcal{Q}_\kappa$ will contain two types of queries:

1. There will be one query for each function $\{f_s\}_{s \in \{0,1\}^\kappa}$ in the family. A universe element $(a, b) \in \mathcal{X}$ satisfies the query s if and only if $f_s(a) = b$.

2. There will be a relatively small number, say κ, truly random queries. Such a query can be constructed by randomly choosing, for each $(a, b) \in \mathcal{X}$, whether or not (a, b) will satisfy the query.

The hard to syntheticize distribution is generated as follows. First, we select a random string $s \in \{0,1\}^\kappa$, specifying a function in our family. Next, we generate, for $n = \kappa$ distinct values $a_1, \ldots, a_n$ chosen at random from $[\ell]$ without replacement, the universe element $(a, f_s(a))$.

The intuition is simple, relies only on the first type of query, and does not make use of the distinctness of the a_i. Given a database x generated according to our distribution, where the pseudo-random function is given by s, the syntheticizer must create a synthetic database (almost) all of whose rows must satisfy the query s. The intuition is that it can't *reliably* find input-output pairs that do not appear in x. A little more precisely, for an arbitrary element $a \in [\ell]$ such that no row in x is of the form $(a, f_s(a))$, the pseudo-randomness of f_s says that an efficient syntheticizer should have probability at most negligibly more than $1/\ell$ of finding $f_s(a)$. In this sense the pseudo-randomness gives us properties similar to, although somewhat weaker than, what we obtained from digital signatures.

Of course, for any given $a \in [\ell]$, the syntheticizer can indeed guess with probability $1/\ell$ the value $f_s(a)$, so without the second type of query, nothing obvious would stop it from ignoring x, choosing an arbitrary a, and outputting a database of n copies of (a, b), where b is chosen uniformly at random from $[\ell]$. The intuition is now that such a synthetic database would give the wrong fraction — either zero or one, when the right answer should be about $1/2$ — on the truly random queries.

Formally, we have:

Theorem 9.1. Let $f : \{0,1\}^\kappa \to \{0,1\}^\kappa$ be a one-way function. For every $a > 0$, and for every integer $n = \text{poly}(\kappa)$, there exists a query family $\mathcal{Q}$ of size $\exp(\text{poly}(\kappa))$, a data universe $\mathcal{X}$ of size $O(n^{2+2a})$, and a distribution on databases of size n that is $(\mu, \alpha, \beta, 0, \mathcal{Q})$-*hard-to-syntheticize* (i.e., hard to syntheticize for worst-case queries) for $\alpha \leq 1/3$, $\beta \leq 1/10$ and $\mu = 1/40n^{1+a}$.

The above theorem shows hardness of sanitizing with synthetic data. Note, however, that when the query set is small one can always simply release noisy counts for every query. We conclude that sanitizing for small query classes (with large data universes) is a task that separates efficient syntheticizing from efficient synopsis generation (sanitization with arbitrary outputs).

9.2.1 Hardness results for general synopses

The hardness results of the previous section apply only to syntheticizers — offline mechanisms that create synthetic databases. There is a tight connection between hardness for more general forms of privacy-preserving offline mechanisms, which we have been calling *offline query release mechanisms* or synopsis generators, and the existence of *traitor tracing* schemes, a method of content distribution in which (short) key strings are distributed to subscribers in such a way that a sender can broadcast encrypted messages that can be decrypted by any subscriber, and any useful "pirate" decoder constructed by a coalition of malicious subscribers can be traced to at least one colluder.

A (private-key, stateless) traitor-tracing scheme consists of algorithms Setup, Encrypt, Decrypt and Trace. The Setup algorithm generates a key bk for the broadcaster and N subscriber keys $k_1, \ldots, k_N$. The Encrypt algorithm encrypts a given bit using the broadcaster's key bk. The Decrypt algorithm decrypts a given ciphertext using any of the subscriber keys. The Trace algorithm gets the key bk and oracle access to a (pirate, stateless) decryption box, and outputs the index $i \in \{1, \ldots, N\}$ of a key k_i that was used to create the pirate box.

An important parameter of a traitor-tracing scheme is its *collusion-resistance*: a scheme is t-resilient if tracing is guaranteed to work as long as no more than t keys are used to create the pirate decoder. When $t = N$, tracing works even if all the subscribers join forces to try and create a pirate decoder. A more complete definition follows.

Definition 9.3. A scheme (Setup, Encrypt, Decrypt, Trace) as above is a *t-resilient traitor-tracing scheme* if (i) the ciphertexts it generates are semantically secure (roughly speaking, polynomial time algorithms cannot distinguish encryptions of 0 from encryptions of 1), and (ii) no polynomial time adversary A can "win" in the following game with non-negligible probability (over the coins of Setup, A, and Trace):

A receives the number of users N and a security parameter κ and (adaptively) requests the keys of up to t users $\{i_1, \ldots, i_t\}$. The adversary then outputs a pirate decoder Dec. The Trace algorithm is run with the key bk and black-box access[5] to Dec; it outputs the name $i \in [N]$ of a user or the error symbol $\perp$. We say that an adversary A "wins" if it is both the case that Dec has a non-negligible advantage in decrypting ciphertexts (even a weaker condition than creating a usable pirate decryption device), *and* the output of Trace is not in $\{i_1, \ldots, i_t\}$, meaning that the adversary avoided detection.

---

[5]Black-box access to an algorithm means that one has no access to the algorithm's internals; one can only feed inputs to the algorithm and observe its outputs.

The intuition for why traitor-tracing schemes imply hardness results for counting query release is as follows. Fix a traitor tracing scheme. We must describe databases and counting queries for which query release is computationally hard.

For any given $n = \kappa$, the database $x \in \{\{0,1\}^d\}^n$ will contain user keys from the traitor tracing scheme of a colluding set of n users; here d is the length of the decryption keys obtained when the Setup algorithm is run on input 1^κ. The query family $\mathcal{Q}_\kappa$ will have a query q_c for each possible ciphertext c asking "For what fraction of the rows $i \in [n]$ does c decrypt to 1 under the key in row i?" Note that, since every user can decrypt, if the sender distributes an encryption c of the bit 1, the answer will be 1: all the rows decrypt c to 1, so the fraction of such rows is 1. If instead the sender distributes an encryption c' of the bit 0, the answer will be 0: since no row decrypts c' to 1, the fraction of rows decrypting c' to 1 is 0. Thus, the exact answer to a query q_c, where c is an encryption of a 1-bit messages b, is b itself.

Now, suppose there were an efficient offline differentially private query release mechanism for queries in $\mathcal{Q}$. The colluders could use this algorithm to efficiently produce a synopsis of the database enabling a data analyst to efficiently compute approximate answers to the queries q_c. If these approximations are at all non-trivial, then the analyst can use these to correctly decrypt. That is, the colluders could use this to form a pirate decoder box. But traitor tracing ensures that, for any such box, the Trace algorithm can recover the key of at least one user, i.e., a row of the database. This violates differential privacy, contradicting the assumption that there is an efficient differentially private algorithm for releasing $\mathcal{Q}$.

This direction has been used to rule out the existence of efficient offline sanitizers for a particular class of $2^{\tilde{O}(\sqrt{n})}$ counting queries; this can be extended to rule out the existence of efficient *on-line* sanitizers answering $\tilde{\Theta}(n^2)$ counting queries drawn adaptively from a second (large) class.

The intuition for why hardness of offline query release for counting queries implies traitor tracing is that failure to protect privacy immediately yields some form of traceability; that is, the *difficulty* of providing an object that yields (approximate) functional equivalence for a set of rows (decryption keys) while preserving privacy of each individual row (decryption key) — that is, the difficulty of producing an untraceable decoder — is precisely what we are looking for in a traitor tracing scheme.

In a little more detail, given a hard-to-sanitize database distribution and family of counting queries, a randomly drawn n-item database can act like a "master key," where the secret used to decrypt messages is the *counts* of random queries on this database. For a randomly chosen subset S of polylog(n) queries, a random set of polylog(n) rows drawn from the database (very likely) yields good approximation to all queries in S. Thus, individual user keys can be obtained by randomly partitioning the database into n/polylog(n) sets of polylog(n) rows and assigning each set to a different user. These sets are large enough that with overwhelming probability their counts on a random collection of say polylog(n) queries are *all* close to the counts of the original database.

To complete the argument, one designs an encryption scheme in which decryption is equivalent to computing approximate counts on small sets of random queries. Since by definition a pirate decryption box can decrypt, the a pirate box can be used to compute approximate counts. If we view this box as a sanitization of the database we conclude (because sanitizing is hard) that the decryption box can be "traced" to the keys (database items) that were used to create it.

9.3 Polynomial time adversaries

Definition 9.4 (Computational Differential Privacy). A randomized algorithm $C_\kappa : \mathcal{X}^n \to Y$ is ε-*computationally differentially private* if and only if for all databases x, y differing in a single row, and for all nonuniform polynomial (in κ) algorithms T,

$$\Pr[T(C_\kappa(x)) = 1] \le e^\varepsilon \Pr[T(C_\kappa(y)) = 1] + \nu(\kappa),$$

where $\nu(\cdot)$ is any function that grows more slowly than the inverse of any polynomial and the agorithm C_κ runs in time polynomial in n, $\log |\mathcal{X}|$, and κ.

Intuitively, this says that if the adversary is restricted to polynomial time then computationally differentially private mechanisms provide the same degree of privacy as do $(\varepsilon, \nu(\kappa))$-differentially private algorithms. In general there is no hope of getting rid of the $\nu(\kappa)$ term; for example, when encryption is involved there is always some (neglibly small) chance of guessing the decryption key.

Once we assume the adversary is restricted to polynomial time, we can use the powerful techniques of *secure multiparty computation* to provide *distributed* online query release algorithms, replacing the trusted server with a distributed protocoal that simulates a trusted curator. Thus, for example, a set of hospitals, each holding the data of many patients, can collaboratively carry out statistical analyses of the union of their patients, while ensuring differential privacy for each patient. A more radical implication is that individuals can maintain their own data, opting in or out of each specific statistical query or study, all the while ensuring differential privacy of their own data.

We have already seen one distributed solution, at least for the problem of computing a sum of n bits: randomized response. This solution requires no computational assumptions, and has an expected error of $\Theta(\sqrt{n})$. In contrast, the use of cryptographic assumptions permits much more accurate and extensive analyses, since by simulating the curator it can run a distributed implementation of the Laplace mechanism, which has constant expected error.

This leads to the natural question of whether there is some other approach, not relying on cryptographic assumptions, that yields better accuracy in the distributed setting than does randomized response. Or more generally, is there a separation between what can be accomplished with computational differential privacy and what can be achieved with "traditional" differential privacy? That is, does cryptography provably buy us something?

In the multiparty setting the answer is yes. Still confining our attention to summing n bits, we have:

Theorem 9.2. For $\varepsilon < 1$, every n-party $(\varepsilon, 0)$-differentially private protocol for computing the sum of n bits (one per party) incurs error $\Omega(n^{1/2})$ with high probability.

A similar theorem holds for (ε, δ)-differential privacy provided $\delta \in o(1/n)$.

Proof. (sketch) Let $X_1, \ldots, X_n$ be uniform independent bits. The transcript T of the protocol is a random variable $T = T(P_1(X_1), \ldots, P_n(X_n))$, where for $i \in [n]$ the protocol of player i is denoted P_i. Conditioned on $T = t$, the bits $X_1, \ldots, X_n$ are still independent bits, each with bias $O(\varepsilon)$. Further, by differential privacy, the uniformity of the X_i, and Bayes' Law we have:

$$\frac{\Pr[X_i = 1 | T = t]}{\Pr[X_i = 0 | T = t]} = \frac{\Pr[T = t | X_i = 1]}{\Pr[T = t | X_i = 0]} \leq e^{\varepsilon} < 1 + 2\varepsilon.$$

To finish the proof we note that the sum of n independent bits, each with constant bias, falls outside any interval of size $o(\sqrt{n})$ with high probability. Thus, with high probability, the sum $\sum_i X_i$ is not in the interval $[\text{output}(\mathrm{T}) - o(n^{1/2}), \text{output}(\mathrm{T}) + o(n^{1/2})]$. $\qquad\square$

A more involved proof shows a separation between computational differential privacy and ordinary differential privacy even for the two-party case. It is a fascinating open question whether computational assumptions buy us anything in the case of the trusted curator. Initial results are negative: for *small* numbers of *real-valued* queries, i.e., for a number of queries that does not grow with the security parameter, there is a natural class of utility measures, including L_p distances and mean-squared errors, for which any computationally private mechanism can be converted to a statistically private mechanism that is roughly as efficient and achieves almost the same utility.

9.4   Bibliographic notes

The negative results for polynomial time bounded curators and the connection to traitor tracing are due to Dwork et al. [28]. The connection to traitor tracing was further investigated by Ullman [82], who showed that, assuming the existence of 1-way functions, it is computationally hard to answer $n^{2+o(1)}$ arbitrary linear queries with differential privacy (even if without privacy the answers are easy to compute). In "Our Data, Ourselves," Dwork, Kenthapadi, McSherry, Mironov, and

Naor considered a distributed version of the precursor of differential privacy, using techniques from secure function evaluation in place of the trusted curator [21]. A formal study of *computational* differential privacy was initiated in [64], and the separation between the accuracy that can be achieved with $(\varepsilon, 0)$-differential privacy in the multiparty and single curator cases in Theorem 9.2 is due to McGregor et al. [58]. The initial results regarding whether computational assumptions on the adversary buys anything in the case of a trusted curator are due to Groce et al. [37].

Construction of pseudorandom functions from any one-way function is due to Håstad et al. [40].

10

Differential Privacy and Mechanism Design

One of the most fascinating areas of game theory is mechanism design, which is the science of designing incentives to get people to do what you want them to do. Differential privacy has proven to have interesting connections to mechanism design in a couple of unexpected ways. It provides a tool to quantify and control privacy loss, which is important if the people the mechanism designer is attempting to manipulate care about privacy. However, it also provides a way to limit the sensitivity of the outcome of a mechanism to the choices of any single person, which turns out to be a powerful tool even in the absence of privacy concerns. In this section, we give a brief survey of some of these ideas.

Mechanism Design is the problem of *algorithm design* when the inputs to the algorithm are controlled by individual, self-interested agents, rather than the algorithm designer himself. The algorithm maps its reported inputs to some outcome, over which the agents have preferences. The difficulty is that the agents may mis-report their data if doing so will cause the algorithm to output a different, preferred outcome, and so the mechanism designer must design the algorithm so that the agents are always incentivized to report their true data.

The concerns of mechanism design are very similar to the concerns of private algorithm design. In both cases, the inputs to the algorithm are thought of as belonging to some third party[1] which has preferences over the outcome. In mechanism design, we typically think of individuals as getting some explicit value from the outcomes of the mechanism. In private algorithm design, we typically think of the individual as experiencing some explicit harm from (consequences of) outcomes of the mechanism. Indeed, we can give a utility-theoretic definition of differential privacy which is equivalent to the standard definition, but makes the connection to individual utilities explicit:

Definition 10.1. An algorithm $A : \mathbb{N}^{|\mathcal{X}|} \to R$ is ϵ-differentially private if for every function $f : R \to \mathbb{R}_+$, and for every pair of neighboring databases $x, y \in \mathbb{N}^{|\mathcal{X}|}$:

$$\exp(-\epsilon)\mathbb{E}_{z \sim A(y)}[f(z)] \leq \mathbb{E}_{z \sim A(x)}[f(z)] \leq \exp(\epsilon)\mathbb{E}_{z \sim A(y)}[f(z)].$$

We can think of f as being some function mapping outcomes to an arbitrary agent's utility for those outcomes. With this interpretation, a mechanism is ϵ-differentially private, if for every agent it promises that their participation in the mechanism cannot affect their expected future utility by more than a factor of $\exp(\epsilon)$ *independent of what their utility function might be.*

Let us now give a brief definition of a problem in mechanism design. A mechanism design problem is defined by several objects. There are n agents $i \in [n]$, and a set of outcomes $\mathcal{O}$. Each agent has a type, $t_i \in \mathcal{T}$ which is known only to her, and there is a utility function over outcomes $u : \mathcal{T} \times \mathcal{O} \to [0, 1]$. The utility that agent i gets from an outcome $o \in \mathcal{O}$ is $u(t_i, o)$, which we will often abbreviate as $u_i(o)$. We will write $t \in \mathcal{T}^n$ to denote vectors of all n agent types, with t_i denoting the type of agent i, and $t_{-i} \equiv (t_1, \ldots, t_{i-1}, t_{i+1}, \ldots, t_n)$ denoting the vector of types of all agents *except* agent i. The type of an agent i completely specifies her utility over outcomes — that is, two agents $i \neq j$ such that $t_i = t_j$ will evaluate each outcome identically: $u_i(o) = u_j(o)$ for all $o \in \mathcal{O}$.

---

[1]In the privacy setting, the database administrator (such as a hospital) might already have access to the data itself, but is nevertheless acting so as to protect the interests of the agents who own the data when it endeavors to protect privacy.

A mechanism M takes as input a set of reported types, one from each player, and selects an outcome. That is, a mechanism is a mapping $M : \mathcal{T}^n \to \mathcal{O}$. Agents will choose to report their types strategically so as to optimize their utility, possibly taking into account what (they think) the other agents will be doing. In particular, they need not report their true types to the mechanism. If an agent is always incentivized to report some type, no matter what her opponents are reporting, then reporting that type is called a *dominant strategy*. If reporting one's true type is a dominant strategy for every agent, then the mechanism is called *truthful*, or equivalently, *dominant strategy truthful*.

Definition 10.2. Given a mechanism $M : \mathcal{T}^n \to \mathcal{O}$, truthful reporting is an ϵ-approximate *dominant strategy* for player i if for every pair of types $t_i, t'_i \in T$, and for every vector of types t_{-i}:

$$u(t_i, M(t_i, t_{-i})) \geq u(t_i, M(t'_i, t_{-i})) - \epsilon.$$

If truthful reporting is an ϵ-approximate dominant strategy for every player, we say that M is ϵ-approximately dominant strategy truthful. If $\epsilon = 0$, then M is *exactly truthful*.

That is, a mechanism is truthful if no agent can improve her utility by misrepresenting her type, no matter what the other players report.

Here we can immediately observe a syntactic connection to the definition of differential privacy. We may identify the type space T with the data universe X. The input to the mechanism therefore consists of a database of size n, consisting of the reports of each agent. In fact, when an agent is considering whether she should truthfully report her type t_i or lie, and misreport her type as t'_i, she is deciding which of two databases the mechanism should receive: $(t_1, \ldots, t_n)$, or $(t_1, \ldots, t_{i-1}, t'_i, t_{i+1}, \ldots, t_n)$. Note that these two databases differ only in the report of agent i! That is, they are *neighboring databases*. Thus, differential privacy gives a guarantee of approximate truthfulness!

10.1 Differential privacy as a solution concept

One of the starting points for investigating the connection between differential privacy and game theory is observing that differential privacy is a *stronger* condition than approximate truthfulness. Note that for $\epsilon \leq 1$, $\exp(\epsilon) \leq 1 + 2\epsilon$ and so the following proposition is immediate.

Proposition 10.1. If a mechanism M is ϵ-differentially private, then M is also 2ϵ-approximately dominant strategy truthful.

As a solution concept, this has several robustness properties that strategy proof mechanisms do not. By the composition property of differential privacy, the composition of 2 ϵ-differentially private mechanisms remains 4ϵ-approximately dominant strategy truthful. In contrast, the incentive properties of general strategy proof mechanisms may not be preserved under composition.

Another useful property of differential privacy as a solution concept is that it generalizes to group privacy: suppose that t and $t' \in \mathcal{T}^n$ are not neighbors, but instead differ in k indices. Recall that by group privacy we then have for any player i: $\mathbb{E}_{o \sim M(t)}[u_i(o)] \leq \exp(k\epsilon)\mathbb{E}_{o \sim M(t')}[u_i(o)]$. That is, changes in up to k types changes the expected output by at most $\approx (1 + k\epsilon)$, when $k \ll 1/\epsilon$. Therefore, differentially private mechanisms make truthful reporting a $2k\epsilon$-approximate dominant strategy *even for coalitions of k agents* — i.e., differential privacy automatically provides robustness to collusion. Again, this is in contrast to general dominant-strategy truthful mechanisms, which in general offer no guarantees against collusion.

Notably, differential privacy allows for these properties in very general settings *without the use of money!* In contrast, the set of exactly dominant strategy truthful mechanisms when monetary transfers are not allowed is extremely limited.

We conclude with a drawback of using differential privacy as a solution concept as stated: not only is truthfully reporting one's type an approximate dominant strategy, *any report* is an approximate dominant strategy! That is, differential privacy makes the outcome approximately independent of any single agent's report. In some settings, this shortcoming can be alleviated. For example, suppose that M is a differentially private mechanism, but that agent utility functions are defined to be functions both of the outcome of the mechanism, *and* of the reported type t'_i of the agent: formally, we view the outcome space as $\mathcal{O}' = \mathcal{O} \times T$. When the agent reports type t'_i to the mechanism, and the mechanism selects outcome $o \in \mathcal{O}$, then the utility experienced by the agent is controlled by the outcome $o' = (o, t'_i)$. Now consider the underlying utility function $u : T \times \mathcal{O}' \rightarrow [0, 1]$. Suppose we have that *fixing* a selection o of the mechanism, truthful reporting is a dominant strategy — that is, for all types t_i, t'_i, and for all outcomes $o \in \mathcal{O}$:

$$u(t_i, (o, t_i)) \geq u(t_i, (o, t'_i)).$$

Then it remains the fact that truthful reporting to an ϵ-differentially private mechanism $M : T^n \rightarrow \mathcal{O}$ remains a 2ϵ approximate dominant strategy, because for any misreport t'_i that player i might consider, we have:

$$
\begin{aligned}
u(t_i, (M(t), t_i)) &= \mathbb{E}_{o \sim M(t)}[u(t_i, (o, t_i))] \\
&\geq (1 + 2\epsilon)\mathbb{E}_{o \sim M(t'_i, t_{-i})}[u(t_i, (o, t_i))] \\
&\geq \mathbb{E}_{o \sim M(t'_i, t_{-i})}[u(t_i, (o, t'_i))] \\
&= u(t_i, (M(t'_i, t_{-i}), t'_i)).
\end{aligned}
$$

However, we no longer have that every report is an approximate dominant strategy, because player i's utility can depend arbitrarily on $o' = (o, t'_i)$, and only o (and not player i's report t'_i itself) is differentially private. This will be the case in all examples we consider here.

10.2 Differential privacy as a tool in mechanism design

In this section, we show how the machinery of differential privacy can be used as a tool in designing novel mechanisms.

10.2.1 Warmup: digital goods auctions

To warm up, let us consider a simple special case of the first application of differential privacy in mechanism design. Consider a *digital goods auction,* i.e., one where the seller has an unlimited supply of a good with zero marginal cost to produce, for example a piece of software or other digital media. There are n unit demand buyers for this good, each with unknown valuation $v_i \in [0, 1]$. Informally, the valuation v_i of a bidder i represents the maximum amount of money that buyer i

would be willing to pay for a good. There is no prior distribution on the bidder valuations, so a natural revenue benchmark is the revenue of the *best fixed price*. At a price $p \in [0,1]$, each bidder i with $v_i \geq p$ will buy. Therefore the total revenue of the auctioneer is

$$\text{Rev}(p,v) = p \cdot |\{i : v_i \geq p\}|.$$

The optimal revenue is the revenue of the best fixed price: $\text{OPT} = \max_p \text{Rev}(p,v)$. This setting is well studied: the best known result for exactly dominant strategy truthful mechanisms is a mechanism which achieves revenue at least $\text{OPT} - O(\sqrt{n})$.

We show how a simple application of the exponential mechanism achieves revenue at least $\text{OPT} - O\left(\frac{\log n}{\epsilon}\right)$. That is, the mechanism trades exact for approximate truthfulness, but achieves an exponentially better revenue guarantee. Of course, it also inherits the benefits of differential privacy discussed previously, such as resilience to collusion, and composability.

The idea is to select a price from the exponential mechanism, using as our "quality score" the revenue that this price would obtain. Suppose we choose the range of the exponential mechanism to be $\mathcal{R} = \{\alpha, 2\alpha, \ldots, 1\}$. The size of the range is $|\mathcal{R}| = 1/\alpha$. What have we lost in potential revenue if we restrict ourselves to selecting a price from $\mathcal{R}$? It is not hard to see that

$$\text{OPT}_{\mathcal{R}} \equiv \max_{p \in \mathcal{R}} \text{Rev}(p,v) \geq \text{OPT} - \alpha n.$$

This is because if p^* is the price that achieves the optimal revenue, and we use a price p such that $p^* - \alpha \leq p \leq p^*$, every buyer who bought at the optimal price continues to buy, and provides us with at most α less revenue per buyer. Since there are at most n buyers, the total lost revenue is at most αn.

So how do we parameterize the exponential mechanism? We have a family of discrete ranges $\mathcal{R}$, parameterized by α. For a vector of values v and a price $p \in \mathcal{R}$, we define our quality function to be $q(v,p) = \text{Rev}(v,p)$. Observe that because each value $v_i \in [0,1]$, we can restrict attention to prices $p \leq 1$ and hence, the *sensitivity* of q is $\Delta = 1$: changing one bidder valuation can only change the revenue at a fixed price by at most $v_i \leq 1$. Therefore, if we require ϵ-differential privacy, by Theorem 3.11, we get that with high probability, the exponential mechanism returns some price p such that

$$\text{Rev}(p, v) \geq (\text{OPT} - \alpha n) - O\left(\frac{1}{\epsilon} \ln\left(\frac{1}{\alpha}\right)\right).$$

Choosing our discretization parameter α to minimize the two sources of error, we find that this mechanism with high probability finds us a price that achieves revenue

$$\text{Rev}(p, v) \geq \text{OPT} - O\left(\frac{\log n}{\epsilon}\right).$$

What is the right level to choose for the privacy parameter ϵ? Note that here, we do not necessarily view privacy itself as a goal of our computation. Rather, ϵ is a way of trading off the revenue guarantee with an upper bound on agent's incentives to deviate. In the literature on large markets in economics, a common goal when exact truthfulness is out of reach is "asymptotic truthfulness" – that is, the maximum incentive that any agent has to deviate from his truthful report tend to 0 as the size of the market n grows large. To achieve a result like that here, all we need to do is set ϵ to be some diminishing function in the number of agents n. For example, if we take $\epsilon = 1/\log(n)$, then we obtain a mechanism that is asymptotically exactly truthful (i.e., as the market grows large, the approximation to truthfulness becomes exact). We can also ask what our approximation to the optimal revenue is as n grows large. Note that our approximation to the optimal revenue is only additive, and so even with this setting of ϵ, we can still guarantee revenue at least $(1 - o(1))\text{OPT}$, so long as OPT grows more quickly than $\log(n)^2$ with the size of the population n.

Finally, notice that we could make the reported value v_i of each agent i binding. In other words, we could allocate an item to agent i and extract payment of the selected posted price p whenever $v_i \geq p$. If we do this, the mechanism is approximately truthful, because the price is picked using a differentially private mechanism. Additionally, it is not the case that *every* report is an approximate dominant strategy: if an agent over-reports, she may be forced to buy the good at a price higher than her true value.

10.2.2   Approximately truthful equilibrium selection mechanisms

We now consider the problem of approximately truthful equilibrium selection. We recall the definition of a *Nash Equilibrium*: Suppose each player has a set of actions $\mathcal{A}$, and can choose to play any action $a_i \in \mathcal{A}$. Suppose, moreover, that *outcomes* are merely choices of actions that the agents might choose to play, and so agent utility functions are defined as $u : \mathcal{T} \times \mathcal{A}^n \to [0, 1]$. Then:

Definition 10.3. A set of actions $a \in \mathcal{A}^n$ is an ϵ-approximate Nash equilibrium if for all players i and for all actions a_i':

$$u_i(a) \geq u_i(a_i', a_{-i}) - \epsilon$$

In other words, every agent is simultaneously playing an (approximate) best response to what the other agents are doing, assuming they are playing according to a.

Roughly speaking, the problem is as follows: suppose we are given a game in which each player knows their own payoffs, but not others' payoffs (i.e., the players do not know what the types are of the other agents). The players therefore do not know the equilibrium structure of this game. Even if they did, there might be multiple equilibria, with different agents preferring different equilibria. Can a mechanism offered by an intermediary incentivize agents to truthfully report their utilities and follow the equilibrium it selects?

For example, imagine a city in which (say) Google Navigation is the dominant service. Every morning, each person enters their starting point and destination, receives a set of directions, and chooses his/her route according to those directions. Is it possible to design a navigation service such that: Each agent is incentivized to both (1) report truthfully, and (2) then follow the driving directions provided? Both misreporting start and end points, and truthfully reporting start and end points, but then following a different (shorter) path are to be disincentivized.

Intuitively, our two desiderata are in conflict. In the commuting example above, if we are to guarantee that every player is incentivized to truthfully follow their suggested route, then we must compute an equilibrium of the game in question given players' reports. On the other hand, to do so, our suggested route to some player i must depend on the reported location/destination pairs of other players. This tension will pose a problem in terms of incentives: if we compute an equilibrium of the game given the reports of the players, an agent can potentially benefit by misreporting, causing us to compute an equilibrium of the wrong game.

This problem would be largely alleviated, however, if the report of agent i only has a tiny effect on the actions of agents $j \neq i$. In this case, agent i could hardly gain an advantage through his effect on other players. Then, assuming that everyone truthfully reported their type, the mechanism would compute an equilibrium of the correct game, and by definition, each agent i could do no better than follow the suggested equilibrium action. In other words, if we could compute an approximate equilibrium of the game under the constraint of *differential privacy*, then truthful reporting, followed by taking the suggested action of the coordination device would be a Nash equilibrium. A moment's reflection reveals that the goal of privately computing an equilibrium is not possible in small games, in which an agent's utility is a highly sensitive function of the actions (and hence utility functions) of the other agents. But what about in large games?

Formally, suppose we have an n player game with action set $\mathcal{A}$, and each agent with type t_i has a utility function $u_i : \mathcal{A}^n \to [0, 1]$. We say that this game is Δ-large if for all players $i \neq j$, vectors of actions $a \in \mathcal{A}^n$, and pairs of actions $a_j, a'_j \in \mathcal{A}$:

$$\left| u_i(a_j, a_{-j}) - u_i(a'_j, a_{-j}) \right| \leq \Delta.$$

In other words, if some agent j unilaterally changes his action, then his affect on the payoff of any other agent $i \neq j$ is at most Δ. Note that if agent j changes his own action, then his payoff can change arbitrarily. Many games are "large" in this sense. In the commuting example above, if Alice changes her route to work she may substantially increase or decrease her commute time, but will only have a minimal impact on the commute time of any other agent Bob. The results in this section are strongest for $\Delta = O(1/n)$, but hold more generally.

First we might ask whether we need privacy at all— could it be the case that in a large game, any algorithm which computes an equilibrium of a game defined by reported types has the stability property that we want? The answer is no. As a simple example, consider n people who must each choose whether to go to the beach (B) or the mountains (M). People privately know their types— each person's utility depends on his own type, his action, and the fraction of other people p who go to the beach. A Beach type gets a payoff of $10p$ if he visits the beach, and $5(1 - p)$ if he visits the mountain. A mountain type gets a payoff $5p$ from visiting the beach, and $10(1-p)$ from visiting the mountain. Note that this is a large (i.e., low sensitivity) game — each player's payoffs are insensitive in the actions of others. Further, note that "everyone visits beach" and "everyone visits mountain" are both equilibria of the game, regardless of the realization of types. Consider the mechanism that attempts to implement the following social choice rule— "if the number of beach types is less than half the population, send everyone to the beach, and vice versa." It should be clear that if mountain types are just in the majority, then each mountain type has an incentive to misreport as a beach type; and vice versa. As a result, even though the game is "large" and agents' actions do not affect others' payoffs significantly, simply computing equilibria from reported type profiles does not in general lead to even approximately truthful mechanisms.

Nevertheless, it turns out to be possible to give a mechanism with the following property: it elicits the type t_i of each agent, and then computes an α-approximate correlated equilibrium of the game defined by the reported types.[2] (In some cases, it is possible to strengthen this result to compute an approximate *Nash equilibrium* of the underlying game.) It draws an action profile $a \in \mathcal{A}^n$ from the correlated equilibrium, and reports action a_i to each agent i. The algorithm has the guarantee that simultaneously for all players i, the joint distribution a_{-i} on reports to all players *other than* i is differentially private in

---

[2]A correlated equilibrium is defined by a joint distribution on profiles of actions, $\mathcal{A}^n$. For an action profile a drawn from the distribution, if agent i is told only a_i, then playing action a_i is a best response given the induced conditional distribution over a_{-i}. An α-approximate correlated equilibrium is one where deviating improves an agent's utility by at most α.

the reported type of agent i. When the algorithm computes a correlated equilibrium of the underlying game, this guarantee is sufficient for a restricted form of approximate truthfulness: agents who have the option to opt-in or opt-out of the mechanism (but not to misreport their type if they opt-in) have no disincentive to opt-out, because no agent i can substantially change the distribution on actions induced on *the other players* by opting out. Moreover, given that he opts in, no agent has incentive not to follow his suggested action, as his suggestion is part of a correlated equilibrium. When the mechanism computes a Nash equilibrium of the underlying game, then the mechanism becomes truthful even when agents have the ability to mis-report their type to the mechanism when they opt in.

More specifically, when these mechanisms compute an α-approximate Nash equilibrium while satisfying ϵ-differential privacy, every agent following the honest behavior (i.e., first opting in and reporting their true type, then following their suggested action) forms an $(2\epsilon + \alpha)$-approximate Nash equilibrium. This is because, by privacy, reporting your true type is a 2ϵ-approximate dominant strategy, and given that everybody reports their true type, the mechanism computes an α-approximate equilibrium of the true game, and hence by definition, following the suggested action is an α-approximate best response. There exist mechanisms for computing and α-approximate equilibrium in large games with $\alpha = O\left(\frac{1}{\sqrt{n}\epsilon}\right)$. Therefore, by setting $\epsilon = O\left(\frac{1}{n^{1/4}}\right)$, this gives an η-approximately truthful equilibrium selection mechanism for

$$\eta = 2\epsilon + \alpha = O\left(\frac{1}{n^{1/4}}\right).$$

In other words, it gives a mechanism for coordinating equilibrium behavior in large games that is asymptotically truthful in the size of the game, all without the need for monetary transfers.

10.2.3   Obtaining exact truthfulness

So far we have discussed mechanisms that are *asymptotically truthful* in large population games. However, what if we want to insist on mechanisms that are *exactly* dominant strategy truthful, while maintaining some of the nice properties enjoyed by our mechanisms so far: for example, that the mechanisms do not need to be able to extract monetary payments? Can differential privacy help here? It can—in this section, we discuss a framework which uses differentially private mechanisms as a building block toward designing exactly truthful mechanisms without money.

The basic idea is simple and elegant. As we have seen, the exponential mechanism can often give excellent utility guarantees while preserving differential privacy. This doesn't yield an exactly truthful mechanism, but it gives every agent very little incentive to deviate from truthful behavior. What if we could pair this with a second mechanism which need not have good utility guarantees, but gives each agent a strict positive incentive to report truthfully, i.e., a mechanism that essentially only punishes non-truthful behavior? Then, we could randomize between running the two mechanisms. If we put enough weight on the punishing mechanism, then we inherit its strict-truthfulness properties. The remaining weight that is put on the exponential mechanism contributes to the utility properties of the final mechanism. The hope is that since the exponential mechanism is approximately strategy proof to begin with, the randomized mechanism can put small weight on the strictly truthful punishing mechanism, and therefore will have good utility properties.

To design punishing mechanisms, we will have to work in a slightly non-standard environment. Rather than simply picking an outcome, we can model a mechanism as picking an outcome, and then an agent as choosing a *reaction* to that outcome, which together define his utility. Mechanisms will then have the power to *restrict the reactions allowed by the agent based on his reported type*. Formally, we will work in the following framework:

Definition 10.4 (The Environment). An environment is a set N of n players, a set of types $t_i \in \mathcal{T}$, a finite set $\mathcal{O}$ of outcomes, a set of reactions R and a utility function $u : T \times \mathcal{O} \times R \to [0, 1]$.

We write $r_i(t, s, \hat{R}_i) \in \arg\max_{r \in \hat{R}_i} u_i(t, s, r)$ to denote is optimal reaction among choices $\hat{R}_i \subseteq R$ to alternative s if he is of type t.

A direct revelation mechanism $\mathcal{M}$ defines a game which is played as follows:

1. Each player i reports a type $t'_i \in \mathcal{T}$.
2. The mechanism chooses an alternative $s \in \mathcal{O}$ and a subset $\hat{R}_i \subseteq R$ of reactions, for each player i.
3. Each player i chooses a reaction $r_i \in \hat{R}_i$ and experiences utility $u(t_i, s, r_i)$.

Agents play so as to maximize their own utility. Note that since there is no further interaction after the 3rd step, rational agents will pick $r_i = r_i(t_i, s, \hat{R}_i)$, and so we can ignore this as a strategic step. Let $\mathcal{R} = 2^R$. Then a mechanism is a randomized mapping $\mathcal{M} : \mathcal{T} \to \mathcal{O} \times \mathcal{R}^n$.

Let us consider the utilitarian welfare criterion: $F(t, s, r) = \frac{1}{n}\sum_{i=1}^{n} u(t_i, s, r_i)$, Note that this has sensitivity $\Delta = 1/n$, since each agent's utility lies in the range $[0, 1]$. Hence, if we simply choose an outcome s and allow each agent to play their best response reaction, the exponential mechanism is an ϵ-differentially private mechanism, which by Theorem 3.11, achieves social welfare at least $\text{OPT} - O\left(\frac{\log |\mathcal{O}|}{\epsilon n}\right)$ with high probability. Let us denote this instantiation of the exponential mechanism, with quality score F, range $\mathcal{O}$ and privacy parameter ϵ, as $\mathcal{M}_\epsilon$.

The idea is to randomize between the exponential mechanism (with good social welfare properties) and a strictly truthful mechanism which punishes false reporting (but with poor social welfare properties). If we mix appropriately, then we will get an exactly truthful mechanism with reasonable social welfare guarantees.

Here is one such punishing mechanism which is simple, but not necessarily the best for a given problem:

Definition 10.5. The commitment mechanism $M^P(t')$ selects $s \in \mathcal{O}$ uniformly at random and sets $\hat{R}_i = \{r_i(t'_i, s, R_i)\}$, i.e., it picks a random outcome and forces everyone to react as if their reported type was their true type.

Define the *gap* of an environment as

$$\gamma = \min_{i, t_i \neq t'_i, t_{-i}} \max_{s \in \mathcal{O}} \left(u(t_i, s, r_i(t_i, s, R_i)) - u(t_i, s, r_i(t'_i, s, R_i)) \right),$$

i.e., γ is a lower bound over players and types of the worst-case cost (over s) of mis-reporting. Note that for each player, this worst-case is realized with probability at least $1/|\mathcal{O}|$. Therefore we have the following simple observation:

Lemma 10.2. For all i, t_i, t_i', t_{-i}:

$$u(t_i, \mathcal{M}^P(t_i, t_{-i})) \geq u(t_i, \mathcal{M}^P(t_i', t_{-i})) + \frac{\gamma}{|\mathcal{O}|}.$$

Note that the commitment mechanism is strictly truthful: every individual has at least a $\frac{\gamma}{|\mathcal{O}|}$ incentive not to lie.

This suggests an exactly truthful mechanism with good social welfare guarantees:

Definition 10.6. The punishing exponential mechanism $\mathcal{M}_\epsilon^P(t)$ defined with parameter $0 \leq q \leq 1$ selects the exponential mechanism $\mathcal{M}_\epsilon(t)$ with probability $1 - q$ and the punishing mechanism $\mathcal{M}^P(t)$ with complementary probability q.

Observe that by linearity of expectation, we have for all t_i, t_i', t_{-i}:

$$
\begin{aligned}
u(t_i, \mathcal{M}_\epsilon^P(t_i, t_{-i})) &= (1-q) \cdot u(t_i, \mathcal{M}_\epsilon(t_i, t_{-i})) + q \cdot u(t_i, \mathcal{M}^P(t_i, t_{-i})) \\
&\geq (1-q)\left(u(t_i, \mathcal{M}_\epsilon(t_i', t_{-i})) - 2\epsilon\right) \\
&\quad + q\left(u(t_i, \mathcal{M}^P(t_i', t_{-i})) + \frac{\gamma}{|\mathcal{O}|}\right) \\
&= u(t_i, \mathcal{M}_\epsilon^P(t_i', t_{-i})) - (1-q)2\epsilon + q\frac{\gamma}{|\mathcal{O}|} \\
&= u(t_i, \mathcal{M}_\epsilon^P(t_i', t_{-i})) - 2\epsilon + q\left(2\epsilon + \frac{\gamma}{|\mathcal{O}|}\right).
\end{aligned}
$$

The following two theorems show incentive and social welfare properties of this mechanism.

Theorem 10.3. If $2\epsilon \leq \frac{q\gamma}{|\mathcal{O}|}$ then $\mathcal{M}_\epsilon^P$ is strictly truthful.

Note that we also have utility guarantees for this mechanism. Setting the parameter q so that we have a truthful mechanism:

$$\mathbb{E}_{s,\hat{R}\sim\mathcal{M}_\epsilon^P}[F(t,s,r(t,s,\hat{R}))]$$

$$\geq (1-q) \cdot \mathbb{E}_{s,\hat{R}\sim\mathcal{M}_\epsilon}[F(t,s,r(t,s,\hat{R}))]$$

$$= \left(1 - \frac{2\epsilon|\mathcal{O}|}{\gamma}\right) \cdot \mathbb{E}_{s,\hat{R}\sim\mathcal{M}_\epsilon}[F(t,s,r(t,s,\hat{R}))]$$

$$\geq \left(1 - \frac{2\epsilon|\mathcal{O}|}{\gamma}\right) \cdot \left(\max_{t,s,r} F(t,s,r) - O\left(\frac{1}{\epsilon n}\log|\mathcal{O}|\right)\right)$$

$$\geq \max_{t,s,r} F(t,s,r) - \frac{2\epsilon|\mathcal{O}|}{\gamma} - O\left(\frac{1}{\epsilon n}\log|\mathcal{O}|\right).$$

Setting

$$\epsilon \in O\left(\sqrt{\frac{\log|\mathcal{O}|\gamma}{|\mathcal{O}|n}}\right)$$

we find:

$$\mathbb{E}_{s,\hat{R}\sim\mathcal{M}_\epsilon^P}[F(t,s,r(t,s,\hat{R}))] \geq \max_{t,s,r} F(t,s,r) - O\left(\sqrt{\frac{|\mathcal{O}|\log|\mathcal{O}|}{\gamma n}}\right).$$

Note that in this calculation, we assume that $\epsilon \leq \gamma/(2|\mathcal{O}|)$ so that $q = \frac{2\epsilon|\mathcal{O}|}{\gamma} \leq 1$ and the mechanism is well defined. This is true for sufficiently large n. That is, we have shown:

Theorem 10.4. For sufficiently large n, M_ϵ^P achieves social welfare at least

$$\text{OPT} - O\left(\sqrt{\frac{|\mathcal{O}|\log|\mathcal{O}|}{\gamma n}}\right).$$

Note that this mechanism is truthful without the need for payments!

Let us now consider an application of this framework: the facility location game. Suppose that a city wants to build k hospitals to minimize the average distance between each citizen and their closest hospital. To simplify matters, we make the mild assumption that the city is built on a discretization of the unit line.[3] Formally, let

---

[3]If this is not the case, we can easily raze and then re-build the city.

$L(m) = \{0, \frac{1}{m}, \frac{2}{m}, \ldots, 1\}$ denote the discrete unit line with step-size $1/m$. $|L(m)| = m+1$. Let $\mathcal{T} = R_i = L(m)$ for all i and let $|\mathcal{O}| = L(m)^k$. Define the utility of agent i to be:

$$u(t_i, s, r_i) = \begin{cases} -|t_i - r_i|, & \text{If } r_i \in s; \\ -1, & \text{otherwise.} \end{cases}$$

In other words, agents are associated with points on the line, and an outcome is an assignment of a location on the line to each of the k facilities. Agents can react to a set of facilities by deciding which one to go to, and their cost for such a decision is the distance between their own location (i.e., their type) and the facility that they have chosen. Note that $r_i(t_i, s)$ is here the closest facility $r_i \in s$.

We can instantiate Theorem 10.4. In this case, we have: $|\mathcal{O}| = (m+1)^k$ and $\gamma = 1/m$, because any two positions $t_i \neq t_i'$ differ by at least $1/m$. Hence, we have:

Theorem 10.5. M_ϵ^P instantiated for the facility location game is strictly truthful and achieves social welfare at least:

$$\text{OPT} - O\left(\sqrt{\frac{km(m+1)^k \log m}{n}}\right).$$

This is already very good for small numbers of facilities k, since we expect that $\text{OPT} = \Omega(1)$.

10.3 Mechanism design for privacy aware agents

In the previous section, we saw that differential privacy can be useful as a tool to design mechanisms, *for agents who care only about the outcome chosen by the mechanism.* We here primarily viewed privacy as a tool to accomplish goals in traditional mechanism design. As a side affect, these mechanisms also preserved the privacy of the reported player types. Is this itself a worthy goal? *Why* might we want our mechanisms to preserve the privacy of agent types?

A bit of reflection reveals that agents might care about privacy. Indeed, basic introspection suggests that in the real world, agents value the ability to keep certain "sensitive" information private, for example, health information or sexual preferences. In this section, we consider the question of how to model this value for privacy, and various approaches taken in the literature.

Given that agents might have preferences for privacy, it is worth considering the design of mechanisms that preserve privacy *as an additional goal*, even for tasks such as welfare maximization that we can already solve non-privately. As we will see, it is indeed possible to generalize the VCG mechanism to *privately* approximately optimize social welfare in *any* social choice problem, with a smooth trade-off between the privacy parameter and the approximation parameter, all while guaranteeing exact dominant strategy truthfulness.

However, we might wish to go further. In the presence of agents with preferences for privacy, if we wish to design truthful mechanisms, we must somehow model their preferences for privacy in their utility function, and then design mechanisms which are truthful with respect to these new "privacy aware" utility functions. As we have seen with differential privacy, it is most natural to model privacy as a property of the mechanism itself. Thus, our utility functions are not merely functions of the outcome, but functions of the outcome and of the mechanism itself. In almost all models, agent utilities for outcomes are treated as linearly separable, that is, we will have for each agent i,

$$u_i(o, \mathcal{M}, t) \equiv \mu_i(o) - c_i(o, \mathcal{M}, t).$$

Here $\mu_i(o)$ represents agent is utility for outcome o and $c_i(o, \mathcal{M}, t)$ the (privacy) cost that agent i experiences when outcome o is chosen with mechanism $\mathcal{M}$.

We will first consider perhaps the simplest (and most naïve) model for the privacy cost function c_i. Recall that for $\epsilon \ll 1$, differential privacy promises that for each agent i, and for every possible utility function f_i, type vector $t \in \mathcal{T}^n$, and deviation $t_i' \in \mathcal{T}$:

$$|\mathbb{E}_{o \sim M(t_i, t_{-i})}[f_i(o)] - \mathbb{E}_{o \sim M(t_i', t_{-i})}[f_i(o)]| \leq 2\epsilon \mathbb{E}_{o \sim M(t)}[f_i(o)].$$

If we view f_i as representing the "expected future utility" for agent i, it is therefore natural to model agent i's cost for having his data used in an ϵ-differentially private computation as being linear in ϵ. That is, we think of agent i as being parameterized by some value $v_i \in \mathbb{R}$, and take:

$$c_i(o, \mathcal{M}, t) = \epsilon v_i,$$

where ϵ is the smallest value such that $\mathcal{M}$ is ϵ-differentially private. Here we imagine v_i to represent a quantity like $\mathbb{E}_{o \sim M(t)}[f_i(o)]$. In this setting, c_i does not depend on the outcome o or the type profile t.

Using this naïve privacy measure, we discuss a basic problem in private data analysis: how to collect the data, when the owners of the data value their privacy and insist on being compensated for it. In this setting, there is no "outcome" that agents value, other than payments, there is only dis-utility for privacy loss. We will then discuss shortcomings of this (and other) measures of the dis-utility for privacy loss, as well as privacy in more general mechanism design settings when agents *do* have utility for the outcome of the mechanism.

10.3.1 A private generalization of the VCG mechanism

Suppose we have a general social choice problem, defined by an outcome space $\mathcal{O}$, and a set of agents N with arbitrary preferences over the outcomes given by $u_i : \mathcal{O} \to [0, 1]$. We might want to choose an outcome $o \in \mathcal{O}$ to maximize the *social welfare* $F(o) = \frac{1}{n} \sum_{i=1}^{n} u_i(o)$. It is well known that in any such setting, the *VCG* mechanism can implement the outcome o^* which exactly maximizes the social welfare, while charging payments that make truth-telling a dominant strategy. What if we want to achieve the same result, while also preserving privacy? How must the privacy parameter ϵ trade off with our approximation to the optimal social welfare?

Recall that we could use the exponential mechanism to choose an outcome $o \in \mathcal{O}$, with quality score F. For privacy parameter ϵ, this would give a distribution $\mathcal{M}_\epsilon$ defined to be $\Pr[\mathcal{M}_\epsilon = o] \propto \exp\left(\frac{\epsilon F(o)}{2n}\right)$. Moreover, this mechanism has good social welfare properties: with probability $1 - \beta$, it selects some o such that: $F(o) \geq F(o^*) - \frac{2}{\epsilon n}\left(\ln \frac{|\mathcal{O}|}{\beta}\right)$. But as we saw, differential privacy only gives ϵ-approximate truthfulness.

However, it can be shown that $\mathcal{M}_\epsilon$ is the solution to the following exact optimization problem:

$$\mathcal{M}_\epsilon = \arg\max_{\mathcal{D} \in \Delta \mathcal{O}} \left(\mathbb{E}_{o \sim \mathcal{D}}[F(o)] + \frac{2}{\epsilon n} H(\mathcal{D}) \right),$$

where H represents the *Shannon Entropy* of the distribution $\mathcal{D}$. In other words, the exponential mechanism is the distribution which exactly maximizes the expected social welfare, *plus* the entropy of the distribution weighted by $2/(\epsilon n)$. This is significant for the following reason: it is known that any mechanism that *exactly* maximizes expected player utilities in any finite range (known as maximal in distributional range mechanisms) can be paired with payments to be made exactly dominant strategy truthful. The exponential mechanism is the distribution that *exactly* maximizes expected social welfare, plus entropy. In other words, if we imagine that we have added a single additional player whose utility is exactly the entropy of the distribution, then the exponential mechanism is maximal in distributional range. Hence, it can be paired with payments that make truthful reporting a dominant strategy for all players — in particular, for the n real players. Moreover, it can be shown how to charge payments in such a way as to preserve privacy. The upshot is that for any social choice problem, the social welfare can be approximated in a manner that both preserves differential privacy, and is exactly truthful.

10.3.2 The sensitive surveyor's problem

In this section, we consider the problem of a data analyst who wishes to conduct a study using the private data of a collection of individuals. However, he must *convince* these individuals to hand over their data! Individuals experience costs for privacy loss. The data analyst can mitigate these costs by guaranteeing differential privacy and compensating them for their loss, while trying to get a representative sample of data.

Consider the following stylized problem of the sensitive surveyor Alice. She is tasked with conducting a survey of a set of n individuals N, to determine what proportion of the individuals $i \in N$ satisfy some property $P(i)$. Her ultimate goal is to discover the true value of this statistic, $s = \frac{1}{n}|\{i \in N : P(i)\}|$, but if that is not possible, she will be satisfied with some estimate $\hat{s}$ such that the error, $|\hat{s} - s|$, is minimized. We will adopt a notion of accuracy based on large deviation bounds, and say that a surveying mechanism is α-accurate if $\Pr[|\hat{s} - s| \geq \alpha] \leq \frac{1}{3}$. The inevitable catch is that individuals value their privacy and will not participate in the survey for free. Individuals experience some *cost* as a function of their loss in privacy when they interact with Alice, and must be compensated for this loss. To make matters worse, these individuals are rational (i.e., selfish) agents, and are apt to misreport their costs to Alice if doing so will result in a financial gain. This places Alice's problem squarely in the domain of mechanism design, and requires Alice to develop a scheme for trading off statistical accuracy with cost, all while managing the incentives of the individuals.

As an aside, this stylized problem is broadly relevant to any organization that makes use of collections of potentially sensitive data. This includes, for example, the use of search logs to provide search query completion and the use of browsing history to improve search engine ranking, the use of social network data to select display ads and to recommend new links, and the myriad other data-driven services now available on the web. In all of these cases, value is being derived from the statistical properties of a collection of sensitive data in exchange for some payment.[4]

Collecting data in exchange for some fixed price could lead to a biased estimate of population statistics, because such a scheme will result in collecting data only from those individuals who value their privacy less than the price being offered. However, without interacting with the agents, we have no way of knowing what price we can offer so that we will have broad enough participation to guarantee that the answer we collect has only small bias. To obtain an accurate estimate of the statistic, it is therefore natural to consider buying private data using an auction — as a means of discovering this price. There are two obvious obstacles which one must confront when conducting an auction for private data, and an additional obstacle which is less obvious but more insidious. The first obstacle is that one must have a quantitative

---

[4]The payment need not be explicit and/or dollar denominated — for example, it may be the use of a "free" service.

formalization of "privacy" which can be used to measure agents' costs under various operations on their data. Here, differential privacy provides an obvious tool. For small values of ϵ, because $\exp(\epsilon) \approx (1 + \epsilon)$, and so as discussed earlier, a simple (but possibly naive) first cut at a model is to view each agent as having some *linear* cost for participating in a private study. We here imagine that each agent i has an unknown value for privacy v_i, and experiences a cost $c_i(\epsilon) = \epsilon v_i$ when his private data is used in an ϵ-differentially private manner.[5] The second obstacle is that our objective is to trade off with *statistical accuracy*, and the latter is not well-studied objective in mechanism design.

The final, more insidious obstacle, is that an individual's cost for privacy loss may be highly correlated with his private data itself! Suppose we only know Bob has a high value for privacy of his AIDS status, but do not explicitly know his AIDS status itself. This is already disclosive because Bob's AIDS status is likely correlated with his value for privacy, and knowing that he has a high cost for privacy lets us update our belief about what his private data might be. More to the point, suppose that in the first step of a survey of AIDS prevalence, we ask each individual to report their value for privacy, with the intention of then running an auction to choose which individuals to buy data from. If agents report truthfully, we may find that the reported values naturally form two clusters: low value agents, and high value agents. In this case, we may have learned something about the population statistic even before collecting any data or making any payments— and therefore, the agents will have already experienced a cost. As a result, the agents may misreport their value, which could introduce a bias in the survey results. This phenomenon makes direct revelation mechanisms problematic, and distinguishes this problem from classical mechanism design.

Armed with a means of quantifying an agent i's loss for allowing his data to be used by an ϵ-differentially-private algorithm $(c_i(\epsilon) = \epsilon v_i)$, we are almost ready to describe results for the sensitive surveyor's problem. Recall that a differentially private algorithm is some mapping $M : \mathcal{T}^n \to \mathcal{O}$, for a general type space $\mathcal{T}$. It remains to define what

---

[5]As we will discuss later, this assumption can be problematic.

exactly the type space $\mathcal{T}$ is. We will consider two models. In both models, we will associate with each individual a bit $b_i \in \{0,1\}$ which represents whether they satisfy the sensitive predicate $P(i)$, as well as a value for privacy $v_i \in \mathbb{R}^+$.

1. In the *insensitive value model*, we calculate the ϵ parameter of the private mechanism by letting the type space be $\mathcal{T} = \{0,1\}$: i.e., we measure privacy cost only with respect to how the mechanism treats the sensitive bit b_i, and ignore how it treats the reported values for privacy, v_i.[6]

2. In the *sensitive value model*, we calculate the ϵ parameter of the private mechanism by letting the type space be $\mathcal{T} = (\{0,1\} \times \mathbb{R}^+)$: i.e., we measure privacy with respect to how it treats the pair (b_i, v_i) for each individual.

Intuitively, the insensitive value model treats individuals as ignoring the potential privacy loss due to correlations between their values for privacy and their private bits, whereas the sensitive value model treats individuals as assuming these correlations are worst-case, i.e., their values v_i are just as disclosive as their private bits b_i. It is known that in the insensitive value model, one can derive approximately optimal direct revelation mechanisms that achieve high accuracy and low cost. By contrast, in the *sensitive value model*, no individually rational direct revelation mechanism can achieve any non-trivial accuracy.

This leaves a somewhat unsatisfying state of affairs. The sensitive value model captures the delicate issues that we really want to deal with, and yet there we have an impossibility result! Getting around this result in a satisfying way (e.g., by changing the model, or the powers of the mechanism) remains an intriguing open question.

10.3.3 Better measures for the cost of privacy

In the previous section, we took the naive modeling assumption that the cost experienced by participation in an ϵ-differentially private mechanism M was $c_i(o, \mathcal{M}, t) = \epsilon v_i$ for some numeric value v_i. This measure

---

[6]That is, the part of the mapping dealing with reported values need not be differentially private.

is problematic for several reasons. First, although differential privacy promises that any agent's loss in utility is *upper bounded* by a quantity that is (approximately) linear in ϵ, there is no reason to believe that agents' costs are *lower bounded* by such a quantity. That is, while taking $c_i(o, \mathcal{M}, t) \leq \epsilon v_i$ is well motivated, there is little support for making the inequality an equality. Second, (it turns out) *any* privacy measure which is a deterministic function only of ϵ (not just a linear function) leads to problematic behavioral predictions.

So how else might we model c_i? One natural measure is the *mutual information* between the reported type of agent i, and the outcome of the mechanism. For this to be well defined, we must be in a world where each agent's type t_i is drawn from a known prior, $t_i \sim \mathcal{T}$. Each agent's strategy is a mapping $\sigma_i : \mathcal{T} \to \mathcal{T}$, determining what type he reports, given his true type. We could then define

$$c_i(o, \mathcal{M}, \sigma) = I(\mathcal{T}; \mathcal{M}(t_{-i}, \sigma(\mathcal{T})),$$

where I is the mutual information between the random variable $\mathcal{T}$ representing the prior on agent is type, and $\mathcal{M}(t_{-i}, \sigma(\mathcal{T}))$, the random variable representing the outcome of the mechanism, given agent is strategy.

This measure has significant appeal, because it represents how "related" the output of the mechanism is to the true type of agent i. However, in addition to requiring a prior over agent types, observe an interesting paradox that results from this measure of privacy loss. Consider a world in which there are two kinds of sandwich breads: Rye (R), and Wheat (W). Moreover, in this world, sandwich preferences are highly embarrassing and held private. The prior on types $\mathcal{T}$ is uniform over R and W, and the mechanism $\mathcal{M}$ simply gives agent i a sandwich of the type that he purports to prefer. Now consider two possible strategies, σ_{truthful} and σ_{random}. σ_{truthful} corresponds to truthfully reporting sandwich preferences (and subsequently leads to eating the preferred sandwich type), while σ_{random} randomly reports independent of true type (and results in the preferred sandwich only half the time). The cost of using the random strategy is $I(\mathcal{T}; \mathcal{M}(t_{-i}, \sigma_{\text{random}}(\mathcal{T}))) = 0$, since the output is independent of agent i's type. On the other hand, the cost of truthfully reporting is $I(\mathcal{T}; \mathcal{M}(t_{-i}, \sigma_{\text{truthful}}(\mathcal{T}))) = 1$, since the sandwich outcome is now the identity function on agent is type. However, from the perspective of any outside observer, the two strategies are indistinguishable! In both cases, agent i receives a uniformly random sandwich. Why then should anyone choose the random strategy? So long as an adversary *believes* they are choosing randomly, they should choose the honest strategy.

Another approach, which does not need a prior on agent types, is as follows. We may model agents as having a cost function c_i that satisfies:

$$|c_i(o, \mathcal{M}, t)| = \ln \left(\max_{t_i, t_i' \in \mathcal{T}} \frac{\Pr[\mathcal{M}(t_i, t_{-i}) = o]}{\Pr[\mathcal{M}(t_i', t_{-i}) = o]} \right).$$

Note that if $\mathcal{M}$ is ϵ-differentially private, then

$$\max_{t \in \mathcal{T}^n} \max_{o \in \mathcal{O}} \max_{t_i, t_i' \in \mathcal{T}} \ln \left(\frac{\Pr[\mathcal{M}(t_i, t_{-i}) = o]}{\Pr[\mathcal{M}(t_i', t_{-i}) = o]} \right) \leq \epsilon.$$

That is, we can view differential privacy as bounding the *worst-case* privacy loss over all possible outcomes, whereas the measure proposed here considers only the privacy loss for the outcome o (and type vector t) actually realized. Thus, for any differentially private mechanism $\mathcal{M}$, $|c_i(o, \mathcal{M}, t)| \leq \epsilon$ for all o, t, but it will be important that the cost can vary by outcome.

We can then consider the following allocation rule for maximizing social welfare $F(o) = \sum_{i=1}^n u_i(o)$.[7] We discuss the case when $|\mathcal{O}| = 2$ (which does not require payments), but it is possible to analyze the general case (with payments), which privately implements the VCG mechanism for any social choice problem.

1. For each outcome $o \in \mathcal{O}$, choose a random number r_o from the distribution $\Pr[r_o = x] \propto \exp(-\epsilon|x|)$.
2. Output $o^* = \arg \max_{o \in \mathcal{O}} (F(o) + r_o)$.

The above mechanism is ϵ-differentially private, and that it is truthful for privacy aware agents, so long as for each agent i, and for the two outcomes $o, o' \in \mathcal{O}$, $|\mu_i(o) - \mu_i(o')| > 2\epsilon$. Note that this will be true

---

[7]This allocation rule is extremely similar to, and indeed can be modified to be identical to the exponential mechanism.

for small enough ϵ so long as agent utilities for outcomes are distinct. The analysis proceeds by considering an arbitrary fixed realization of the random variables r_o, and an arbitrary deviation t_i' from truthful reporting for the ith agent. There are two cases: In the first case, the deviation does not change the outcome o of the mechanism. In this case, *neither* the agent's utility for the outcome μ_i, nor his cost for privacy loss c_i change at all, and so the agent does not benefit from deviating. In the second case, if the outcome changes from o to o' when agent i deviates, it must be that $\mu_i(o') < \mu_i(o) - 2\epsilon$. By differential privacy, however, $|c_i(o, \mathcal{M}, t) - c_i(o', \mathcal{M}, t)| \leq 2\epsilon$, and so the change in privacy cost cannot be enough to make it beneficial.

Finally, the most conservative approach to modeling costs for privacy generally considered is as follows. Given an ϵ-differentially private mechanism $\mathcal{M}$, assume only that

$$c_i(o, \mathcal{M}, t) \leq \epsilon v_i,$$

for some number v_i. This is similar to the linear cost functions that we considered earlier, but crucially, here we assume only an upper bound. This assumption is satisfied by all of the other models for privacy cost that we have considered thus far. It can be shown that many mechanisms that combine a differentially private algorithm with a punishing mechanism that has the ability to restrict user choices, like those that we considered in Section 10.2.3, maintain their truthfulness properties in the presence of agents with preferences for privacy, so long as the values v_i are bounded.

10.4 Bibliographical notes

This section is based off of a survey of Pai and Roth [70] and a survey of Roth [73]. The connections between differential privacy and mechanism design were first suggested by Jason Hartline and investigated by McSherry and Talwar in their seminal work, "Mechanism Design via Differential Privacy" [61], where they considered the application of differential privacy to designing approximately truthful digital goods auctions. The best result for exactly truthful mechanisms in the digital goods setting is due to Balcan et al. [2].

The problem of designing exactly truthful mechanisms using differential privacy as a tool was first explored by Nissim, Smorodinsky, and Tennenholtz in [69], who also first posed a criticism as differential privacy (by itself) used as a solution concept. The example in this section of using differential privacy to obtain exactly truthful mechanisms is taken directly from [69]. The sensitive surveyors problem was first considered by Ghosh and Roth [36], and expanded on by [56, 34, 75, 16]. Fleischer and Lyu [34] consider the Bayesian setting discussed in this section, and Ligett and Roth [56] consider the worst-case setting with take-it-or-leave-it offers, both in an attempt to get around the impossibility result of [36]. Ghosh and Ligett consider a related model in which participation decisions (and privacy guarantees) are determined only in equilibrium [35].

The question of conducting mechanism design in the presence of agents who explicitly value privacy as part of their utility function was first raised by the influential work of Xiao [85], who considered (among other measures for privacy cost) the mutual information cost function. Following this, Chen et al. [15] and Nissim et al. [67] showed how in two distinct models, truthful mechanisms can sometimes be designed even for agents who value privacy. Chen Chong, Kash, Moran, and Vadhan considered the outcome-based cost function that we discussed in this section, and Nissim, Orlandi, and Smorodinsky considered the conservative model of only upper bounding each agent's cost by a linear function in ϵ> The "sandwich paradox" of valuing privacy according to mutual information is due to Nissim, Orlandi, and Smorodinsky.

Huang and Kannan proved that the exponential mechanism could be made exactly truthful with the addition of payments [49]. Kearns Pai, Roth, and Ullman showed how differential privacy could be used to derive asymptotically truthful equilibrium selection mechanisms [54] by privately computing correlated equilibria in large games. These results were strengthened by Rogers and Roth [71], who showed how to privately compute approximate *Nash* equilibria in large congestion games, which leads to stronger incentive properties of the mechanism. Both of these papers use the solution concept of "Joint Differential Privacy," which requires that for every player i, the joint distribution on messages sent to *other* players $j \neq i$ be differentially private in is report. This solution concept has also proven useful in other settings of private mechanism design settings, including an algorithm for computing private matchings by Hsu et al. [47].

11

Differential Privacy and Machine Learning

One of the most useful tasks in data analysis is machine learning: the problem of automatically finding a simple rule to accurately predict certain unknown characteristics of never before seen data. Many machine learning tasks can be performed under the constraint of differential privacy. In fact, the constraint of privacy is not necessarily at odds with the goals of machine learning, both of which aim to extract information from the distribution from which the data was drawn, rather than from individual data points. In this section, we survey a few of the most basic results on private machine learning, without attempting to cover this large field completely.

The goal in machine learning is very often similar to the goal in private data analysis. The *learner* typically wishes to learn some simple rule that explains a data set. However, she wishes this rule to generalize — that is, it should be that the rule she learns not only correctly describes the data that she has on hand, but that it should also be able to correctly describe *new* data that is drawn from the same distribution. Generally, this means that she wants to learn a rule that captures distributional information about the data set on hand, in a way that does not depend too specifically on any single data point. Of course, this is exactly the goal of private data analysis — to reveal *distributional information* about the private data set, without revealing too much about any single individual in the dataset. It should come as no surprise then that machine learning and private data analysis are closely linked. In fact, as we will see, we are often able to perform private machine learning *nearly as accurately, with nearly the same number of examples* as we can perform non-private machine learning.

Let us first briefly define the problem of machine learning. Here, we will follow Valiant's *PAC* (Or *Probably Approximately Correct*) model of machine learning. Let $\mathcal{X} = \{0,1\}^d$ be the domain of "unlabeled examples." Think of each $x \in \mathcal{X}$ as a vector containing d boolean attributes. We will think of vectors $x \in \mathcal{X}$ as being paired with *labels* $y \in \{0,1\}$.

Definition 11.1. A *labeled example* is a pair $(x,y) \in \mathcal{X} \times \{0,1\}$: a vector paired with a label.

A learning problem is defined as a distribution $\mathcal{D}$ over labeled examples. The goal will to be to find a function $f : \mathcal{X} \to \{0,1\}$ that correctly labels almost all of the examples drawn from the distribution.

Definition 11.2. Given a function $f : \mathcal{X} \to \{0,1\}$ and a distribution $\mathcal{D}$ over labeled examples, the *error rate* of f on $\mathcal{D}$ is:

$$\mathrm{err}(f, \mathcal{D}) = \Pr_{(x,y) \sim \mathcal{D}}[f(x) \neq y]$$

We can also define the error rate of f over a finite sample D:

$$\mathrm{err}(f, D) = \frac{1}{|D|} |\{(x,y) \in D : f(x) \neq y\}|.$$

A learning *algorithm* gets to observe some number of labeled examples drawn from $\mathcal{D}$, and has the goal of finding a function f with as small an error rate as possible when measured on $\mathcal{D}$. Two parameters in measuring the quality of a learning algorithm are its running time, and the number of examples it needs to see in order to find a good hypothesis.

Definition 11.3. An algorithm A is said to PAC-learn a class of functions C over d dimensions if for every $\alpha, \beta > 0$, there exists an

$m = \text{poly}(d, 1/\alpha, \log(1/\beta))$ such that for every distribution $\mathcal{D}$ over labeled examples, A takes as input m labeled examples drawn from $\mathcal{D}$ and outputs a hypothesis $f \in C$ such that with probability $1 - \beta$:

$$\text{err}(f, \mathcal{D}) \leq \min_{f^* \in C} \text{err}(f^*, \mathcal{D}) + \alpha$$

If $\min_{f^* \in C} \text{err}(f^*, \mathcal{D}) = 0$, the learner is said to operate in the *realizable* setting (i.e., there exists some function in the class which perfectly labels the data). Otherwise, the learner is said to operate in the *agnostic* setting. If A also has run time that is polynomial in $d, 1/\alpha$, and $\log(1/\beta)$, then the learner is said to be *efficient*. If there is an algorithm which PAC-learns C, then C is said to be PAC-learnable.

The above definition of learning allows the learner to have direct access to labeled examples. It is sometimes also useful to consider models of learning in which the algorithm only has oracle access to some noisy information about $\mathcal{D}$.

Definition 11.4. A *statistical query* is some function $\phi : \mathcal{X} \times \{0, 1\} \to [0, 1]$. A *statistical query oracle* for a distribution over labeled examples $\mathcal{D}$ with tolerance τ is an oracle $\mathcal{O}_{\mathcal{D}}^\tau$ such that for every statistical query ϕ:

$$\left| \mathcal{O}_{\mathcal{D}}^\tau(\phi) - \mathbb{E}_{(x,y) \sim \mathcal{D}}[\phi(x, y)] \right| \leq \tau$$

In other words, an SQ oracle takes as input a statistical query ϕ, and outputs some value that is guaranteed to be within $\pm\tau$ of the expected value of ϕ on examples drawn from $\mathcal{D}$.

The statistical query model of learning was introduced to model the problem of learning in the presence of noise.

Definition 11.5. An algorithm A is said to SQ-learn a class of functions C over d dimensions if for every $\alpha, \beta > 0$ there exists an $m = \text{poly}(d, 1/\alpha, \log(1/\beta))$ such that A makes at most m queries of tolerance $\tau = 1/m$ to $\mathcal{O}_{\mathcal{D}}^\tau$, and with probability $1 - \beta$, outputs a hypothesis $f \in C$ such that:

$$\text{err}(f, \mathcal{D}) \leq \min_{f^* \in C} \text{err}(f^*, \mathcal{D}) + \alpha$$

Note that an SQ learning algorithm does not get any access to $\mathcal{D}$ except through the SQ oracle. As with PAC learning, we can talk about an SQ learning algorithm operating in either the realizable or the agnostic setting, and talk about the computational efficiency of the learning algorithm. We say that a class C is SQ learnable if there exists an SQ learning algorithm for C.

11.1 The sample complexity of differentially private machine learning

Perhaps the first question that one might ask, with respect to the relationship between privacy and learning, is "When is it possible to privately perform machine learning"? In other words, you might ask for a PAC learning algorithm that takes as input a dataset (implicitly assumed to be sampled from some distribution $\mathcal{D}$), and then privately output a hypothesis f that with high probability has low error over the distribution. A more nuanced question might be, "How many *additional* samples are required to privately learn, as compared with the number of samples *already required* to learn without the constraint of differential privacy?" Similarly, "How much additional runtime is necessary to privately learn, as compared with the run-time required to learn non-privately?" We will here briefly sketch known results for $(\varepsilon, 0)$-differential privacy. In general, better results for (ε, δ)-differential privacy will follow from using the advanced composition theorem.

A foundational *information theoretic result* in private machine learning is that private PAC learning is possible with a polynomial number of samples if and only if non-private PAC learning is possible with a polynomial number of samples, even in the agnostic setting. In fact, the increase in sample complexity necessary is relatively small — however, this result does not preserve *computational efficiency*. One way to do this is directly via the exponential mechanism. We can instantiate the exponential mechanism with a range $R = C$, equal to the class of queries to be learned. Given a database D, we can use the quality score $q(f, D) = -\frac{1}{|D|}|\{(x, y) \in D : f(x) \neq y\}|$: i.e., we seek to minimize the fraction of misclassified examples in the private dataset. This is clearly a $1/n$ sensitive function of the private data, and so we have via our utility theorem for the exponential mechanism that with probability $1 - \beta$, this mechanism returns a function $f \in C$ that correctly labels an $\text{OPT} - \frac{2(\log |C| + \log \frac{1}{\beta})}{\varepsilon n}$ fraction of the points in the database correctly. Recall, however, that in the learning setting, we view the database D as consisting of n i.i.d. draws from some distribution over labeled examples $\mathcal{D}$. Recall the discussion of sampling bounds in Lemma 4.3. A Chernoff bound combined with a union bound tells us that with high probability, if D consists of n i.i.d. samples drawn from $\mathcal{D}$, then for all $f \in C$: $|\text{err}(f, D) - \text{err}(f, \mathcal{D})| \leq O(\sqrt{\frac{\log |C|}{n}})$. Hence, if we wish to find a hypothesis that has error within α of the optimal error on the distribution $\mathcal{D}$, it suffices to draw a database D consisting of $n \geq \log |C|/\alpha^2$ samples, and learn the best classifier f^* on D.

Now consider the problem of privately PAC learning, using the exponential mechanism as described above. Recall that, by Theorem 3.11, it is highly unlikely that the exponential mechanism will return a function f with utility score that is inferior to that of the optimal f^* by more than an additive factor of $O((\Delta u/\varepsilon) \log |C|)$, where in this case Δu, the sensitivity of the utility function, is $1/n$. That is, with high probability the exponential mechanism will return a function $f \in C$ such that:

$$\text{err}(f, D) \leq \min_{f^* \in C} \text{err}(f^*, D) + O\left(\frac{(\log |C|)}{\varepsilon n}\right)$$

$$\leq \min_{f^* \in C} \text{err}(f^*, \mathcal{D}) + O\left(\sqrt{\frac{\log |C|}{n}}\right) + O\left(\frac{(\log |C|)}{\varepsilon n}\right).$$

Hence, if we wish to find a hypothesis that has error within α of the optimal error on the distribution $\mathcal{D}$, it suffices to draw a database D consisting of:

$$n \geq O\left(\max\left(\frac{\log |C|}{\varepsilon \alpha}, \frac{\log |C|}{\alpha^2}\right)\right),$$

which is not asymptotically any more than the database size that is required for non-private learning, whenever $\varepsilon \geq \alpha$.

A corollary of this simple calculation[1] is that (ignoring computational efficiency), a class of functions C is PAC learnable if and only if it is privately PAC learnable.

Can we say something stronger about a concept class C that is SQ learnable? Observe that if C is efficiently SQ learnable, then the learning algorithm for C need only access the data through an SQ oracle, which is very amenable to differential privacy: note that an SQ oracle answers an expectation query defined over a predicate $\phi(x, y) \in [0, 1]$, $\mathbb{E}_{(x,y)\sim\mathcal{D}}[\phi(x, y)]$, which is only $1/n$ sensitive when estimated on a database D which is a sample of size n from $\mathcal{D}$. Moreover, the learning algorithm does not need to receive the answer exactly, but can be run with any answer a that has the property that: $|\mathbb{E}_{(x,y)\sim\mathcal{D}}[\phi(x, y)]-a| \leq \tau$: that is, the algorithm can be run using *noisy answers* on *low sensitivity queries*. The benefit of this is that we can answer such queries computationally efficiently, using the Laplace mechanism — but at the expense of requiring a potentially large sample size. Recall that the Laplace mechanism can answer m $1/n$ sensitive queries with $(\varepsilon, 0)$-differential privacy and with expected worst-case error $\alpha = O(\frac{m \log m}{\varepsilon n})$. Therefore, an SQ learning algorithm which requires the answers to m queries with accuracy α can be run with a sample size of $n = O(\max(\frac{m \log m}{\varepsilon \alpha}, \frac{\log m}{\alpha^2}))$. Let us compare this to the sample size required for a non-private SQ learner. If the SQ learner needs to make m queries to tolerance α, then by a Chernoff bound and a union bound, a sample size of $O(\log m/\alpha^2)$ suffices. Note that for $\varepsilon = O(1)$ and error $\alpha = O(1)$, the non-private algorithm potentially requires exponentially fewer samples. However, at the error tolerance $\alpha \leq 1/m$ as allowed in the definition of SQ learning, the sample complexity for private SQ learning is no worse than the sample complexity for non-private SQ learning, for $\epsilon = \Theta(1)$.

The upshot is that *information theoretically*, privacy poses very little hinderance to machine learning. Moreover, for any algorithm that accesses the data only though an SQ oracle,[2] then the reduction to

---

[1] Together with corresponding lower bounds that show that for general C, it is not possible to non-privately PAC learn using a sample with $o(\log |C|/\alpha^2)$ points.

[2] And in fact, almost every class (with the lone exception of *parity functions*) of functions known to be PAC learnable is also learnable using only an SQ oracle.

private learning is immediate via the Laplace mechanism, and preserves computational efficiency!

11.2 Differentially private online learning

In this section, we consider a slightly different learning problem, known as the problem of *learning from expert advice*. This problem will appear somewhat different from the classification problems that we discussed in the previous section, but in fact, the simple algorithm presented here is extremely versatile, and can be used to perform classification among many other tasks which we will not discuss here.

Imagine that you are betting on horse races, but unfortunately know nothing about horses! Nevertheless, you have access to the opinions of some k *experts*, who every day make a prediction about which horse is going to win. Each day you can choose one of the experts whose advice you will follow, and each day, following your bet, you learn which horse actually won. How should you decide which expert to follow each day, and how should you evaluate your performance? The experts are not perfect (in fact they might not even be any good!), and so it is not reasonable to expect you to make the correct bet all of the time, or even most of the time if none of the experts do so. However, you might have a weaker goal: can you bet on horses in such a way so that you do almost as well as *the best expert, in hindsight*?

Formally, an online learning algorithm A operates in the following environment:

1. Each day $t = 1, \ldots, T$:

    (a) A chooses an expert $a_t \in \{1, \ldots, k\}$
    (b) A observes a loss $\ell_i^t \in [0, 1]$ for each expert $i \in \{1, \ldots, k\}$ and experiences loss $\ell_{a_t}^t$.

For a sequence of losses $\ell^{\leq T} \equiv \{\ell^t\}_{t=1}^T$, we write:

$$L_i(\ell^{\leq T}) = \frac{1}{T} \sum_{t=1}^{T} \ell_i^t$$

to denote the total average loss of expert i over all T rounds, and write

$$L_A(\ell^{\leq T}) = \frac{1}{T} \sum_{t=1}^{T} \ell_{a_t}^t$$

to denote the total average loss of the algorithm.

The *regret* of the algorithm is defined to be the difference between the loss that it actually incurred, and the loss of the *best* expert in hindsight:

$$\text{Regret}(A, \ell^{\leq T}) = L_A(\ell^{\leq T}) - \min_i L_i(\ell^{\leq T}).$$

The goal in online learning is to design algorithms that have the guarantee that for *all possible loss sequences* $\ell^{\leq T}$, even adversarialy chosen, the regret is guaranteed to tend to zero as $T \to \infty$. In fact, this is possible using the multiplicative weights algorithm (known also by many names, e.g., the Randomized Weighted Majority Algorithm, Hedge, Exponentiated Gradient Descent, and multiplicative weights being among the most popular).

Remark 11.1. We have already seen this algorithm before in Section 4 — this is just the multiplicative weights update rule in another guise! In fact, it would have been possible to derive all of the results about the private multiplicative weights mechanism directly from the regret bound we state in Theorem 11.1.

Algorithm 15 The Multiplicative Weights (or Randomized Weighted Majority (RWM)) algorithm, version 1. It takes as input a stream of losses $\ell^1, \ell^2, \ldots$ and outputs a stream of actions $a_1, a_2, \ldots$. It is parameterized by an update parameter η.

RWM(η):

    For each $i \in \{1, \ldots, k\}$, let $w_i \leftarrow 1$.

    for $t = 1, \ldots$ **do**

        Choose action $a_t = i$ with probability proportional to w_i

        Observe ℓ^t and set $w_i \leftarrow w_i \cdot \exp(-\eta \ell_i^t)$, for each $i \in [k]$

    end for

It turns out that this simple algorithm already has a remarkable regret bound.

Theorem 11.1. For any adversarially chosen sequence of losses of length T, $\ell^{\leq T} = (\ell^1, \ldots, \ell^T)$ the Randomized Weighted Majority algorithm with update parameter η has the guarantee that:

$$\mathbb{E}[\text{Regret}(\text{RWM}(\eta), \ell^{\leq T})] \leq \eta + \frac{\ln(k)}{\eta T}, \tag{11.1}$$

where k is the number of experts. Choosing $\eta = \sqrt{\frac{\ln k}{T}}$ gives:

$$\mathbb{E}[\text{Regret}(\text{RWM}(\eta), \ell^{\leq T})] \leq 2\sqrt{\frac{\ln k}{T}}.$$

This remarkable theorem states that even faced with an adversarial sequence of losses, the Randomized Weighted Majority algorithm can do as well, on average, as the best expert among k in hindsight, minus only an additional additive term that goes to zero at a rate of $O(\sqrt{\frac{\ln k}{T}})$. In other words, after at most $T \leq 4\frac{\ln k}{\alpha^2}$ rounds, the regret of the randomized weighted majority algorithm is guaranteed to be at most α! Moreover, this bound is the best possible.

Can we achieve something similar, but under the constraint of differential privacy? Before we can ask this question, we must decide *what is the input database*, and at what granularity we would like to protect privacy? Since the input is the collection of loss vectors $\ell^{\leq T} = (\ell^1, \ldots, \ell^T)$, it is natural to view $\ell^{\leq T}$ as the database, and to view a neighboring database $\hat{\ell}^{\leq T}$ as one that differs in the entire loss vector in any single timestep: i.e., one in which for some fixed timestep t, $\hat{\ell}^i = \ell^i$ for all $i \neq t$, but in which ℓ^t and $\hat{\ell}^t$ can differ arbitrarily. The output of the algorithm is the sequence of actions that it chooses, $a_1, \ldots, a_T$, and it is this that we wish to be output in a differentially private manner.

Our first observation is that the randomized weighted majority algorithm chooses an action at each day t in a familiar manner! We here rephrase the algorithm in an equivalent way:

It chooses an action a_t with probability proportional to: $\exp(-\eta \sum_{j=1}^{t-1} \ell_i^j)$, which is simply the exponential mechanism with quality score $q(i, \ell^{<T}) = \sum_{j=1}^{t-1} \ell_i^j$, and privacy parameter $\varepsilon = 2\eta$. Note that because each $\ell_i^t \in [0, 1]$, the quality function has sensitivity 1. Thus,

---

Algorithm 16 The Multiplicative Weights (or Randomized Weighted Majority (RWM)) algorithm, rephrased. It takes as input a stream of losses $\ell^1, \ell^2, \ldots$ and outputs a stream of actions $a_1, a_2, \ldots$. It is parameterized by an update parameter η.

RWM(η):

    for $t = 1, \ldots$ **do**

        Choose action $a_t = i$ with probability proportional to $\exp(-\eta \sum_{j=1}^{t-1} \ell_i^j)$

        Observe ℓ^t

    end for

---

each round t, the randomized weighted majority algorithm chooses an action a_t in a way that preserves 2η differential privacy, so to achieve privacy ε it suffices to set $\eta = \varepsilon/2$.

Moreover, over the course of the run of the algorithm, it will choose an action T times. If we want the *entire* run of the algorithm to be (ε, δ)-differentially private for some ε and δ, we can thus simply apply our composition theorems. Recall that by Theorem 3.20, since there are T steps in total, if each step of the algorithm is $(\varepsilon', 0)$-differentially private for $\varepsilon' = \varepsilon/\sqrt{8T \ln(1/\delta)}$, then the entire algorithm will be (ε, δ) differentially private. Thus, the following theorem is immediate by setting $\eta = \varepsilon'/2$:

Theorem 11.2. For a sequence of losses of length T, the algorithm RWM(η) with $\eta = \dfrac{\varepsilon}{\sqrt{32T \ln(1/\delta)}}$ is (ε, δ)-differentially private.

Remarkably, we get this theorem *without modifying the original randomized weighted majority algorithm at all*, but rather just by setting η appropriately. In some sense, we are getting privacy for free! We can therefore use Theorem 11.1, the utility theorem for the RWM algorithm, without modification as well:

Theorem 11.3. For any adversarially chosen sequence of losses of length T, $\ell^{\leq T} = (\ell^1, \ldots, \ell^T)$ the Randomized Weighted Majority algorithm with update parameter $\eta = \frac{\varepsilon}{\sqrt{32T \ln(1/\delta)}}$ has the guarantee that:

$$\mathbb{E}[\text{Regret}(\text{RWM}(\eta), \ell^{\leq T})] \leq \frac{\varepsilon}{\sqrt{32T \ln(1/\delta)}} + \frac{\sqrt{32 \ln(1/\delta)} \ln k}{\varepsilon \sqrt{T}}$$

$$\leq \frac{\sqrt{128 \ln(1/\delta)} \ln k}{\varepsilon \sqrt{T}},$$

where k is the number of experts.

Since the per-round loss at each time step t is an independently chosen random variable (over the choices of a_t) with values bounded in $[-1, 1]$, we can also apply a Chernoff bound to get a high probability guarantee:

Theorem 11.4. For any adversarially chosen sequence of losses of length T, $\ell^{\leq T} = (\ell^1, \ldots, \ell^T)$ the Randomized Weighted Majority algorithm with update parameter $\eta = \frac{\varepsilon}{\sqrt{32T \ln(1/\delta)}}$ produces a sequence of actions such that with probability at least $1 - \beta$:

$$\text{Regret}(\text{RWM}(\eta), \ell^{\leq T}) \leq \frac{\sqrt{128 \ln(1/\delta)} \ln k}{\varepsilon \sqrt{T}} + \sqrt{\frac{\ln k/\beta}{T}}$$

$$= O\left(\frac{\sqrt{\ln(1/\delta)} \ln(k/\beta)}{\sqrt{\varepsilon T}}\right).$$

This bound is nearly as good as the best possible bound achievable even without privacy (i.e., the RWM bound) — the regret bound is larger only by a factor of $\Omega(\frac{\sqrt{\ln(k)} \ln(1/\delta)}{\varepsilon})$. (We note that by using a different algorithm with a more careful analysis, we can remove this extra factor of $\sqrt{\ln k}$). Since we are in fact using the same algorithm, efficiency is of course preserved as well. Here we have a powerful example in machine learning where privacy is nearly "free." Notably, just as with the non-private algorithm, our utility bound only gets better the longer we run the algorithm, while keeping the privacy guarantee the same.[3]

---

[3]Of course, we have to set the update parameter appropriately, just as we have to do with the non-private algorithm. This is easy when the number of rounds T is known ahead of time, but can also be done adaptively when the number of rounds is not known ahead of time.

11.3   Empirical risk minimization

In this section, we apply the randomized weighted majority algorithm discussed in the previous section to a special case of the problem of empirical risk minimization to learn a linear function. Rather than assuming an adversarial model, we will assume that *examples* are drawn from some known distribution, and we wish to learn a classifier from some finite number of samples from this distribution so that our loss will be low on *new* samples drawn from the same distribution.

Suppose that we have a distribution $\mathcal{D}$ over *examples* $x \in [-1,1]^d$, and for each such vector $x \in [-1,1]^d$, and for each vector $\theta \in [0,1]^d$ with $\|\theta\|_1 = 1$, we define the loss of θ on example x to be $\text{Loss}(\theta, x) = \langle \theta, x \rangle$. We wish to find a vector θ^* to minimize the *expected* loss over examples drawn from $\mathcal{D}$:

$$\theta^* = \arg \min_{\theta \in [0,1]^d : \|\theta\|_1 = 1} \mathbb{E}_{x \sim \mathcal{D}}[\langle \theta, x \rangle].$$

This problem can be used to model the task of finding a low error linear classifier. Typically our only access to the distribution $\mathcal{D}$ is through some collection of examples $S \subset [-1,1]^d$ drawn i.i.d. from $\mathcal{D}$, which serves as the input to our learning algorithm. We will here think of this sample S as our private database, and will be interested in how well we can privately approximate the error of θ^* as a function of $|S|$ (the *sample complexity* of the learning algorithm).

Our approach will be to reduce the problem to that of learning with expert advice, and apply the private version of the randomized weighted majority algorithm as discussed in the last section:

1. The *experts* will be the d standard basis vectors $\{e_1, \ldots, e_d\}$, where $e_i = (0, \ldots, 0, \underbrace{1}_{i}, 0, \ldots, 0)$.

2. Given an example $x \in [-1,1]^d$, we define a loss vector $\ell(x) \in [-1,1]^d$ by setting $\ell(x)_i = \langle e_i, x \rangle$ for each $i \in \{1, \ldots, d\}$. In other words, we simply set $\ell(x)_i = x_i$.

3. At time t, we choose a loss function ℓ^t by sampling $x \sim \mathcal{D}$ and setting $\ell^t = \ell(x)$.

Note that if we have a sample S from $\mathcal{D}$ of size $|S| = T$, then we can run the RWM algorithm on the sequence of losses as described above for a total of T rounds. This will produce a sequence of outputs $a_1, \ldots, a_T$, and we will define our final classifier to be $\theta^T \equiv \frac{1}{T} \sum_{i=1}^{T} a_i$. (Recall that each a_i is a standard basis vector $a_i \in \{e_1, \ldots, e_d\}$, and so we have $\|\theta^T\|_1 = 1$).

We summarize the algorithm below:

Algorithm 17 An algorithm for learning linear functions. It takes as input a private database of examples $S \subset [-1, 1]^d$, $S = (x_1, \ldots, x_T)$, and privacy parameters ε and δ.

LinearLearner(S, ε, δ):

   Let $\eta \leftarrow \dfrac{\varepsilon}{\sqrt{32T \ln(1/\delta)}}$
   for $t = 1$ to $T = |S|$ **do**
      Choose vector $a_t = e_i$ with probability proportional to $\exp(-\eta \sum_{j=1}^{t-1} \ell_i^j)$
      Let loss vector $\ell^t = (\langle e_1, x_t \rangle, \langle e_2, x_t \rangle, \ldots, \langle e_d, x_t \rangle)$.
   end for
   Output $\theta^T = \frac{1}{T} \sum_{t=1}^{T} a_t$.

We have already seen that LinearLearner is private, since it is simply an instantiation of the randomized weighted majority algorithm with the correct update parameter η:

Theorem 11.5. LinearLearner(S, ε, δ) is (ε, δ)-differentially private.

It remains to analyze the classification accuracy of LinearLearner, which amounts to considering the regret bound of the private RWM algorithm.

Theorem 11.6. If S consists of T i.i.d. samples $x \sim \mathcal{D}$, then with probability at least $1 - \beta$, LinearLearner outputs a vector θ^T such that:

$$\mathbb{E}_{x \sim \mathcal{D}}[\langle \theta^T, x \rangle] \leq \min_{\theta^*} \mathbb{E}_{x \sim \mathcal{D}}[\langle \theta^*, x \rangle] + O\left(\frac{\sqrt{\ln(1/\delta)} \ln(d/\beta)}{\sqrt{\varepsilon T}} \right),$$

where d is the number of experts.

Proof. By Theorem 11.4, we have the following guarantee with probability at least $1 - \beta/2$:

$$\frac{1}{T}\sum_{t=1}^{T}\langle a_t, x_t\rangle \leq \min_{i\in\{1,\dots,d\}}\left\langle e_i, \frac{1}{T}\sum_{t=1}^{T}x_t\right\rangle + O\left(\frac{\sqrt{\ln(1/\delta)}\ln(d/\beta)}{\sqrt{\varepsilon T}}\right)$$

$$= \min_{\theta^*\in[0,1]^d:\|\theta^*\|_1=1}\left\langle\theta^*, \frac{1}{T}\sum_{t=1}^{T}x_t\right\rangle + O\left(\frac{\sqrt{\ln(1/\delta)}\ln(d/\beta)}{\sqrt{\varepsilon T}}\right).$$

In the first equality, we use the fact that the minimum of a linear function over the simplex is achieved at a vertex of the simplex. Noting that each $x_t \sim \mathcal{D}$ independently and that each $\langle x_t, e_i\rangle$ is bounded in $[-1,1]$, we can apply Azuma's inequality twice to bound the two quantities with probability at least $1 - \beta/2$:

$$\left|\frac{1}{T}\sum_{t=1}^{T}\langle a_t, x_t\rangle - \frac{1}{T}\sum_{t=1}^{T}\mathbb{E}_{x\sim\mathcal{D}}\langle a_t, x\rangle\right|$$

$$= \left|\frac{1}{T}\sum_{t=1}^{T}\langle a_t, x_t\rangle - \mathbb{E}_{x\sim\mathcal{D}}\langle\theta^T, x\rangle\right| \leq O\left(\sqrt{\frac{\ln(1/\beta)}{T}}\right)$$

and

$$\max_{i\in\{1,\dots,d\}}\left|\left\langle e_i, \frac{1}{T}\sum_{t=1}^{T}x_t\right\rangle - \mathbb{E}_{x\sim\mathcal{D}}\langle e_i, x\rangle\right| \leq O\left(\sqrt{\frac{\ln(d/\beta)}{T}}\right).$$

Hence we also have:

$$\max_{\theta^*\in[0,1]^d:\|\theta^*\|_1=1}\left|\left\langle\theta^*, \frac{1}{T}\sum_{t=1}^{T}x_t\right\rangle - \mathbb{E}_{x\sim\mathcal{D}}\langle\theta^*, x\rangle\right| \leq O\left(\sqrt{\frac{\ln d/\beta}{T}}\right).$$

Combining these inequalities gives us our final result about the output of the algorithm θ^T:

$$\mathbb{E}_{x\sim\mathcal{D}}\langle\theta^T, x\rangle \leq \min_{\theta^*\in[0,1]^d:\|\theta^*\|_1=1}\mathbb{E}_{x\sim\mathcal{D}}\langle\theta^*, x\rangle + O\left(\frac{\sqrt{\ln(1/\delta)}\ln(d/\beta)}{\sqrt{\varepsilon T}}\right).$$

$\square$

11.4 Bibliographical notes

The PAC model of machine learning was introduced by Valiant in 1984 [83], and the SQ model was introduced by Kearns [53]. The randomized weighted majority algorithm is originally due to Littlestone and War-muth [57], and has been studied in many forms. See Blum and Mansour [9] or Arora et al. [1] for a survey. The regret bound that we use for the randomized weighted majority algorithm is given in [1].

Machine learning was one of the first topics studied in differential privacy, beginning with the work of Blum et al. [7], who showed that algorithms that operate in the SQ-learning framework could be converted into privacy preserving algorithms. The sample complexity of differentially private learning was first considered by Kasiviswanathan, Lee, Nissim, Raskhodnikova, and Smith, "What can we Learn Privately?" [52], which characterize the sample complexity of private learning up to polynomial factors. For more refined analysis of the sample complexity of private learning, see [3, 4, 12, 19].

There is also extensive work on efficient machine learning algorithms, including the well known frameworks of SVMs and empirical risk minimizers [13, 55, 76]. Spectral learning techniques, including PCA and low rank matrix approximation have also been studied [7, 14, 33, 42, 43, 51].

Private learning from expert advice was first considered by Dwork et al. [26]. The fact that the randomized weighted majority algorithm is privacy preserving without modification (when the update parameter is set appropriately) is folklore (following from advanced composition [32]) and has been widely used; for example, in [48]. For a more general study of private online learning, see [50], and for a more general study of empirical risk minimization, see [50, 13].

12

Additional Models

So far, we have made some implicit assumptions about the model of private data analysis. For example, we have assumed that there is some trusted curator who has direct access to the private dataset, and we have assumed that the adversary only has access to the output of the algorithm, not to any of its internal state during its execution. But what if this is not the case? What if we trust no one to look at our data, even to perform the privacy preserving data analysis? What if some hacker might gain access to the internal state of the private algorithm while it is running? In this section, we relax some of our previously held assumptions and consider these questions.

In this section we describe some additional computational models that have received attention in the literature.

- The *local model* is a generalization of randomized response (see Section 2), and is motivated by situations in which individuals do not trust the curator with their data. While this lack of trust can be addressed using secure multiparty computation to simulate the role played by the trusted curator, there are also some techniques that do not require cryptography.

The next two models consider streams of *events*, each of which may be associated with an individual. For example, an event may be a search by a particular person on an arbitrary term. In a given event stream, the (potentially many) events associated with a given individual can be arbitrarily interleaved with events associated with other individuals.

- In *pan-privacy* the curator is trusted, but may be subject to compulsory non-private data release, for example, because of a subpoena, or because the entity holding the information is purchased by another, possibly less trustworthy, entity. Thus, in pan-privacy the *internal state* of the algorithm is also differentially private, as is the joint distribution of the internal state and the outputs.

- The *continual observation* model addresses the question of maintaining privacy when the goal is to continually monitor and report statistics about events, such as purchases of over-the-counter medications that might be indicative of an impending epidemic. Some work addresses pan-privacy under continual observation.

12.1   The local model

So far, we have considered a *centralized* model of data privacy, in which there exists a database administrator who has direct access to the private data. What if there is instead no trusted database administrator? Even if there is a suitable trusted party, there are many reasons not to want private data aggregated by some third party. The very existence of an aggregate database of private information raises the possibility that at some *future time*, it will come into the hands of an untrusted party, either maliciously (via data theft), or as a natural result of organizational succession. A superior model — from the perspective of the owners of private data — would be a local model, in which agents could (randomly) answer questions in a differentially private manner about their own data, without ever sharing it with anyone else. In the context of predicate queries, this seems to severely limit the expressivity of a private mechanism's interaction with the data: The mechanism can ask each user whether or not her data satisfies a given predicate, and the user may flip a coin, answering truthfully only with slightly higher probability than answering falsely. In this model what is possible?

The local privacy model was first introduced in the context of learning. The local privacy model formalizes randomized response: there is no central database of private data. Instead, each individual maintains possession of their own data element (a database of size 1), and answers questions about it only in a differentially private manner. Formally, the database $x \in \mathbb{N}^{|\mathcal{X}|}$ is a collection of n elements from some domain $\mathcal{X}$, and each $x_i \in x$ is held by an individual.

Definition 12.1 (Local Randomizer). An ε-local randomizer $R : \mathcal{X} \to W$ is an ε-differentially private algorithm that takes as input a database of size $n = 1$.

In the local privacy model, algorithms may interact with the database only through a local randomizer oracle:

Definition 12.2 (LR Oracle). An LR oracle $LR_D(\cdot, \cdot)$ takes as input an index $i \in [n]$ and an ε-local randomizer R and outputs a random value $w \in W$ chosen according to the distribution $R(x_i)$, where $x_i \in D$ is the element held by the ith individual in the database.

Definition 12.3 ((Local Algorithm)). An algorithm is ε-local if it accesses the database D via the oracle LR_D, with the following restriction: If $LR_D(i, R_1), \ldots, LR_D(i, R_k)$ are the algorithm's invocations of LR_D on index i, where each R_J is an ε_j-local randomizer, then $\varepsilon_1 + \cdots + \varepsilon_k \leq \varepsilon$.

Because differential privacy is composable, it is easy to see that ε-local algorithms are ε-differentially private.

Observation 12.1. ε-local algorithms are ε-differentially private.

That is to say, an ε-local algorithm interacts with the data using only a sequence of ε-differentially private algorithms, each of which computes only on a database of size 1. Because nobody other than its owner ever touches any piece of private data, the local setting is far more secure: it does not require a trusted party, and there is no central party who might be subject to hacking. Because even the algorithm never sees private data, the internal state of the algorithm is always differentially private as well (i.e., local privacy implies pan privacy, described in the next section). A natural question is how restrictive the local privacy model is. In this section, we merely informally discuss results. The interested reader can follow the bibliographic references at the end of this section for more information. We note that an alternative name for the local privacy model is the *fully distributed* model.

We recall the definition of the statistical query (SQ) model, introduced in Section 11. Roughly speaking, given a database x of size n, the statistical query model allows an algorithm to access this database by making a polynomial (in n) number of noisy linear queries to the database, where the error in the query answers is some inverse polynomial in n. Formally:

Definition 12.4. A *statistical query* is some function $\phi : \mathcal{X} \times \{0,1\} \to [0,1]$. A *statistical query oracle* for a distribution over labeled examples $\mathcal{D}$ with tolerance τ is an oracle $\mathcal{O}_{\mathcal{D}}^{\tau}$ such that for every statistical query ϕ:

$$\left| \mathcal{O}_{\mathcal{D}}^{\tau}(\phi) - \mathbb{E}_{(x,y)\sim\mathcal{D}}[\phi(x,y)] \right| \leq \tau$$

In other words, an SQ oracle takes as input a statistical query ϕ, and outputs some value that is guaranteed to be within $\pm\tau$ of the expected value of ϕ on examples drawn from $\mathcal{D}$.

Definition 12.5. An algorithm A is said to SQ-learn a class of functions C if for every $\alpha, \beta > 0$ there exists an $m = \mathrm{poly}(d, 1/\alpha, \log(1/\beta))$ such that A makes at most m queries of tolerance $\tau = 1/m$ to $\mathcal{O}_{\mathcal{D}}^{\tau}$, and with probability $1 - \beta$, outputs a hypothesis $f \in C$ such that:

$$\mathrm{err}(f, \mathcal{D}) \leq \min_{f^* \in C} \mathrm{err}(f^*, \mathcal{D}) + \alpha$$

More generally, we can talk about an algorithm (for performing any computation) as operating in the SQ model if it accesses the data only through an SQ oracle:

Definition 12.6. An algorithm A is said to operate in the SQ model if there exists an m such that A makes at most m queries of tolerance $\tau = 1/m$ to $\mathcal{O}_{\mathcal{D}}^{\tau}$, and does not have any other access to the database. A is efficient if m is polynomial in the size of the database, D.

It turns out that up to polynomial factors in the size of the database and in the number of queries, any algorithm that can be implemented in the SQ model can be implemented and analyzed for privacy in the local privacy model, and vice versa. We note that there is a distinction between an algorithm being implemented in the SQ model, and its privacy analysis being carried out in the local model: almost all of the algorithms that we have presented in the end access the data using noisy linear queries, and so can be thought of as acting in the SQ model. However, their privacy guarantees are analyzed in the centralized model of data privacy (i.e., because of some "global" part of the analysis, as in the sparse vector algorithm).

In the following summary, we will also recall the definition of PAC learning, also introduced in Section 11:

Definition 12.7. An algorithm A is said to PAC-learn a class of functions C if for every $\alpha, \beta > 0$, there exists an $m = \text{poly}(d, 1/\alpha, \log(1/\beta))$ such that for every distribution $\mathcal{D}$ over labeled examples, A takes as input m labeled examples drawn from $\mathcal{D}$ and outputs a hypothesis $f \in C$ such that with probability $1 - \beta$:

$$\text{err}(f, \mathcal{D}) \leq \min_{f^* \in C} \text{err}(f^*, \mathcal{D}) + \alpha$$

If $\min_{f^* \in C} \text{err}(f^*, \mathcal{D}) = 0$, the learner is said to operate in the *realizable* setting (i.e., there exists some function in the class which perfectly labels the data). Otherwise, the learner is said to operate in the *agnostic* setting. If A also has run time that is polynomial in $d, 1/\alpha$, and $\log(1/\beta)$, then the learner is said to be *efficient*. If there is an algorithm which PAC-learns C, then C is said to be PAC-learnable. Note that the main distinction between an SQ learning algorithm and a PAC learning algorithm, is that the PAC learning algorithm gets direct access to the database of examples, whereas the SQ learning algorithm only has access to the data through a noisy SQ oracle.

What follows is some of our understanding of the limitations of the SQ model and problems which separate it from the centralized model of data privacy.

1. A single sensitivity-1 query can be answered to error $O(1)$ in the centralized model of data privacy using the Laplace mechanism, but requires error $\Theta(\sqrt{n})$ in the local data privacy model.

2. The set of function classes that we can (properly) learn in the local privacy model is exactly the set of function classes that we can properly learn in the SQ model (up to polynomial factors in the database size and query complexity of the algorithm). In contrast, the set of things we can (properly or agnostically) learn in the centralized model corresponds to the set of things we can learn in the PAC model. SQ learning is strictly weaker, but this is not a huge handicap, since parity functions are essentially the only interesting class that is PAC learnable but not SQ learnable. We remark that we refer explicitly to proper learning here (meaning the setting in which there is some function in the class which perfectly labels the data). In the PAC model there is no information theoretic difference between proper and agnostic learning, but in the SQ model the difference is large: see the next point.

3. The set of queries that we can release in the local privacy model are exactly those queries that we can agnostically learn in the SQ model. In contrast, the set of things we can release in the centralized model corresponds to the set of things we can agnostically learn in the PAC model. This is a much bigger handicap — even conjunctions (i.e., marginals) are not agnostically learnable in the SQ model. This follows from the information theoretic reduction from agnostic learning (i.e., *distinguishing*) to query release that we saw in Section 5 using the iterative construction mechanism.

We note that if we are only concerned about computationally bounded adversaries, then in principle distributed agents can use *secure multiparty computation* to simulate private algorithms in the centralized setting. While this does not actually give a differential privacy guarantee, the result of such simulations will be indistinguishable from the result of differentially private computations, from the point of view of a computationally bounded adversary. However, general secure multiparty computation protocols typically require huge amounts of message passing (and hence sometimes have unreasonably large run times), whereas algorithms in the local privacy model tend to be extremely simple.

12.2 Pan-private streaming model

The goal of a pan-private algorithm is to remain differentially private even against an adversary that can, on rare occasions, observe the algorithm's internal state. Intrusions can occur for many reasons, including hacking, subpoena, or *mission creep*, when data collected for one purpose are used for a different purpose ("Think of the children!"). Pan-private streaming algorithms provide protection against all of these. Note that ordinary streaming algorithms do *not* necessarily provide privacy against intrusions, as even a low-memory streaming algorithm can hold a small number of data items in memory, which would be completely exposed in an intrusion. On the technical side, intrusions can be *known* to the curator (subpoena) or unknown (hacking). These can have very different effects, as a curator aware of an intrusion can take protective measures, such as re-randomizing certain variables.

12.2.1 Definitions

We assume a data stream of unbounded length composed of elements in a universe $\mathcal{X}$. It may be helpful to keep in mind as motivation data analysis on a query stream, in which queries are accompanied by the IP address of the issuer. For now, we ignore the query text itself; the universe $\mathcal{X}$ is the universe of potential IP addresses. Thus, intuitively, *user-level* privacy protects the presence or absence of an IP address in the stream, indpendent of the number of times it arises, should it actually be present at all. In contrast, *event-level* privacy merely protects the privacy of individual accesses. For now, we focus on user-level privacy.

As usual in differentially private algorithms, the adversary can have arbitrary control of the input stream, and may have arbitrary auxiliary knowledge obtained from other sources. It can also have arbitrary computational power.

We assume the algorithm runs until it receives a special signal, at which point it produces (observable) outputs. The algorithm may optionally continue to run and produce additional outputs later, again in response to a special signal. Since outputs are obvservable we do not provide privacy for the special signals.

A streaming algorithm experiences a sequence of internal states. and produces a (possibly unbounded) sequence of outputs. Let I denote the set of possible internal states of the algorithm, and σ the set of possible output sequences. We assume that the adversary can only observe internal states and the output sequence; it cannot see the data in the stream (although it may have auxiliary knowledge about some of these data) and it has no access to the *length* of the input sequence.

Definition 12.8 ($\mathcal{X}$-Adjacent Data Streams). We think of data streams as being of unbounded length; *prefixes* have finite length. Data streams S and S' are $\mathcal{X}$-adjacent if they differ only in the presence or absence of *all* occurrences of a single element $u \in \mathcal{X}$. We define $\mathcal{X}$-adjacency for stream prefixes analogously.

User-Level Pan-Privacy. An algorithm **Alg** mapping data stream prefixes to the range $\mathrm{I} \times \sigma$, is *pan-private against a single intrusion* if for all sets $\mathrm{I}' \subseteq \mathrm{I}$ of internal states and $\sigma' \subseteq \sigma$ of output sequences, and for all pairs of adjacent data stream prefixes S, S'

$$\Pr[\mathbf{Alg}(S) \in (\mathrm{I}', \sigma')] \le e^{\varepsilon} \Pr[\mathbf{Alg}(S') \in (\mathrm{I}', \sigma')],$$

where the probability spaces are over the coin flips of the algorithm **Alg**.

This definition speaks only of a single intrusion. For multiple intrusions we must consider interleavings of observations of internal states and outputs.

The relaxation to *event-level privacy* is obtained by modifying the notion of adjacency so that, roughly speaking, two streams are event-adjacent if they differ in a single instance of a single element in $\mathcal{X}$; that is, one instance of one element is deleted/added. Clearly, event-level privacy is a much weaker guarantee than user-level privacy.

Remark 12.1. If we assume the existence of a very small amount of secret storage, not visible to the adversary, then many problems for which we have been unable to obtain pan-private solutions have (non-pan-) private streaming solutions. However, the *amount* of secret storage is not so important as its *existence*, since secret storage is vulnerable to the social pressures against which pan-privacy seeks to protect the data (and the curator).

Pan-Private Density Estimation. Quite surprisingly, pan-privacy can be achieved even for *user-level* privacy of many common streaming computations. As an example, consider the problem of *density estimation*: given a universe $\mathcal{X}$ of data elements and a stream σ, the goal is to estimate the fraction of $\mathcal{X}$ that acutally appears in the stream. For example, the universe consists of all teenagers in a given community (represented by IP addresses), and the goal is to understand what fraction visit the Planned Parenthood website.

Standard low-memory streaming solutions for density estimation involve recording the results of deterministic computations of at least some input items, an approach that is inherently not pan-private. Here is a simple, albeit high-memory, solution inspired by randomized response. The algorithm maintains a bit b_a for each IP address a (which may appear any number of times in the stream), initialized uniformly at random. The stream is processed one element at a time. On input a the algorithm flips a bit biased to 1; that is, the biased bit will take value 0 with probability $1/2 - \varepsilon$, and value 1 with probability $1/2 + \varepsilon$. The algorithm follows this procedure independent of the number of times IP address a appears in the data stream. This algorithm is $(\varepsilon, 0)$-differentially private. As with randomized response, we can estimate the fraction of "real" 1's by $z = 2(y - |\mathcal{X}|/2)/|\mathcal{X}|$, where y is the actual number of 1's in the table after the stream is processed. To ensure pan-privacy, the algorithm publishes a noisy version of z. As with randomized response, the error will be on the order of $1/\sqrt{|\mathcal{X}|}$, yielding meaningful results when the density is high.

Other problems enjoying user-level pan-private algorithms include:

- Estimating, for any t, the fraction of elements appearing exactly t times;

- Estimating the *t-cropped mean*: roughly, the average, over all elements, of the minimum of t and the number of occurrences of the element in the data stream;
- Estimating the fraction of k-heavy hitters (elements of $\mathcal{X}$ that appear at least k times in the data stream).

Variants of these problems can also be defined for *fully dynamic* data, in which counts can be decremented as well as incremented. For example, density estimation (what fraction appeared in the stream?) becomes "How many (or what fraction) of elements have a (net) count equal to zero?" These, too, can be solved with user-level pan-privacy, using differentially private variations of *sketching* techniques from the streaming literature.

12.3   Continual observation

Many applications of data analysis involve repeated computations, either because the entire goal is one of monitoring of, for example, traffic conditions, search trends, or incidence of influenza. In such applications the system is required to continually produce outputs. We therefore need techniques for achieving *differential privacy under continual observation*.

As usual, differential privacy will require having essentially the same distribution on outputs for each pair of adjacent databases, but how should we define adjacency in this setting? Let us consider two example scenarios.

Suppose the goal is to monitor public health by analyzing statistics from an H1N1 self-assessment Web site.[1] Individuals can interact with the site to learn whether symptoms they are experiencing may be indicative of the H1N1 flu. The user fills in some demographic data (age, zipcode, sex), and responds to queries about his symptoms (fever over 100.4°F?, sore throat?, duration of symptoms?). We would expect a given individual to interact very few times with the H1N1 self-assessment site (say, if we restrict our attention to a six-month

---

[1]https://h1n1.cloudapp.net provided such a service during the winter of 2010; user-supplied data were stored for analysis with the user's consent.

period). For simplicity, let us say this is just once. In such a setting, it is sufficient to ensure *event-level* privacy, in which the privacy goal is to hide the presence or absence of a single event (interaction of one user with the self-assessment site).

Suppose again that the goal is to monitor public health, this time by analyzing search terms submitted to a medical search engine. Here it may no longer be safe to assume an individual has few interactions with the Web site, even if we restrict attention to a relatively short period of time. In this case we would want *user-level* privacy, ensuring that the entire set of a user's search terms is protected simultaneously.

We think of continual observation algorithms as taking steps at discrete time intervals; at each step the algorithm receives an input, computes, and produces output. We model the data as arriving in a stream, at most one data element in each time interval. To capture the fact that, in real life, there are periods of time in which nothing happens, null events are modeled by a special symbol in the data stream. Thus, the intuitive notion of "t time periods" corresponds to processing a sequence of t elements in the stream.

For example, the motivation behind the counter primitive below is to count the number of times that something has occurred since the algorithm was started (the counter is very general; we don't specify *a priori* what it is counting). This is modeled by an input stream over $\{0, 1\}$. Here, "0" means "nothing happened," "1" means the event of interest occurred, and for $t = 1, 2, \ldots, T$ the algorithm outputs an approximation to the number of 1s seen in the length t prefix of the stream.

There are three natural options:

1. Use randomized response for each time period and add this randomized value to the counter;
2. Add noise distributed according to $\mathrm{Lap}(1/\varepsilon)$ to the true value for each time step and add this perturbed value to the counter;
3. Compute the true count at each time step, add noise distributed according to $\mathrm{Lap}(T/\varepsilon)$ to the count, and release this noisy count.

All of these options result in noise on the order of at least $\Omega(\sqrt{T}/\varepsilon)$. The hope is to do much better by exploiting structure of the query set.

Let $\mathcal{X}$ be the universe of possible input symbols. Let S and S' be stream prefixes (i.e., finite streams) of symbols drawn from $\mathcal{X}$. Then $\text{Adj}(S, S')$ ("S is adjacent to S'") if and only if there exist $a, b \in \mathcal{X}$ so that if we change some of the instances of a in S to instances of b, then we get S'. More formally, $\text{Adj}(S, S')$ iff $\exists a, b \in \mathcal{X}$ and $\exists R \subseteq [|S|]$, such that $S|_{R:a \to b} = S'$. Here, R is a set of indices in the stream prefix S, and $S|_{R:a \to b}$ is the result of replacing all the occurrences of a at these indices with b. Note that adjacent prefixes are always of the same length.

To capture event-level privacy, we restrict the definition of adjacency to the case $|R| \le 1$. To capture user-level privacy we do not constrain the size of R in the definition of adjacency.

As noted above, one option is to publish a noisy count at each time step; the count published at time t reflects the approximate number of 1s in the length t prefix of the stream. The privacy challenge is that early items in the stream are subject to nearly T statistics, so for $(\varepsilon, 0)$-differential privacy we would be adding noise scaled to T/ε, which is unacceptable. In addition, since the 1s are the "interesting" elements of the stream, we would like that the distortion be scaled to the number of 1s seen in the stream, rather than to the length of the stream. This rules out applying randomized response to each item in the stream independently.

The algorithm below follows a classical approach for converting static algorithms to dynamic algorithms.

Assume T is a power of 2. The intervals are the natural ones corresponding to the labels on a complete binary tree with T leaves, where the leaves are labeled, from left to right, with the intervals $[0,0], [1,1], \ldots, [T-1, T-1]$ and each parent is labeled with the interval that is the union of the intervals labeling its children. The idea is to compute and release a noisy count for each label $[s, t]$; that is, the released value corresponding to the label $[s, t]$ is a noisy count of the number of 1s in positions $s, s+1, \ldots, t$ of the input stream. To learn the approximate cumulative count at time $t \in [0, T-1]$ the analyst uses the binary representation of t to determine a set of at most $\log_2 T$

Counter (T, ε)

Initialization. Initialize $\xi = \log_2 T/\varepsilon$, and sample Counter $\sim \mathrm{Lap}(\xi)$.

Intervals. For $i \in \{1, \ldots, \log T\}$, associate with each string $s \in \{0, 1\}^i$ the time interval S of $2^{\log T - i}$ time periods $\{s \circ 0^{\log T - i}, \ldots s \circ 1^{\log T - i}\}$. The interval *begins in time* $s \circ 0^{\log T - i}$ and *ends in time* $s \circ 1^{\log T - i}$.

Processing. In time period $t \in \{0, 1, \ldots, T - 1\}$, let $x_t \in \{0, 1\}$ be the t-th input bit:

1. For every interval I beginning at time t, initialize c_I to an independent random draw: $c_I \leftarrow \mathrm{Lap}((\log_2 T)/\varepsilon)$;

2. For every interval I containing t, add x_t to c_I: $c_I \leftarrow c_I + x_t$;

3. For every interval I that ends in time t, output c_I.

Figure 12.1: Event-level private counter algorithm (not pan-private).

disjoint intervals whose union is $[0, t]$, and computes the sum of the corresponding released noisy counts.[2] See Figure 12.1.

Each stream position $t \in [0, T - 1]$ appears in at most $1 + \log_2 T$ intervals (because the height of the tree is $\log_2 T$), and so each element in the stream affects at most $1 + \log_2 T$ released noisy counts. Thus, adding noise to each interval count distributed according to $\mathrm{Lap}((1 + \log_2 T)/\varepsilon)$ ensures $(\varepsilon, 0)$-differential privacy. As for accuracy, since the binary representation of any index $t \in [0, T - 1]$ yields a disjoint set of at most $\log_2 T$ intervals whose union is $[0, t]$ we can apply Lemma 12.2 below to conclude that the expected error is tightly concentrated around $(\log_2 T)^{3/2}$. The maximum expected error, over all times t, is on the order of $(\log_2 T)^{5/3}$.

Lemma 12.2. Let Let $Y_1, \ldots, Y_k$ be independent variables with distribution $\mathrm{Lap}(b_i)$. Let $Y = \sum_i Y_i$ and $b_{\max} = \max_i b_i$. Let $\nu \geq \sqrt{\sum_i (b_i)^2}$, and $0 < \lambda < \frac{2\sqrt{2}\nu^2}{b_{\max}}$. Then

$$\Pr[Y > \lambda] \leq \exp\left(-\frac{\lambda^2}{8\nu^2}\right).$$

---

[2]This algorithm can be optimized slightly (for example, we never use the count corresponding to the root, eliminating one level from the tree), and it can be modified to handle the case in which T is not a power of 2 and, more interestingly, when T is not known *a priori*.

Proof. The moment generating function of Y_i is $\mathbb{E}[\exp(hY_i)] = 1/(1 - h^2b_i^2)$, where $|h| < 1/b_i$. Using the inequality $(1 - x)^{-1} \leq 1 + 2x \leq \exp(2x)$ for $0 \leq x < 1/2$, we have $\mathbb{E}[\exp(hY_i)] \leq \exp(2h^2b_i^2)$, if $|h| < 1/2b_i$. We now calculate, for $0 < h < 1/\sqrt{2}b_{\max}$:

$$\begin{aligned}
\Pr[Y > \lambda] &= \Pr[\exp(hY) > \exp(h\lambda)] \\
&\leq \exp(-h\lambda)\mathbb{E}[\exp(hY)] \\
&= \exp(-h\lambda) \prod_i \mathbb{E}[\exp(hY_i)] \\
&\leq \exp(-h\lambda + 2h^2\nu^2).
\end{aligned}$$

By assumption, $0 < \lambda < \frac{2\sqrt{2}\nu^2}{b_{\max}}$. We complete the proof by setting $h = \lambda/4\nu^2 < 1/\sqrt{2}b_{\max}$. $\qquad\square$

Corollary 12.3. Let $Y, \nu, \{b_i\}_i, b_{\max}$ be as in Lemma 12.2. For $\delta \in (0, 1)$ and $\nu > \max\{\sqrt{\sum_i b_i^2}, b_{\max}\sqrt{\ln(2/\delta)}\}$, we have that $\Pr[|Y| > \nu\sqrt{8\ln(2/\delta)}] \leq \delta$.

In our case, all the b_i's are the same (e.g., $b = (\log_2 T)/\varepsilon$). Taking $\nu = \sqrt{k}b$ we have the following corollary:

Corollary 12.4. For all $\lambda < \alpha(\sqrt{k}b) < 2\sqrt{2}kb = 2\sqrt{2}k\nu$,

$$\Pr[Y > \lambda] \leq e^{-\alpha^2/8}.$$

Note that we have taken the unusual step of adding noise to the count *before* counting, rather than after. In terms of the outputs it makes no difference (addition is commutative). However, it has an interesting effect on the algorithm's internal states: they are differentially private! That is, suppose the intrusion occurs at time t, and consider any $i \in [0, t]$. Since there are at most $\log_2 T$ intervals containing step i (in the algorithm we abolished the interval corresponding to the root), x_i affects at most $\log_2 T$ of the noisy counts, and so x_i is protected against the intrusion for exactly the same reason that it is protected in the algorithm's outputs. Nevertheless, the algorithm in Figure 12.1 is *not* pan-private even against a single intrusion. This is because, while its internal state and its outputs are each independently differentially private, the joint distribution does not ensure ε-differential privacy. To see why this is so, consider an intruder that sees the internal state at time t and knows the entire data stream except x_{t+1}, and let $I = [a, b]$ be an interval containing both t and $t + 1$. Since the adversary knows $x_{[0,t]}$, it can subtract from c_I the contribution from the stream occurring up through time t (that is, it subtracts off from the observed c_I at time t the values $x_a, x_{a+1}, \ldots, x_t$, all of which it knows). From this the intruder learns the value of the Laplace draw to which c_I was initialized. When c_I is published at the end of step b, the adversary subtracts from the published value this initial draw, together with the contributions of all elements in $x_{[a,b]}$ except x_{t+1}, which it does not know. What remains is the unknown x_{t+1}.

12.3.1 Pan-private counting

Although the algorithm in Figure 12.1 is easily modified to ensure *event-level pan-privacy against a single intrusion*, we give a different algorithm here in order to introduce a powerful *bijection* technique which has proved useful in other applications. This algorithm maintains in its internal state a single noisy counter, or accumulator, as well as noise values for each interval. The output at any given time period t is the sum of the accumulator and the noise values for the intervals containing t. When an interval I ends, its associated noise value, η_I, is erased from memory.

Theorem 12.5. The counter algorithm of Figure 12.2, when run with parameters T, ε, and suffering at most one intrusion, yields an $(\varepsilon, 0)$-pan-private counter that, with probability at least $1 - \beta$ has maximum error, over its T outputs, of $O(\log(1/\beta) \cdot \log^{2.5} T/\varepsilon)$. We note also that in every round *individually* (rather than in all rounds simultaneously), with all but β probability, the error has magnitude at most $O(\log(1/\beta) \cdot \log^{1.5} T/\varepsilon)$.

Proof. The proof of accuracy is the same as that for the algorithm in Figure 12.1, relying on Corollary 12.4. We focus here on the proof of pan-privacy.

During an intrusion between atomic steps t^* and $t^* + 1$, that is, immediately following the processing of element t^* in the input stream

---

Pan-Private Counter (T, ε)

Initialization. Initialize $\xi = (1 + \log T)/\varepsilon$, and sample Counter $\sim \mathrm{Lap}(\xi)$.

Intervals. For $i \in \{1, \ldots, \log T\}$, associate with each string $s \in \{0,1\}^i$ the time interval S of $2^{\log T - i}$ time periods $\{s \circ 0^{\log T - i}, \ldots s \circ 1^{\log T - i}\}$. The interval *begins in time* $s \circ 0^{\log T - i}$ and *ends in time* $s \circ 1^{\log T - i}$.

Processing. In time period $t \in \{0, 1, \ldots, T - 1\}$, let $x_t \in \{0, 1\}$ be the t-th input bit:

  1. Counter $\leftarrow$ Counter $+ x_t$;

  2. For every interval I which begins in time t, sample noise $\eta_I \sim \mathrm{Lap}(\xi)$;

  3. Let $I_1, \ldots, I_{\log T}$ be the $\log T$ intervals that contain t. Output Counter $+ \sum_{i=1}^{\log T} \eta_{I_i}$.

  4. For every interval I that ends in time t, erase η_I.

Figure 12.2: Event-level pan-private counter algorithm.

(recall that we begin numbering the elements with 0), the view of the adversary consists of (1) the noisy cumulative count (in the variable "count"), (2) the interval noise values η_S in memory when the intrusion occurs, and (3) the complete sequence of all of the algorithm's outputs in rounds $0, 1, \ldots, t$. Consider adjacent databases x and x', which differ in time t, say, without loss of generality, $x_t = 1$ and $x'_t = 0$, and an intrusion immediately following time period $t^* \geq t$ (we will discuss the case $t^* < t$ below). We will describe a bijection between the vector of noise values used in executions on x and executions on x', such that corresponding noise values induce identical adversary views on x and x', and the probabilities of adjacent noise values differ only by an e^ε multiplicative factor. This implies ε-differential pan-privacy.

By assumption, the true count just after the time period $t^* \geq t$ is larger when the input is x than it is when the input is x'. Fix an arbitrary execution E_x when the input stream is x. This amounts to fixing the randomness of the algorithm, which in turn fixes the noise values generated. We will describe the corresponding execution $E_{x'}$ by describing how its noise values differ from those in E_x.

The program variable Counter was initialized with Laplace noise. By increasing this noise by 1 in $E_{x'}$ the value of Counter just after step t^* is identical in $E_{x'}$ and E_x. The noise variables in memory immediately following period t^* are independent of the input; these will be unchanged in $E_{x'}$. We will make the sequence of outputs in $E_{x'}$ *identical* to those in E_x by changing a collection of $\log T$ interval noise values η_S that are *not* in memory when the adversary intrudes, so that the sum of *all* noise values in all rounds up through $t - 1$ is unchanged, but the sum from round t on is larger by 1 for database x' than for x. Since we *increased* the initialization noise for Counter, we now need to *decrease* the sum of interval noise values for periods $0, \ldots, t - 1$ by 1, and leave unchanged the sum of interval noise values from period t.

To do this, we find a collection of disjoint intervals whose union is $\{0, \ldots, t-1\}$. There is always such a collection, and it is always of size at most $\log T$. We can construct it iteratively by, for i decreasing from $\lfloor \log(t - 1) \rfloor$ to 0, choosing the interval of size 2^i that is contained in $\{0, \ldots, t - 1\}$ and is not contained in a previously chosen interval (if such an interval exists). Given this set of disjoint intervals, we notice also that they all end by time $t - 1 < t \leq t^*$, and so their noises are not in memory when the adversary intrudes (just following period t^*). In total (taking into account also changing the initial noise value for Counter), the complete view seen by the adversary is identical and the probabilities of the (collection of) noise values used for x and x' differ by at most an e^ε multiplicative factor.

Note that we assumed $t^* \geq t$. If $t^* < t$ then the initial noise added to Counter in $E_{x'}$ will be the same as in E_x, and we need to add 1 to the sum of interval noises in every time period from t through T (the sum of interval noises before time t remains unchanged). This is done as above, by finding a disjoint collection of at most $\log T$ intervals that exactly covers $\{t, \ldots, T - 1\}$. The noise values for these intervals are not yet in memory when the intrusion occurs in time $t^* < t$, and the proof follows similarly. $\square$

12.3.2 A logarithmic (in T) lower bound

Given the upper bound of Theorem 12.5, where the error depends only poly-logarithmically on T, it is natural to ask whether *any* dependence is inherent. In this section we show that a logarithmic dependence on T is indeed inherent.

Theorem 12.6. Any differentially private event-level algorithm for counting over T rounds must have error $\Omega(\log T)$ (even with $\varepsilon = 1$).

Proof. Let $\varepsilon = 1$. Suppose for the sake of contradiction that there exists a differentially private event-level counter for streams of length T that guarantees that with probability at least $2/3$, its count at all time periods is accurate up to a maximum error of $(\log_2 T)/4$. Let $k = (\log_2 T)/4$. We construct a set S of T/k inputs as follows. Divide the T time periods into T/k consecutive phases, each of length k (except, possibly, the last one). For $i = 1, \ldots, T/k$, the i-th input $x^i \in S$ has 0 input bits everywhere except during the ith phase. That is, $x^i = 0^{k \cdot i} \circ 1^k \circ 0^{k \cdot ((T/k)-(i+1))}$.

Fo $1 \leq i \leq T/k$, we say an output *matches* i if just before the ith phase the output is less than $k/2$ and at the end of the ith phase the output is at least $k/2$. By accuracy, on input x^i the output should match i with probability at least $2/3$. By ε differential privacy, this means that for every $i, j \in [T/k]$ such that $i \neq j$, the output on input x^i should match j with probability at least

$$e^{-2\varepsilon \cdot k} = e^{-\varepsilon \log(T^{1/2})}$$
$$= e^{-\log(T^{1/2})} = 1/\sqrt{T}.$$

This is a contradiction, because the events that the output matches j are disjoint for different j, and yet the sum of their probabilities on input x^i exceeds 1. □

12.4 Average case error for query release

In Sections 4 and 5, we considered various mechanisms for solving the private query release problem, where we were interested in *worst case error*. That is, given a class of queries Q, of size $|Q| = k$, we wished to recover a vector of answers $\hat{a} \in \mathbb{R}^k$ such that for *each* query $f_i \in Q$, $|f_i(x) - \hat{a}_i| \leq \alpha$ for some worst-case error rate α. In other words, if we let $a \in \mathbb{R}^k$ denote the vector of *true* answers, with $a_i \equiv f_i(x)$, then we require a bound of the form: $\|a - \hat{a}\|_\infty \leq \alpha$. In this section, we consider a weakened utility guarantee, on the ℓ_2 (rather than ℓ_∞) error: a bound of the form $\|a - \hat{a}\|_2 \leq \alpha$. A bound of this form does not guarantee that we have low error for *every* query, but it does guarantee that on average, we have small error.

Although this sort of bound is weaker than worst-case error, the mechanism is particularly simple, and it makes use of an elegant geometric view of the query release problem that we have not seen until now.

Recall that we can view the database x as a vector $x \in \mathbb{N}^{|\mathcal{X}|}$ with $\|x\|_1 = n$. We can similarly also view the queries $f_i \in \mathcal{Q}$ as vectors $f_i \in \mathbb{N}^{|\mathcal{X}|}$, such that $f_i(x) = \langle f_i, x \rangle$. It will therefore be helpful to view our class of queries $\mathcal{Q}$ as a matrix $A \in \mathbb{R}^{k \times |\mathcal{X}|}$, with the ith row of A being the vector f_i. We can then see that our answer vector $a \in \mathbb{R}^k$ is, in matrix notation:

$$A \cdot x = a.$$

Let's consider the domain and range of A when viewed as a linear map. Write $B_1 = \{x \in \mathbb{R}^{|\mathcal{X}|} : \|x\|_1 = 1\}$ denote the unit ℓ_1 ball in $|\mathcal{X}|$ dimensional space. Observe that $x \in nB_1$, since $\|x\|_1 = n$. We will refer to nB_1 as "Database Space." Write $K = AB_1$. Note similarly that for all $x \in nB_1$, $a = A \cdot x \in nK$. We will refer to nK as "answer space." We make a couple of observations about K: Note that because B_1 is centrally symmetric, so is K — that is, $K = -K$. Note also that $K \subset \mathbb{R}^k$ is a convex polytope with vertices $\pm A^1, \dots, \pm A^{|\mathcal{X}|}$ equal to the columns of A, together with their negations.

The following algorithm is extremely simple: it simply answers every query independently with the Laplace mechanism, and then *projects back into answer space*. In other words, it adds independent Laplace noise to every query, which as we have seen, by itself leads to distortion that is linear in k (or at least $\sqrt{k}$, if we relax to (ε, δ)-differential privacy). However, the resulting vector $\tilde{a}$ of answers is likely not consistent with *any* database $y \in nB_1$ in database space. Therefore, rather than returning $\tilde{a}$, it instead returns some consistent answer vector $\hat{a} \in nK$ that is as close to $\tilde{a}$ as possible. As we will see, this projection step improves the accuracy of the mechanism, while having no effect on privacy (since it is just post-processing!)

We first observe that Project is differentially private.

Theorem 12.7. For any $A \in [0,1]^{k \times |\mathcal{X}|}$, **Project**$(x, A, \varepsilon)$ preserves (ε, δ)-differential privacy.

Algorithm 18 The K-Projected Laplace Mechanism. It takes as input a matrix $A \in [0,1]^{k \times |\mathcal{X}|}$, a database $x \in nB_1$, and a privacy parameters ε and δ.

Project$(x, A, \varepsilon, \delta)$:

  Let $a = A \cdot x$
  For each $i \in [k]$, sample $\nu_i \sim \text{Lap}(\sqrt{8k\ln(1/\delta)}/\varepsilon)$, and let $\tilde{a} = a + \nu$.
  Output $\hat{a} = \arg\min_{\hat{a} \in nK} \|\hat{a} - \tilde{a}\|_2^2$.

Proof. We simply note that $\tilde{a}$ is the output of the Laplace mechanism on k sensitivity 1 queries, which is (ε, δ)-differentially private by Theorems 3.6 and 3.20 . Finally, since $\hat{a}$ is derived from $\tilde{a}$ without any further access to the private data, the release of $\hat{a}$ is differentially private by the post-processing guarantee of differential privacy, Proposition 2.1. $\square$

Theorem 12.8. For any class of linear queries A and database x, let $a = A \cdot x$ denote the true answer vector. Let $\hat{a}$ denote the output of the mechanism **Project**: $\hat{a} = $ **Project**(x, A, ε). With probability at least $1 - \beta$:

$$\|a - \hat{a}\|_2^2 \leq \frac{kn\sqrt{192\ln(1/\delta)\ln(2|\mathcal{X}|/\beta)}}{\varepsilon}.$$

To prove this theorem, we will introduce a couple of simple concepts from convex geometry. For a convex body $K \subset \mathbb{R}^k$, its *polar body* is $K°$ defined to be $K° = \{y \in \mathbb{R}^k : \langle y, x \rangle \leq 1 \text{ for all } x \in K\}$. The *Minkowski Norm* defined by a convex body K is

$$\|x\|_K \equiv \min\{r \in \mathbb{R} \text{ such that } x \in rK\}.$$

The *dual norm* of $\|x\|_K$ is the Minkowski norm induced by the polar body of K, i.e., $\|x\|_{K°}$. This norm also has the following form:

$$\|x\|_{K°} = \max_{y \in K} \langle x, y \rangle.$$

The key fact we will use is *Holder's Inequality*, which is satisfied by all centrally symmetric convex bodies K:

$$|\langle x, y \rangle| \leq \|x\|_K \|y\|_{K°}.$$

Proof of Theorem 12.8. The proof will proceed in two steps. First we will show that: $\|a - \hat{a}\|_2^2 \leq 2\langle \hat{a} - a, \tilde{a} - a \rangle$, and then we will use Holder's inequality to bound this second quantity.

Lemma 12.9.

$$\|a - \hat{a}\|_2^2 \leq 2\langle \hat{a} - a, \tilde{a} - a \rangle$$

Proof. We calculate:

$$
\begin{aligned}
\|\hat{a} - a\|_2^2 &= \langle \hat{a} - a, \hat{a} - a \rangle \\
&= \langle \hat{a} - a, \tilde{a} - a \rangle + \langle \hat{a} - a, \hat{a} - \tilde{a} \rangle \\
&\leq 2\langle \hat{a} - a, \tilde{a} - a \rangle.
\end{aligned}
$$

The inequality follows from calculating:

$$
\begin{aligned}
\langle \hat{a} - a, \tilde{a} - a \rangle &= \|\tilde{a} - a\|_2^2 + \langle \hat{a} - \tilde{a}, \tilde{a} - a \rangle \\
&\geq \|\hat{a} - a\|_2^2 + \langle \hat{a} - \tilde{a}, \tilde{a} - a \rangle \\
&= \langle \hat{a} - \tilde{a}, \hat{a} - a \rangle,
\end{aligned}
$$

Where the final inequality follows because by choice of $\hat{a}$, for all $a' \in nK$: $\|\tilde{a} - \hat{a}\|_2^2 \leq \|\tilde{a} - a'\|_2^2$. □

We can now complete the proof. Recall that by definition, $\tilde{a} - a = \nu$, the vector of i.i.d. Laplace noise added by the Laplace mechanism. By Lemma 12.9 and Holder's inequality, we have:

$$
\begin{aligned}
\|a - \hat{a}\|_2^2 &\leq 2\langle \hat{a} - a, \nu \rangle \\
&\leq 2\|\hat{a} - a\|_K \|\nu\|_{K^\circ}.
\end{aligned}
$$

We bound these two terms separately. Since by definition $\hat{a}, a \in nK$, we have $\max(\|\hat{a}\|_K, \|a\|_K) \leq n$, and so by the triangle inequality, $\|\hat{a} - a\|_K \leq 2n$.

Next, observe that since $\|\nu\|_{K^\circ} = \max_{y \in K} \langle y, \nu \rangle$, and since the maximum of a linear function taken over a polytope is attained at a vertex, we have: $\|\nu\|_{K^\circ} = \max_{i \in [|\mathcal{X}|]} |\langle A^i, \nu \rangle|$.

Because each $A^i \in \mathbb{R}^k$ is such that $\|A^i\|_\infty \leq 1$, and recalling that for any scalar q, if $Z \sim \mathrm{Lap}(b)$, then $qZ \sim \mathrm{Lap}(qb)$, we can apply Lemma by

Lemma 12.2 to bound the weighted sums of Laplace random variables $\langle A^i, \nu \rangle$. Doing so, we have that with probability at least $1 - \beta$:

$$\max_{i \in [|\mathcal{X}|]} |\langle A^i, \nu \rangle| \leq \frac{8k\sqrt{\ln(1/\delta)\ln(|\mathcal{X}|/\beta)}}{\epsilon}.$$

Combining all of the above bounds, we get that with probability $1 - \beta$:

$$\|a - \hat{a}\|_2^2 \leq \frac{16nk\sqrt{\ln(1/\delta)\ln(|\mathcal{X}|/\beta)}}{\epsilon}. \qquad \square$$

Let's interpret this bound. Observe that $\|a - \hat{a}\|_2^2 = \sum_{i=1}^k (a_i - \hat{a}_i)^2$, and so this is a bound on the sum of squared errors over all queries. Hence, the *average* per-query squared error of this mechanism is only:

$$\frac{1}{k}\sum_{i=1}^k (a_i - \hat{a}_i)^2 \leq \frac{16n\sqrt{\ln(1/\delta)\ln(|\mathcal{X}|/\beta)}}{\epsilon}.$$

In contrast, the private multiplicative weights mechanism guarantees that $\max_{i \in [k]} |a_i - \hat{a}_i| \leq \tilde{O}(\sqrt{n}\log|\mathcal{X}|^{1/4}/\epsilon^{1/2})$, and so matches the average squared error guarantee of the projected Laplace mechanism, with a bound of: $\tilde{O}(n\sqrt{\log|\mathcal{X}|}/\varepsilon)$. However, the multiplicative weights mechanism (and especially its privacy analysis) its much more complex than the Projected Laplace mechanism! In particular, the *private* part of the K-Projected Laplace mechanism is simply the Laplace mechanism itself, and requires no coordination between queries. Interestingly — and, it turns out, necessarily — coordination occurs in the projection phase. Since projection is in post-precessing, it incurs no further privacy loss; indeed, it can be carrie out (online, if necessary) by the data analyst himself.

12.5   Bibliographical notes

The local model of data privacy has its roots in randomized response, as first proposed by Warner in 1965 [84]. The local model was formalized by Kasiviswanathan et al. [52] in the context of learning, who proved that private learning in the local modal is equivalent to non-private learning in the statistical query (SQ) model. The set of queries which can be *released* in the local model was shown to be exactly equal to the set of queries that can be *agnostically learned* in the SQ model by Gupta et al. [38].

Pan-Privacy was introduced by Dwork et al. [27], and further explored by Mir et al. [62]. The pan-private density estimation, as well as a low-memory variant using hashing, appear in [27].

Privacy under continual observation was introduced by Dwork et al. [26]; our algorithm for counting under continual observation is from that paper, as is the lower bound on error. Similar algorithms were given by Chan et al. [11]. The proof of concentration of measure inequality for the sums of Laplace random variables given in Lemma 12.2 is from [11].

The Projected Laplace mechanism for achieving low average error was given by Nikolov et al.[66], who also give *instance optimal* algorithms for the (average error) query release problem for any class of queries. This work extends a line of work on the connections between differential privacy and geometry started by Hardt and Talwar [45], and extended by Bhaskara et al. [5] and Dwork et al. [30].

Dwork, Naor, and Vadhan proved an exponential gap between the number of queries that can be answered (with non-trivial error) by stateless and stateful differentially private mechanisms [29]. The lesson learned — that coordination is essential for accurately and privately answering very large numbers of queries — seems to rule out the independent noise addition in the Projected Laplace mechanism. The statefulness of that algorithm appears in the projection step, resolving the paradox.

13

Reflections

13.1 Toward practicing privacy

Differential Privacy was designed with internet-scale data sets in mind. Reconstruction attacks along the lines of those in Section 8 can be carried out by a *polynomial time* bounded adversary asking only $O(n)$ queries on databases of size n. When n is on the order of hundreds of millions, and each query requires a linear amount of computation, such an attack is unrealistic, even thought the queries can be parallelized. This observation led to the earliest steps toward differential privacy: If the adversary is restricted to a *sublinear* number of counting queries, then $o(\sqrt{n})$ noise per query — less than the sampling error! — is sufficient for preserving privacy (Corollary 3.21).

To what extent can differential privacy be brought to bear on smaller data sets, or even targeted attacks that isolate a small subset of a much larger database, without destroying statistical utility? First, an analysis may require a number of queries that begins to look something like the size of this smaller set. Second, letting n now denote the size of the smaller set or small database, and letting k be the number of queries, fractional errors on the order of $\sqrt{k}/n$ are harder to ignore when n is small. Third, the $\sqrt{\ln(1/\delta)}/\varepsilon$ factor in the advanced

261

composition theorem becomes significant. Keeping in mind the reconstruction attacks when noise is $o(\sqrt{n})$, there appears to be little room to maneuver for arbitrary sets of $k \approx n$ low-sensitivity queries.

There are several promising lines of research for addressing these concerns.

The Query Errors Don't Tell the Whole Story. As an example of this phenomenon, consider the problem of linear regression. The input is a collection of labeled data points of the form (x, y), where $x \in \mathbb{R}^d$ and $y \in \mathbb{R}$, for arbitrary dimension d. The goal is to find $\theta \in \mathbb{R}^d$ that "predicts" y "as well as possible," given x, under the assumption that the relationship is linear. If the goal is simply to "explain" the given data set, differential privacy may well introduce unacceptable error. Certainly the specific algorithm that simply computes

$$\text{argmin}_\theta | \sum_{i=1}^{n} \theta \cdot x_i - y_i |^2$$

and adds appropriately scaled Laplace noise independently to each coordinate of θ may produce a $\tilde{\theta}$ that differs substantially from θ. But if the goal is to learn a predictor that will do well for *future, unseen* inputs (x, y) then a slightly different computation is used to avoid overfitting, and the (possibly large) difference between the private and non-private coefficient vectors does *not* translate into a gap in classification error! A similar phenomenon has been observed in model fitting.

Less Can Be More. Many analyses ask for more than they actually use. Exploitation of this principle is at the heart of Report Noisy Max, where for the accuracy "price" of one measurement we learn one of the largest of many measurements. By asking for "less" (that is, not requiring that all noisy measurements be released, but rather only asking for the largest one), we obtain "more" (better accuracy). A familiar principle in privacy is to *minimize* collection and reporting. Here we see this play out in the realm of what must be *revealed*, rather than what must be used in the computation.

Quit When You are NOT Ahead. This is the philosophy behind Propose-Test-Release, in which we test in a privacy-preserving way that small noise is sufficient for a particular intended computation on the given data set.

Algorithms with Data-Dependent Accuracy Bounds. This can be viewed as a generalization of Quit When You are Not Ahead. Algorithms with data-dependent accuracy bounds can deliver excellent results on "good" data sets, as in Propose-Test-Release, and the accuracy can degrade gradually as the "goodness" decreases, an improvement over Propose-Test-Release.

Exploit "Nice" Query Sets. When (potentially large) sets of linear queries are presented as a batch it is possible, by analyzing the geometry of the query *matrix* to obtain higher quality answers than would be obtained were the queries answered independently[1].

Further Relaxation of Differential Privacy We have seen that (ϵ, δ)-differential privacy is a meaningful relaxation of differential privacy that can provide substantially improved accuracy bounds. Moreover, such a relaxation can be essential to these improvements. For example, Propose-Test-Release algorithms can only offer (ε, δ)-differential privacy for $\delta > 0$. What about other, but still meaningful, relaxations of differential privacy? *Concentrated Differential Privacy* is such a relaxation that is incomparable to (ε, δ)-differential privacy and that permits better accuracy. Roughly speaking, it ensures that large privacy loss happens with very small probability; for example, for all k the probability of privacy loss $k\varepsilon$ falls exponentially in k^2. In contrast, (ε, δ)-differential privacy is consistent with having *infinite* privacy loss with probability δ; on the other hand, privacy lost 2ε can happen in concentrated differential privacy with constant probability, while in (ε, δ)-differential privacy it will only occur with probability bounded by δ, which we typically take to be cryptographically small.

Why might we feel comfortable with this relaxation? The answer lies in behavior under composition. As an individual's data participate

---

[1]More accurately, the analysis is of the object $K = AB_1^k$, where A is the query matrix and B_1^k is the k-dimensional L_1 ball; note that K is the feasible region in answer space when the database has one element.

in many databases and many different computations, perhaps the real worry is the combined threat of multiple exposures. This is captured by privacy under composition. Concentrated differential privacy permits better accuracy while yielding the same behavior under composition as (ε, δ) (and $(\varepsilon, 0)$) differential privacy.

Differential privacy also faces a number of cultural challenges. One of the most significant is non-algorithmic thinking. Differential privacy is a property of an algorithm. However, many people who work with data describe their interactions with the data in fundamentally non-algorithmic terms, such as, "First, I *look at* the data." Similarly, data cleaning is often described in non-algorithmic terms. If data are reasonably plentiful, and the analysts are energetic, then the "Raw Data" application of the Subsample and Aggregate methodology described in Example 7.3 suggests a path toward enabling non-algorithmic, interactions by trusted analysts who will follow directions. In general, it seems plausible that on high-dimensional and on internet-scale data sets non-algorithmic interactions will be the exception.

What about ε? In Example 3.7 we applied Theorem 3.20 to conclude that to bound the cumulative lifetime privacy loss at $\varepsilon = 1$ with probability $1 - e^{-32}$, over participation in $10,000$ databases, it is sufficient that each database be $(1/801, 0)$-differentially private. While $k = 10,000$ may be an overestimate, the dependence on k is fairly weak ($\sqrt{k}$), and in the worst case these bounds are tight, ruling out a more relaxed bound than $\varepsilon_0 = 1/801$ for each database *over the lifetime of the database*. This is simply too strict a requirement in practice.

Perhaps we can ask a different question: Fix ε, say, $\varepsilon = 1$ or $\varepsilon = 1/10$; now ask: How can multiple ε's be apportioned? Permitting ε privacy loss *per query* is too weak, and ε loss over the lifetime of the database is too strong. Something in between, say, ε per study or ε per researcher, may make sense, although this raises the questions of who is a "researcher" and what constitutes a "study." This affords substantially more protection against accidental and intentional privacy compromise than do current practices, from enclaves to confidentiality contracts.

A different proposal is less prescriptive. This proposal draws from second-generation regulatory approaches to reducing environmental degradation, in particular pollution release registries such as the Toxic Release Inventory that have been found to encourage better practices through transparency. Perhaps a similar effect could arise with private data analysis: an Epsilon Registry describing data uses, granularity of privacy protection, a "burn rate" of privacy loss per unit time, and a cap on total privacy loss permitted before data are retired, when accompanied with a financial penalty for infinite (or very large) loss, can lead to innovation and competition, deploying the talents and resources of a larger set of researchers and privacy professionals in the search for differentially private algorithms.

13.2 The differential privacy lens

An online etymological dictionary describes the original 18th century meaning of the term of the word "statistics" as "science dealing with data about the condition of a state or community." This resonates with differential privacy in the breach: if the presence or absence of the data of a small number of individuals changes the outcome of an analysis then in some sense the outcome is "about" these few individuals, and is not describing the condition of the community as a whole. Put differently, stability to small perturbations in the data is both the hallmark of differential privacy and the essence of a common conception of the term "statistical." Differential privacy is enabled by stability (Section 7) and ensures stability (by definition). In some sense it forces all queries to be statistical in nature. As stability is also increasingly understood to be a key necessary and sufficient condition for learnability, we observe a tantalizing moral equivalence between learnability, differential privacy, and stability.

With this in mind, it is not surprising that differential privacy is also a means to ends other than privacy, and indeed we saw this with game theory in Section 10. The power of differential privacy comes from its amenability to composition. Just as composition allows us to build complex differentially private algorithms from smaller differentially private building blocks, it provides a programming language for constructing stable algorithms for complex analytical tasks. Consider, for example, the problem of eliciting a set of bidder values, and using them to price a collection of goods that are for sale. Informally, *Walrasian equilib-rium prices* are prices such that every individual can simultaneously purchase their *favorite* bundle of goods *given the prices*, while ensuring that demand exactly equals the supply of each good. It would seem at first blush, then, that simply computing these prices, and assigning each person their favorite bundle of goods given the prices would yield a mechanism in which agents were incentivized to tell the truth about their valuation function — since how could any agent do better than receiving their favorite bundle of goods? However, this argument fails — because in a Walrasian equilibrium, agents receive their favorite bundle of goods *given the prices*, but the prices are computed as a function of the reported valuations, so an industrious but dishonest agent could potentially gain by manipulating the computed prices. However, this problem is solved (and an approximately truthful mechanism results) if the equilibrium prices are computed using a differentially private algorithm — precisely because individual agents have almost no effect on the distribution of prices computed. Note that this application is made possible by the use of the tools of differential privacy, but is completely orthogonal to privacy concerns. More generally, this connection is more fundamental: computing *equilibria* of various sorts using algorithms that have the stability property guaranteed by differential privacy leads to approximately truthful mechanisms implementing these equilibrium outcomes.

Differential privacy also helps in ensuring generalizability in adaptive data analysis. Adaptivity means that the questions asked and hypotheses tested depend on outcomes of earlier questions. Generalizability means that the outcome of a computation or a test on the data set is close to the ground truth of the distribution from which the data are sampled. It is known that the naive paradigm of answering queries with the exact empirical values on a fixed data set fails to generalize even under a limited amount of adaptive questioning. Remarkably, answering with differential privacy not only ensures privacy, but with high probability it ensures generalizability even for exponentially many adaptively chosen queries. Thus, the deliberate introduction of noise using the techniques of differential privacy has profound and promising implications for the validity of traditional scientific inquiry.

Appendices

A

The Gaussian Mechanism

Let $f : \mathbb{N}^{|\mathcal{X}|} \to \mathbb{R}^d$ be an arbitrary d-dimensional function, and define its ℓ_2 sensitivity to be $\Delta_2 f = \max_{\text{adjacent} x,y} \|f(x) - f(y)\|_2$. The *Gaussian Mechanism with parameter* σ adds noise scaled to $\mathcal{N}(0, \sigma^2)$ to each of the d components of the output.

Theorem A.1. Let $\varepsilon \in (0, 1)$ be arbitrary. For $c^2 > 2\ln(1.25/\delta)$, the Gaussian Mechanism with parameter $\sigma \geq c\Delta_2 f/\varepsilon$ is (ε, δ)-differentially private.

Proof. There is a database D and a query f, and the mechanism will return $f(D)+\eta$, where the noise is normally distributed. We are adding noise $\mathcal{N}(0, \sigma^2)$. For now, assume we are talking about real-valued functions, so

$$\Delta f = \Delta_1 f = \Delta_2 f.$$

We are looking at

$$\left| \ln \frac{e^{(-1/2\sigma^2)x^2}}{e^{(-1/2\sigma^2)(x+\Delta f)^2}} \right|. \tag{A.1}$$

We are investigating the probability, given that the database is D, of observing an output that occurs with a very different probability

269

under D than under an adjacent database D', where the probability space is the noise generation algorithm. The numerator in the ratio above describes the probability of seeing $f(D) + x$ when the database is D, the denominator corresponds the probability of seeing *this same value* when the database is D'. This is a ratio of probabilities, so it is always positive, but the logarithm of the ratio may be negative. Our random variable of interest — the privacy loss — is

$$\ln \frac{e^{(-1/2\sigma^2)x^2}}{e^{(-1/2\sigma^2)(x+\Delta f)^2}}$$

and we are looking at its absolute value.

$$\left| \ln \frac{e^{(-1/2\sigma^2)x^2}}{e^{(-1/2\sigma^2)(x+\Delta f)^2}} \right| = \left| \ln e^{(-1/2\sigma^2)[x^2-(x+\Delta f)^2]} \right|$$

$$= \left| -\frac{1}{2\sigma^2}[x^2 - (x^2 + 2x\Delta f + \Delta f^2)] \right|$$

$$= \left| \frac{1}{2\sigma^2}(2x\Delta f + (\Delta f)^2) \right|. \qquad (A.2)$$

This quantity is bounded by ε whenever $x < \sigma^2\varepsilon/\Delta f - \Delta f/2$. To ensure privacy loss bounded by ε with probability at least $1 - \delta$, we require

$$\Pr[|x| \geq \sigma^2\varepsilon/\Delta f - \Delta f/2] < \delta,$$

and because we are concerned with $|x|$ we will find σ such that

$$\Pr[x \geq \sigma^2\varepsilon/\Delta f - \Delta f/2] < \delta/2.$$

We will assume throughout that $\varepsilon \leq 1 \leq \Delta f$.

We will use the tail bound

$$\Pr[x > t] \leq \frac{\sigma}{\sqrt{2\pi}}e^{-t^2/2\sigma^2}.$$

We require:

$$\frac{\sigma}{\sqrt{2\pi}}\frac{1}{t}e^{-t^2/2\sigma^2} < \delta/2$$

$$\Leftrightarrow \sigma\frac{1}{t}e^{-t^2/2\sigma^2} < \sqrt{2\pi}\delta/2$$

$$\Leftrightarrow \frac{t}{\sigma}e^{t^2/2\sigma^2} > 2/\sqrt{2\pi}\delta$$

$$\Leftrightarrow \ln(t/\sigma) + t^2/2\sigma^2 > \ln(2/\sqrt{2\pi}\delta).$$

Taking $t = \sigma^2\varepsilon/\Delta f - \Delta f/2$, we get

$$\ln((\sigma^2\varepsilon/\Delta f - \Delta f/2)/\sigma) + (\sigma^2\varepsilon/\Delta f - \Delta f/2)^2/2\sigma^2 > \ln(2/\sqrt{2\pi}\delta)$$

$$= \ln\left(\sqrt{\frac{2}{\pi}\frac{1}{\delta}}\right).$$

Let us write $\sigma = c\Delta f/\varepsilon$; we wish to bound c. We begin by finding the conditions under which the first term is non-negative.

$$\frac{1}{\sigma}\left(\sigma^2\frac{\varepsilon}{\Delta f} - \frac{\Delta f}{2}\right) = \frac{1}{\sigma}\left[\left(c^2\frac{(\Delta f)^2}{\varepsilon^2}\right)\frac{\varepsilon}{\Delta f} - \frac{\Delta f}{2}\right]$$

$$= \frac{1}{\sigma}\left[c^2\left(\frac{\Delta f}{\varepsilon}\right) - \frac{\Delta f}{2}\right]$$

$$= \frac{\varepsilon}{c\Delta f}\left[c^2\left(\frac{\Delta f}{\varepsilon}\right) - \frac{\Delta f}{2}\right]$$

$$= c - \frac{\varepsilon}{2c}.$$

Since $\varepsilon \leq 1$ and $c \geq 1$, we have $c - \varepsilon/(2c) \geq c - 1/2$. So $\ln(\frac{1}{\sigma}(\sigma^2\frac{\varepsilon}{\Delta f} - \frac{\Delta f}{2})) > 0$ provided $c \geq 3/2$. We can therefore focus on the t^2/σ^2 term.

$$\left(\frac{1}{2\sigma^2}\frac{\sigma^2\varepsilon}{\Delta f} - \frac{\Delta f}{2}\right)^2 = \frac{1}{2\sigma^2}\left[\Delta f\left(\frac{c^2}{\varepsilon} - \frac{1}{2}\right)\right]^2$$

$$= \left[(\Delta f)^2\left(\frac{c^2}{\varepsilon} - \frac{1}{2}\right)\right]^2\left[\frac{\varepsilon^2}{c^2(\Delta f)^2}\right]\frac{1}{2}$$

$$= \frac{1}{2}\left(\frac{c^2}{\varepsilon} - \frac{1}{2}\right)^2\frac{\varepsilon^2}{c^2}$$

$$= \frac{1}{2}(c^2 - \varepsilon + \varepsilon^2/4c^2).$$

Since $\varepsilon \leq 1$ the derivative of $(c^2 - \varepsilon + \varepsilon^2/4c^2)$ with respect to c is positive in the range we are considering ($c \geq 3/2$), so $c^2 - \varepsilon + \varepsilon^2/4c^2 \geq c^2 - 8/9$ and it suffices to ensure

$$c^2 - 8/9 > 2\ln\left(\sqrt{\frac{2}{\pi}\frac{1}{\delta}}\right).$$

In other words, we need that

$$c^2 > 2\ln(\sqrt{2/\pi}) + 2\ln(1/\delta) + \ln(e^{8/9}) = \ln(2/\pi) + \ln(e^{8/9}) + 2\ln(1/\delta),$$

which, since $(2/\pi)e^{8/9} < 1.55$, is satisfied whenever $c^2 > 2\ln(1.25/\delta)$.

Let us parition $\mathbb{R}$ as $\mathbb{R} = R_1 \cup R_2$, where $R_1 = \{x \in \mathbb{R} : |x| \le c\Delta f/\varepsilon\}$ and $R_2 = \{x \in \mathbb{R} : |x| > c\Delta f/\varepsilon\}$. Fix any subset $S \subseteq \mathbb{R}$, and define

$$S_1 = \{f(x) + x \,|\, x \in R_1\}$$
$$S_2 = \{f(x) + x \,|\, x \in R_2\}.$$

We have

$$\Pr_{x \sim \mathcal{N}(0,\sigma^2)}[f(x) + x \in S] = \Pr_{x \sim \mathcal{N}(0,\sigma^2)}[f(x) + x \in S_1]$$

$$+ \Pr_{x \sim \mathcal{N}(0,\sigma^2)}[f(x) + x \in S_2]$$

$$\le \Pr_{x \sim \mathcal{N}(0,\sigma^2)}[f(x) + x \in S_1] + \delta$$

$$\le e^{\varepsilon} \left(\Pr_{x \sim \mathcal{N}(0,\sigma^2)}[f(y) + x \in S_1] \right) + \delta,$$

yielding (ε, δ)-differential privacy for the Gaussian mechanism in one dimension.

High Dimension.   To extend this to functions in R^m, define $\Delta f = \Delta_2 f$. We can now repeat the argument, using Euclidean norms. Let v be any vector satisfying $\|v\| \le \Delta f$. For a fixed pair of databases x, y we are interested in $v = f(x) - f(y)$, since this is what our noise must obscure. As in the one dimensional, case we seek conditions on σ under which the privacy loss

$$\left| \ln \frac{e^{(-1/2\sigma^2)\|x-\mu\|^2}}{e^{(-1/2\sigma^2)\|x+v-\mu\|^2}} \right|$$

is bounded by ε; here x is chosen from $\mathcal{N}(0, \Sigma)$, where (Σ) is a diagonal matrix with entries σ^2, whence $\mu = (0, \ldots, 0)$.

$$\left| \ln \frac{e^{(-1/2\sigma^2)\|x-\mu\|^2}}{e^{(-1/2\sigma^2)\|x+v-\mu\|^2}} \right| = \left| \ln e^{(-1/2\sigma^2)[\|x-\mu\|^2 - \|x+v-\mu\|^2]} \right|$$

$$= \left| \frac{1}{2\sigma^2}(\|x\|^2 - \|x+v\|^2)) \right|.$$

We will use the fact that the distribution of a spherically symmetric normal is independent of the orthogonal basis from which its constituent normals are drawn, so we may work in a basis that is alligned with v. Fix such a basis $b_1, \ldots, b_m$, and draw x by first drawing signed lengths $\lambda_i \sim \mathcal{N}(0, \sigma^2)$, for $i \in [m]$, then defining $x^{[i]} = \lambda_i b_i$, and finally letting $x = \sum_{i=1}^m x^{[i]}$. Assume without loss of generality that b_1 is parallel to v. We are interested in $\left| \|x\|^2 - \|x+v\|^2 \right|$.

Consider the right triangle with base $v + x^{[1]}$ and edge $\sum_{i=2}^m x^{[i]}$ orthogonal to v. The hypotenuse of this triangle is $x + v$.

$$\|x + v\|^2 = \|v + x^{[1]}\|^2 + \sum_{i=2}^m \|x^{[i]}\|^2$$

$$\|x\|^2 = \sum_{i=1}^m \|x^{[i]}\|^2.$$

Since v is parallel to $x^{[1]}$ we have $\|v + x^{[1]}\|^2 = (\|v\| + \lambda_1)^2$. Thus, $\|x + v\|^2 - \|x\|^2 = \|v\|^2 + 2\lambda_1 \cdot \|v\|$. Recall that $\|v\| \le \Delta f$, and $\lambda \sim \mathcal{N}(0, \sigma)$, so we are now exactly back in the one-dimensional case, writing λ_1 instead of x in Equation (A.2):

$$\left| \frac{1}{2\sigma^2}(\|x\|^2 - \|x+v\|^2)) \right| \le \left| \frac{1}{2\sigma^2}(2\lambda_1 \Delta f - (\Delta f)^2) \right|$$

and the rest of the argument proceeds as above. $\qquad \square$

The argument for the high dimensional case highlights a weakness of (ε, δ)-differential privacy that does not exist for $(\varepsilon, 0)$-differential privacy. Fix a database x. In the $(\varepsilon, 0)$-case, the guarantee of indistinguishability holds for all adjacent databases *simultaneously*. In the

(ε, δ) case indistinguishability only holds "prospectively," i.e., for any fixed y adjacent to x, the probability that the mechanism will allow the adversary to distinguish x from y is small. In the proof above, this is manifested by the fact that we fixed $v = f(x) - f(y)$; we did not have to argue about all possible directions of v simultaneously, and indeed we cannot, as once we have fixed our noise vector $x \sim \mathcal{N}(0, \Sigma)$, so that the output on x is $o = f(x) + x$, there may exist an adjacent y such that output $o = f(x) + x$ is much more likely when the database is y than it is on x.

A.1   Bibliographic notes

Theorem A.1 is folklore initially observed by the authors of [23]. A generalization to non-spherical gaussian noise appears in [66].

B

Composition Theorems for (ε, δ)-DP

B.1 Extension of Theorem 3.16

Theorem B.1. Let $T_1(D) : D \mapsto T_1(D) \in \mathcal{C}_1$ be an (ϵ, δ)-d.p. function, and for any $s_1 \in \mathcal{C}_1$, $T_2(D, s_1) : (D, s_1) \mapsto T_2(D, s_1) \in \mathcal{C}_2$ be an (ϵ, δ)-d.p. function given the second input s_1. Then we show that for any neighboring D, D', for any $S \subseteq \mathcal{C}_2 \times \mathcal{C}_1$, we have, using the notation in our paper

$$P((T_2, T_1) \in S) \le e^{2\epsilon} P'((T_2, T_1) \in S) + 2\delta. \tag{B.1}$$

Proof. For any $C_1 \subseteq \mathcal{C}_1$, define

$$\mu(C_1) = \left(P(T_1 \in C_1) - e^{\epsilon} P'(T_1 \in C_1)\right)_+,$$

then μ is a measure on $\mathcal{C}_1$ and $\mu(\mathcal{C}_1) \le \delta$ since T_1 is (ϵ, δ)-d.p. As a result, we have for all $s_1 \in \mathcal{C}_1$,

$$P(T_1 \in ds_1) \le e^{\epsilon} P'(T_1 \in ds_1) + \mu(ds_1). \tag{B.2}$$

Also note that by the definition of (ϵ, δ)-d.p., for any $s_1 \in \mathcal{C}_1$,

$$P((T_2, s_1) \in S) \le \left(e^{\epsilon} P'((T_2, s_1) \in S) + \delta\right) \wedge 1$$
$$\le \left(e^{\epsilon} P'((T_2, s_1) \in S)\right) \wedge 1 + \delta. \tag{B.3}$$

275

Then (B.2) and (B.3) give (B.1):

$$P((T_2, T_1) \in S) \le \int_{S_1} P((T_2, s_1) \in S) P(T_1 \in ds_1)$$

$$\le \int_{S_1} \left((e^\epsilon P'((T_2, s_1) \in S)) \wedge 1 + \delta\right) P(T_1 \in ds_1)$$

$$\le \int_{S_1} \left((e^\epsilon P'((T_2, s_1) \in S)) \wedge 1\right) P(T_1 \in ds_1) + \delta$$

$$\le \int_{S_1} \left((e^\epsilon P'((T_2, s_1) \in S)) \wedge 1\right)$$
$$\times \left(e^\epsilon P'(T_1 \in ds_1) + \mu(ds_1)\right) + \delta$$

$$\le e^{2\epsilon} \int_{S_1} P'((T_2, s_1) \in S) P'(T_1 \in ds_1) + \mu(S_1) + \delta$$

$$\le e^{2\epsilon} P'((T_2, T_1) \in S) + 2\delta. \tag{B.4}$$

In the equations above, S_1 denotes the projection of S onto $\mathcal{C}_1$. The event $\{(T_2, s_1) \in S\}$ refers to $\{(T_2(D, s_1), s_1) \in S\}$ (or $\{(T_2(D', s_1), s_1) \in S\}$). $\qquad\square$

Using induction, we have:

Corollary B.2 (general composition theorem for (ϵ, δ)-d.p. algorithms). Let $T_1 : D \mapsto T_1(D)$ be (ϵ, δ)-d.p., and for $k \ge 2$, $T_k : (D, s_1, \ldots, s_{k-1}) \mapsto T_k(D, s_1, \ldots, s_{k-1}) \in \mathcal{C}_k$ be (ϵ, δ)-d.p., for all given $(s_{k-1}, \ldots, s_1) \in \otimes_{j=1}^{k-1} \mathcal{C}_j$. Then for all neighboring D, D' and all $S \subseteq \otimes_{j=1}^{k} \mathcal{C}_j$

$$P((T_1, \ldots, T_k) \in S) \le e^{k\epsilon} P'((T_1, \ldots, T_k) \in S) + k\delta.$$

Acknowledgments

We would like to thank many people for providing careful comments and corrections on early drafts of this book, including Vitaly Feldman, Justin Hsu, Katrina Ligett, Dong Lin, David Parkes, Ryan Rogers, Guy Rothblum, Jon Ullman, Salil Vadhan, Zhiwei Steven Wu, and the anonymous referees. This book was used in a course taught by Salil Vadhan and Jon Ullman, whose students also provided careful feedback. This book has also benefited from conversations with many other colleagues, including Moritz Hardt, Ilya Mironov, Sasho Nikolov, Kobbi Nissim, Mallesh Pai, Benjamin Pierce, Adam Smith, Abhradeep Thakurta, Abhishek Bhowmick, Kunal Talwar, and Li Zhang. We are grateful to Madhu Sudan for proposing this monograph.

References

[1] S. Arora, E. Hazan, and S. Kale. The multiplicative weights update method: A meta-algorithm and applications. *Theory of Computing*, 8(1):121–164, 2012.

[2] M.-F. Balcan, A. Blum, J. D. Hartline, and Y. Mansour. Mechanism design via machine learning. In *Foundations of Computer Science, 2005. FOCS 2005. 46th Annual IEEE Symposium on*, pages 605–614. IEEE, 2005.

[3] A. Beimel, S. P. Kasiviswanathan, and K. Nissim. Bounds on the sample complexity for private learning and private data release. In *Theory of Cryptography*, pages 437–454. Springer, 2010.

[4] A. Beimel, K. Nissim, and U. Stemmer. Characterizing the sample complexity of private learners. In *Proceedings of the Conference on Innovations in Theoretical Computer Science*, pages 97–110. Association for Computing Machinery, 2013.

[5] A. Bhaskara, D. Dadush, R. Krishnaswamy, and K. Talwar. Unconditional differentially private mechanisms for linear queries. In H. J. Karloff and T. Pitassi, editors, *Proceedings of the Symposium on Theory of Computing Conference, Symposium on Theory of Computing, New York, NY, USA, May 19–22, 2012*, pages 1269–1284. 2012.

[6] A. Blum, C. Dwork, F. McSherry, and K. Nissim. Practical privacy: the SuLQ framework. In Chen Li, editor, *Principles of Database Systems*, pages 128–138. ACM, 2005.

[7] A. Blum, C. Dwork, F. McSherry, and K. Nissim. Practical privacy: the sulq framework. In *Principles of Database Systems*. 2005.

[8] A. Blum, K. Ligett, and A. Roth. A learning theory approach to non-interactive database privacy. In Cynthia Dwork, editor, *Symposium on Theory of Computing*, pages 609–618. Association for Computing Machinery, 2008.

[9] A. Blum and Y. Monsour. Learning, regret minimization, and equilibria, 2007.

[10] J. L. Casti. *Five Golden Rules: Great Theories of 20th-Century Mathematics and Why They Matter*. Wiley, 1996.

[11] T. H. Hubert Chan, E. Shi, and D. Song. Private and continual release of statistics. In *Automata, Languages and Programming*, pages 405–417. Springer, 2010.

[12] K. Chaudhuri and D. Hsu. Sample complexity bounds for differentially private learning. In *Proceedings of the Annual Conference on Learning Theory (COLT 2011)*. 2011.

[13] K. Chaudhuri, C. Monteleoni, and A. D. Sarwate. Differentially private empirical risk minimization. *Journal of machine learning research: JMLR*, 12:1069, 2011.

[14] K. Chaudhuri, A. Sarwate, and K. Sinha. Near-optimal differentially private principal components. In *Advances in Neural Information Processing Systems 25*, pages 998–1006. 2012.

[15] Y. Chen, S. Chong, I. A. Kash, T. Moran, and S. P. Vadhan. Truthful mechanisms for agents that value privacy. *Association for Computing Machinery Conference on Electronic Commerce*, 2013.

[16] P. Dandekar, N. Fawaz, and S. Ioannidis. Privacy auctions for recommender systems. In *Internet and Network Economics*, pages 309–322. Springer, 2012.

[17] A. De. Lower bounds in differential privacy. In *Theory of Cryptography Conference*, pages 321–338. 2012.

[18] I. Dinur and K. Nissim. Revealing information while preserving privacy. In *Proceedings of the Association for Computing Machinery SIGACT-SIGMOD-SIGART Symposium on Principles of Database Systems*, pages 202–210. 2003.

[19] J. C. Duchi, M. I. Jordan, and M. J. Wainwright. Local privacy and statistical minimax rates. *arXiv preprint arXiv:1302.3203*, 2013.

[20] C. Dwork. Differential privacy. In *Proceedings of the International Colloquium on Automata, Languages and Programming (ICALP)(2)*, pages 1–12. 2006.

[21] C. Dwork, K. Kenthapadi, F. McSherry, I. Mironov, and M. Naor. Our data, ourselves: Privacy via distributed noise generation. In *EURO-CRYPT*, pages 486–503. 2006.

[22] C. Dwork and J. Lei. Differential privacy and robust statistics. In *Proceedings of the 2009 International Association for Computing Machinery Symposium on Theory of Computing (STOC)*. 2009.

[23] C. Dwork, F. McSherry, K. Nissim, and A. Smith. Calibrating noise to sensitivity in private data analysis. In *Theory of Cryptography Conference '06*, pages 265–284. 2006.

[24] C. Dwork, F. McSherry, and K. Talwar. The price of privacy and the limits of lp decoding. In *Proceedings of the Association for Computing Machinery Symposium on Theory of Computing*, pages 85–94. 2007.

[25] C. Dwork and M. Naor. On the difficulties of disclosure prevention in statistical databases or the case for differential privacy. *Journal of Privacy and Confidentiality*, 2010.

[26] C. Dwork, M. Naor, T. Pitassi, and G. N. Rothblum. Differential privacy under continual observation. In *Proceedings of the Association for Computing Machinery Symposium on Theory of Computing*, pages 715–724. Association for Computing Machinery, 2010.

[27] C. Dwork, M. Naor, T. Pitassi, G. N. Rothblum, and Sergey Yekhanin. Pan-private streaming algorithms. In *Proceedings of International Conference on Super Computing*. 2010.

[28] C. Dwork, M. Naor, O. Reingold, G. N. Rothblum, and S. P. Vadhan. On the complexity of differentially private data release: Efficient algorithms and hardness results. In *Symposium on Theory of Computing '09*, pages 381–390. 2009.

[29] C. Dwork, M. Naor, and S. Vadhan. The privacy of the analyst and the power of the state. In *Foundations of Computer Science*. 2012.

[30] C. Dwork, A. Nikolov, and K. Talwar. Efficient algorithms for privately releasing marginals via convex relaxations. In *Proceedings of the Annual Symposium on Computational Geometry (SoCG)*. 2014.

[31] C. Dwork and K. Nissim. Privacy-preserving datamining on vertically partitioned databases. In *Proceedings of Cryptology 2004*, vol. 3152, pages 528–544. 2004.

[32] C. Dwork, G. N. Rothblum, and S. P. Vadhan. Boosting and differential privacy. In *Foundations of Computer Science*, pages 51–60. 2010.

[33] C. Dwork, K. Talwar, A. Thakurta, and L. Zhang. Analyze gauss: Optimal bounds for privacy-preserving pca. In *Symposium on Theory of Computing*. 2014.

[34] L. Fleischer and Y.-H. Lyu. Approximately optimal auctions for selling privacy when costs are correlated with data. In *Association for Computing Machinery Conference on Electronic Commerce*, pages 568–585. 2012.

[35] A. Ghosh and K. Ligett. Privacy and coordination: Computing on databases with endogenous participation. In *Proceedings of the fourteenth ACM conference on Electronic commerce (EC)*, pages 543–560, 2013.

[36] A. Ghosh and A. Roth. Selling privacy at auction. In *Association for Computing Machinery Conference on Electronic Commerce*, pages 199–208. 2011.

[37] A. Groce, J. Katz, and A. Yerukhimovich. Limits of computational differential privacy in the client/server setting. In *Proceedings of the Theory of Cryptography Conference*. 2011.

[38] A. Gupta, M. Hardt, A. Roth, and J. Ullman. Privately releasing conjunctions and the statistical query barrier. In *Symposium on Theory of Computing '11*, pages 803–812. 2011.

[39] A. Gupta, A. Roth, and J. Ullman. Iterative constructions and private data release. In *Theory of Cryptography Conference*, pages 339–356. 2012.

[40] J. Håstad, R. Impagliazzo, L. Levin, and M. Luby. A pseudorandom generator from any one-way function. *SIAM Journal of Computing*, 28, 1999.

[41] M. Hardt, K. Ligett, and F. McSherry. A simple and practical algorithm for differentially private data release. In *Advances in Neural Information Processing Systems 25*, pages 2348–2356. 2012.

[42] M. Hardt and A. Roth. Beating randomized response on incoherent matrices. In *Proceedings of the Symposium on Theory of Computing*, pages 1255–1268. Association for Computing Machinery, 2012.

[43] M. Hardt and A. Roth. Beyond worst-case analysis in private singular vector computation. In *Proceedings of the Symposium on Theory of Computing*. 2013.

[44] M. Hardt and G. N. Rothblum. A multiplicative weights mechanism for privacy-preserving data analysis. In *Foundations of Computer Science*, pages 61–70. IEEE Computer Society, 2010.

[45] M. Hardt and K. Talwar. On the geometry of differential privacy. In *Proceedings of the Association for Computing Machinery Symposium on Theory of Computing*, pages 705–714. Association for Computing Machinery, 2010.

[46] N. Homer, S. Szelinger, M. Redman, D. Duggan, W. Tembe, J. Muehling, J. Pearson, D. Stephan, S. Nelson, and D. Craig. Resolving individuals contributing trace amounts of dna to highly complex mixtures using high-density snp genotyping microarrays. *PLoS Genet*, 4, 2008.

[47] J. Hsu, Z. Huang, A. Roth, T. Roughgarden, and Z. S. Wu. Private matchings and allocations. arXiv preprint arXiv:1311.2828, 2013.

[48] J. Hsu, A. Roth, and J. Ullman. Differential privacy for the analyst via private equilibrium computation. In *Proceedings of the Association for Computing Machinery Symposium on Theory of Computing (STOC)*, pages 341–350, 2013.

[49] Z. Huang and S. Kannan. The exponential mechanism for social welfare: Private, truthful, and nearly optimal. In *IEEE Annual Symposium on the Foundations of Computer Science (FOCS)*, pages 140–149. 2012.

[50] P. Jain, P. Kothari, and A. Thakurta. Differentially private online learning. *Journal of Machine Learning Research — Proceedings Track*, 23:24.1–24.34, 2012.

[51] M. Kapralov and K. Talwar. On differentially private low rank approximation. In Sanjeev Khanna, editor, *Symposium on Discrete Algorthims*, pages 1395–1414. SIAM, 2013.

[52] S. P. Kasiviswanathan, H. K. Lee, Kobbi Nissim, S. Raskhodnikova, and A. Smith. What can we learn privately? *SIAM Journal on Computing*, 40(3):793–826, 2011.

[53] M. Kearns. Efficient noise-tolerant learning from statistical queries. *Journal of the Association for Computing Machinery (JAssociation for Computing Machinery)*, 45(6):983–1006, 1998.

[54] M. Kearns, M. Pai, A. Roth, and J. Ullman. Mechanism design in large games: Incentives and privacy. In *Proceedings of the 5th conference on Innovations in theoretical computer science (ITCS)*, 2014.

[55] D. Kifer, A. Smith, and A. Thakurta. Private convex empirical risk minimization and high-dimensional regression. *Journal of Machine Learning Research*, 1:41, 2012.

[56] K. Ligett and A. Roth. Take it or leave it: Running a survey when privacy comes at a cost. In *Internet and Network Economics*, pages 378–391. Springer, 2012.

[57] N. Littlestone and M. K. Warmuth. The weighted majority algorithm. In *Annual Symposium on Foundations of Computer Science, 1989*, pages 256–261. IEEE, 1989.

[58] A. McGregor, I. Mironov, T. Pitassi, O. Reingold, K. Talwar, and S. P. Vadhan. The limits of two-party differential privacy. In *Foundations of Computer Science*, pages 81–90. IEEE Computer Society, 2010.

[59] F. McSherry. Privacy integrated queries (codebase). Available on Microsoft Research downloads website. See also the Proceedings of SIG-MOD 2009.

[60] F. McSherry and K. Talwar. Mechanism design via differential privacy. In *Foundations of Computer Science*, pages 94–103. 2007.

[61] F. McSherry and K. Talwar. Mechanism design via differential privacy. In *Foundations of Computer Science*, pages 94–103. 2007.

[62] D. Mir, S. Muthukrishnan, A. Nikolov, and R. N. Wright. Pan-private algorithms via statistics on sketches. In *Proceedings of the Association for Computing Machinery SIGMOD-SIGACT-SIGART Symposium on Principles of Database Systems*, pages 37–48. Association for Computing Machinery, 2011.

[63] I. Mironov. On significance of the least significant bits for differential privacy. In T. Yu, G. Danezis, and V. D. Gligor, editors, *Association for Computing Machinery Conference on Computer and Communications Security*, pages 650–661. Association for Computing Machinery, 2012.

[64] I. Mironov, O. Pandey, O. Reingold, and S. P. Vadhan. Computational differential privacy. In *Proceedings of CRYPTOLOGY*, pages 126–142. 2009.

[65] A. Narayanan and V. Shmatikov. Robust de-anonymization of large sparse datasets (how to break anonymity of the netflix prize dataset). In *Proceedings of IEEE Symposium on Security and Privacy*. 2008.

[66] A. Nikolov, K. Talwar, and L. Zhang. The geometry of differential privacy: the sparse and approximate cases. *Symposium on Theory of Computing*, 2013.

[67] K. Nissim, C. Orlandi, and R. Smorodinsky. Privacy-aware mechanism design. In *Association for Computing Machinery Conference on Electronic Commerce*, pages 774–789. 2012.

[68] K. Nissim, S. Raskhodnikova, and A. Smith. Smooth sensitivity and sampling in private data analysis. In *Proceedings of the Association for Computing Machinery Symposium on Theory of Computing*, pages 75–84. 2007.

[69] K. Nissim, R. Smorodinsky, and M. Tennenholtz. Approximately optimal mechanism design via differential privacy. In *Innovations in Theoretical Computer Science*, pages 203–213. 2012.

[70] M. Pai and A. Roth. Privacy and mechanism design. *SIGecom Exchanges*, 2013.

[71] R. Rogers and A. Roth. Asymptotically truthful equilibrium selection in large congestion games. arXiv preprint arXiv:1311.2625, 2013.

[72] A. Roth. Differential privacy and the fat-shattering dimension of linear queries. In *Approximation, Randomization, and Combinatorial Optimization, Algorithms and Techniques*, pages 683–695. Springer, 2010.

[73] A. Roth. Buying private data at auction: the sensitive surveyor's problem. *Association for Computing Machinery SIGecom Exchanges*, 11(1):1–8, 2012.

[74] A. Roth and T. Roughgarden. Interactive privacy via the median mechanism. In *Symposium on Theory of Computing '10*, pages 765–774. 2010.

[75] A. Roth and G. Schoenebeck. Conducting truthful surveys, cheaply. In *Proceedings of the ACM Conference on Electronic Commerce*, pages 826–843. 2012.

[76] B. I. P. Rubinstein, P. L. Bartlett, L. Huang, and N. Taft. Learning in a large function space: Privacy-preserving mechanisms for svm learning. arXiv preprint arXiv:0911.5708, 2009.

[77] R. Schapire. The boosting approach to machine learning: An overview. In D. D. Denison, M. H. Hansen, C. Holmes, B. Mallick, and B. Yu, editors, *Nonlinear Estimation and Classification*. Springer, 2003.

[78] R. Schapire and Y. Singer. Improved boosting algorithms using confidence-rated predictions. *Machine Learning*, 39:297–336, 1999.

[79] R. E. Schapire and Y. Freund. *Boosting: Foundations and Algorithms*. MIT Press, 2012.

[80] A. Smith and A. G. Thakurta. Differentially private feature selection via stability arguments, and the robustness of the lasso. In *Proceedings of Conference on Learning Theory*. 2013.

[81] L. Sweeney. Weaving technology and policy together to maintain confidentiality. *Journal of Law, Medicines Ethics*, 25:98–110, 1997.

[82] J. Ullman. Answering $n^{\{2+o(1)\}}$ counting queries with differential privacy is hard. In D. Boneh, T. Roughgarden, and J. Feigenbaum, editors, *Symposium on Theory of Computing*, pages 361–370. Association for Computing Machinery, 2013.

[83] L. G. Valiant. A theory of the learnable. *Communications of the Association for Computing Machinery*, 27(11):1134–1142, 1984.

[84] S. L. Warner. Randomized response: A survey technique for eliminating evasive answer bias. *Journal of the American Statistical Association*, 60(309):63–69, 1965.

[85] D. Xiao. Is privacy compatible with truthfulness? In *Proceedings of the Conference on Innovations in Theoretical Computer Science*, pages 67–86. 2013.